中国社会科学院—格鲁吉亚理工大学：中国研究中心
CASS-GTU：RESEARCH INSTITUTE OF CHINA STUDIES

中国与格鲁吉亚："一带一路"建设与发展

China and Georgia: the Belt and Road Construction and Development

张翼 马峰 等著

中国社会科学出版社

图书在版编目（CIP）数据

中国与格鲁吉亚："一带一路"建设与发展 / 张翼等著. —北京：中国社会科学出版社，2021.6
ISBN 978-7-5203-7675-4

Ⅰ.①中… Ⅱ.①张… Ⅲ.①"一带一路"—国际合作—中国、格鲁吉亚 Ⅳ.①F125.536.7

中国版本图书馆 CIP 数据核字（2021）第 068007 号

出 版 人	赵剑英
责任编辑	刘凯琳
责任校对	侯聪睿
责任印制	王　超

出　　版	中国社会科学出版社
社　　址	北京鼓楼西大街甲 158 号
邮　　编	100720
网　　址	http://www.csspw.cn
发 行 部	010-84083685
门 市 部	010-84029450
经　　销	新华书店及其他书店

印　　刷	北京明恒达印务有限公司
装　　订	廊坊市广阳区广增装订厂
版　　次	2021 年 6 月第 1 版
印　　次	2021 年 6 月第 1 次印刷

开　　本	710×1000　1/16
印　　张	18
字　　数	260 千字
定　　价	99.00 元

凡购买中国社会科学出版社图书，如有质量问题请与本社营销中心联系调换
电话：010-84083683
版权所有　侵权必究

目　　录

第一篇　中国经济社会发展

第一章　新中国社会发展历程与展望 …………………… 张　翼（3）
第二章　中国经济结构分析与预测 ……………………… 娄　峰（24）

第二篇　格鲁吉亚经济社会发展

第三章　格鲁吉亚经济发展与前景 …………………… 欧阳向英（45）
第四章　格鲁吉亚社会发展：现状与展望 ……………… 马　峰（52）

第三篇　中国与格鲁吉亚的交流与合作

第五章　"一带一路"倡议框架下中格旅游合作前景
　　　　与展望 ……………………………………… 张艳璐（77）
第六章　中格两国文学在"一带一路"语境下的交流
　　　　和研究 ……………………………………… 王玉欢（88）
第七章　中国与格鲁吉亚在"一带一路"建设中的文化
　　　　交流与合作 ………………………………… 王　辉（101）

Contents

Part 1 China's Economic and Social Development

Chapter 1 China's Social Development History and
　　　　　Prospect ·· Zhang Yi (125)
Chapter 2 Analysis and Forecast of China's Economic
　　　　　Structure ·· Lou Feng (156)

Part 2 Georgia's Economic and Social Development

Chapter 3 Georgia's Economic Development and
　　　　　Prospect ···················· Ouyang Xiangying (183)
Chapter 4 Georgia's Social Development: Status Quo
　　　　　and Prospects ·· Ma Feng (194)

Part 3 Communication and Cooperation between China and Georgia

Chapter 5 Prospects of China – Georgia Tourism
　　　　　Cooperation under the Belt and Road
　　　　　Initiative Framework ···················· Zhang Yanlu (225)

Chapter 6　Exchanges and Studies of Chinese and Georgian Literature in the Belt and Road Context ·················· Wang Yuhuan （240）

Chapter 7　Cultural Exchange and Cooperation between China and Georgia in Belt and Road Initiative ·················· Wang Hui （257）

第一篇
中国经济社会发展

第一章

新中国社会发展历程与展望

张 翼

中国社会科学院社会发展战略研究院院长、研究员

中国社会的发展，首先表现为人口规模的增长与就业区域的变化，继之出现波澜壮阔的城镇化与三次产业结构从业人员比重的梯次推移，最后发生了阶层结构的优化、消费水平的升级和家庭人均住房面积的扩大。中国划时代地从贫困社会转变为全面小康社会，同时，提升了人均受教育程度、延长了人均预期寿命。中国在整体上已经从普及9年制义务教育阶段转变到大众化高等教育阶段，已经从新中国成立初期的低预期寿命阶段转变到高预期寿命阶段——2018年的人均预期寿命已达77岁——居所有发展中国家之首。

在绝大多数社会科学的解释中，社会发展暗含着社会结构、社会组织方式、社会生产方式和社会生活方式从相对较低水平向相对较高水平的转变过程。自工业社会以来，发展总是被书写为人类从农业社会向工业社会再向后工业社会的转型，或者总是被现代化过程所解释。[1] 不管是在宏观社会层面，还是在微观社区与组织层面，中国的社会发展都充满了自上而下或自下而上日常生活意义的工业化、现代

---

[1] 王元、孔伟艳：《未来30年中国社会发展趋势及促进共享发展的建议》，《宏观经济研究》2019年第5期。

化的词义表达。

中国现代化意义上的发展在客观上表现为经济增长拉动之下的社会各领域的变化过程。经济增长又与人口增长纽结在一起。少儿人口、劳动力人口与老年人口的结构变化，从积累与消费的分配比例上影响着经济增速及其增长方式。所以，新中国成立70多年来的社会建设与社会发展，首先表现为人口增速与经济增速之辨证变化中的人口转型过程。

一 人口规模的扩大与人均预期寿命的延长

新中国成立以来，人口就作为预设变量影响着经济发展与社会发展。从土地改革平均地权到合作化，再到以人民公社为基础的三级所有体制的建立，以及城市企业的国有化和集体化运动，在一定程度上解决了人民"能够吃上饭"的问题，也在一定程度上提升了人民安定生活的水平与医疗水平，由此导致了人口的迅速增长。[①] 而人口的快速增长反过来又给经济与社会发展带来压力。为克服人口增速快于经济增速所带来的压力，国家开始施行计划生育的政策，提倡一对夫妇只生育一个孩子，力图在2000年将人口规模控制在12亿内。2001年出台了《中华人民共和国人口与计划生育法》，以立法方式控制人口增长对国民经济与社会发展的影响。

经过多年努力，中国人口增长方式，从高出生率、低死亡率、高增长率阶段逐步过渡到21世纪的低出生率、低死亡率、低增长率阶段。但由于受庞大人口基数的影响，每年新增长的人口依旧十分可观，所以，人口数量屡屡向上突破。新中国成立之初实际人口已突破"四万万五千万"，1960年达到6.6亿，1970年达到8.3亿，1980年达到9.8亿，1990年达到11.4亿，2000年达到12.6亿，2010年达到13.4亿，2018年年底达到13.95亿。

---

① 除1959年到1961年的"三年困难时期"，其他历史时期人口都呈现增长态势。

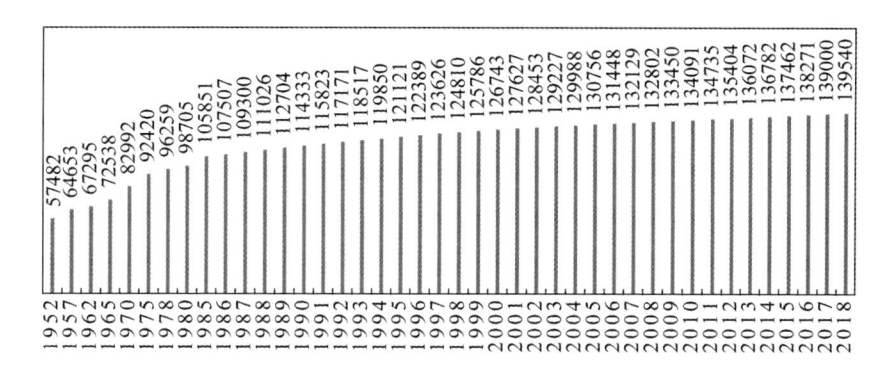

图1—1 新中国成立70年中国人口增长趋势

资料来源：2017年及以前人口数据来自2018年《中国统计年鉴》表2—1。2018年人口数据来自《2018年国民经济和社会发展统计公报》。

计划经济时期，由于生产效率低下，土地产出的增量难以供应人口增量带来的粮食消费需求。改革开放之后，不管是农村还是城市，都在充分解放生产力的同时，改善了生产关系和上层建筑，使其与日益发展的生产力相适应，从而焕发了人民的生产积极性。中国的粮食产量历史性地、长足地增长。中国的农民也以农民工的方式转变了自己的劳动职业，离开家乡到城市务工经商，既满足城市之劳动力所需，也以打工赚钱的形式反哺农业，从根本上改变了乡村与城镇的传统模样。

从理论和实践来看，在生产力水平较低的情况下，人多、口多、吃饭多，粮食产量难以"养活"或"养好"存量人口。但在改革使生产力与生产关系逐渐协调、在家庭联产承包责任制逐步实施、在增人不增地减人不减地的制度配置中，在劳动力流动的约束逐步解除、在户籍制度不得不适时改革、在乡镇企业和民营企业逐步壮大的经济格局中，人口总量的上涨、劳动力数量的增长却与生活条件的改善同步向前。中国在5亿多人口、6亿多人口、7亿多人口、8亿多人口、9亿多人口阶段遇到的饥饿问题，在10亿以上人口的增长实践中，几乎未曾遇到。越来越多的事实表明，人口增加同时也伴随着生活质量的提升。计划经济时期为保证粮食供应而设计的粮票、布票、肉票、油票等配给制度，随着改革开放之后的经济发展逐步走入历史。价格双轨制，也同样如此。

在生产力构成中，科学技术是最积极的进步因素。改革开放之前，生产队、生产大队或人民公社的农业生产，都维持在人力与畜力相结合的再生产结构之中。在土地肥力既定的情况下，农业劳动力的"内卷化"投入所提供的粮食增量极其有限。1952年，第一产业就业人数占全国劳动就业人数的83.5%，在1978年改革开放之初，仍然有70.5%的就业人员生存于第一产业。也就是说，在农业科学技术缓慢发展、在生产关系难以解放生产力的情况下，即使将全国70%以上劳动就业人员投放在第一产业，其生产的粮食也难以满足人口的需要。但在改革开放之后，伴随农村开放搞活，伴随家庭联产承包责任制的推行，一方面是农业产量大幅提升，另外一方面是农村剩余劳动力大量进入城市打工。中国早期的计划生育，减少了家庭子女数量，减少了家庭照顾子女的时间和父母的家庭劳动量，先是丈夫解放出来进城务工，接着是妻子携带孩子进城务工。取之不尽、用之不竭的廉价劳动力，与外来资本的结合，将中国迅速转变为制造业大国，同时也增加了国际与国内市场的商品供应，极大改善了消费品市场，并以人口红利增进了经济与社会发展动力。应该说，改革开放以来，中国维持了年均9.5%左右的高速增长，推进了社会建设和社区建设，大幅提高了人民的生活水平。同时，中国第一产业从业人员的比重迅速降低，在1990年降低到60.1%，在2000年降低到50%，到2017年降低到27%。中国用27%左右的劳动就业人员生产的粮食，就养活了近14亿人口，而且还大幅度提高了中国人的食品消费水平。2017年，中国人均粮食的消费量已经降低到每年约130.1公斤，但肉类消费量却增加到年均26.7公斤，奶类消费量增加到12.1公斤，干鲜瓜果类消费量增加到45.6公斤。①

营养状况的改善及医疗保障水平的提高,迅速延长了中国人口的平均预期寿命。在新中国成立之初的1949年,中国人口的平均预期寿命仅仅为35岁,1957年延长到57岁,1964年达到64岁。实践证明,只要消除战乱并形成相对公平的生产生活环境,人口预期寿命就会迅速延长。改革开放之后,中国人的平均预期寿命得到长足增长,1981年达到68岁,1990年达到69岁,1996年达到71岁,2005年达到73岁,2010年达到75岁,2015年超过76岁,2018年达到77岁。②

在人均预期寿命的增长中,女性相对男性更多发挥出了生存优势。1990年第四次人口普查时,女性人口的平均预期寿命为70.5岁,男性为66.8岁。2000年第五次人口普查时,女性平均预期寿命为73.3岁,男性为69.6岁。2010年第六次人口普查时,女性人口的平均预期寿命为77.4岁,男性为72.4岁。2015年女性人口的平均预期寿命为79.4岁,男性为73.6岁。③ 中国社会发展最让世人羡慕之处,便是人口平均预期寿命的延长。人口平均预期寿命的延长速度反过来也验证着社会进步与社会发展的共享速度。

二 教育大发展与人力资本的提升

新中国成立以来中国社会发展的最大表征,是国民平均受教育程度的提升。

中国在1949年左右的文盲率高达80%左右。自1949—2000年,中国用50多年致力于提升全民识字率,努力扫除文盲,终于在第一人口大国完成了脱盲任务。早在合作化、集体化和国有化时期,政府就

---

① 数据来源:参见2018年《中国统计年鉴》表6—4。
② 数据来源:参见2018年《中国统计年鉴》表2—4。
③ 亚洲最长寿国家是日本,其女性平均预期寿命达到87.32岁,男性平均预期寿命达到81.25岁。

开始了全民扫盲运动和成人识字率提升运动。各级政府和群团组织在工厂、农村、街道、部队等广泛举办夜校和扫盲班,编写识字教材,将识字率的提升与日常生活相结合、与老百姓的互教相结合、与青年人的发展相结合、与妇女解放运动相结合,形成了全民在田间地头、车间厂房、驻地军营等集中学习的热潮。经过多年努力,成人识字率连年提高。在1964年第二次人口普查时,文盲和半文盲人口(13周岁及以上不识字或识字很少的人口)下降到33.58%;到1982年第三次人口普查时,下降到22.81%;[①] 到1990年第四次人口普查时,下降到15.88%。历经将近50年努力,终于在2000年第五次人口普查时,将文盲率下降到6.72%。

在扫除文盲的同时,政府还大力兴办教育,扩展各级教育的招生规模。20世纪50年代初,为适应入学适龄人口的增加,政府在几个合作社或一个乡办一所小学。在人民公社和生产大队成立之后,基层的组织化程度进一步加强。在人民公社领导下,几乎有条件的生产大队都办起了小学。所以,从图1—2可以看出,20世纪50年代和60年代是中国小学招生人数上升最快的时期。

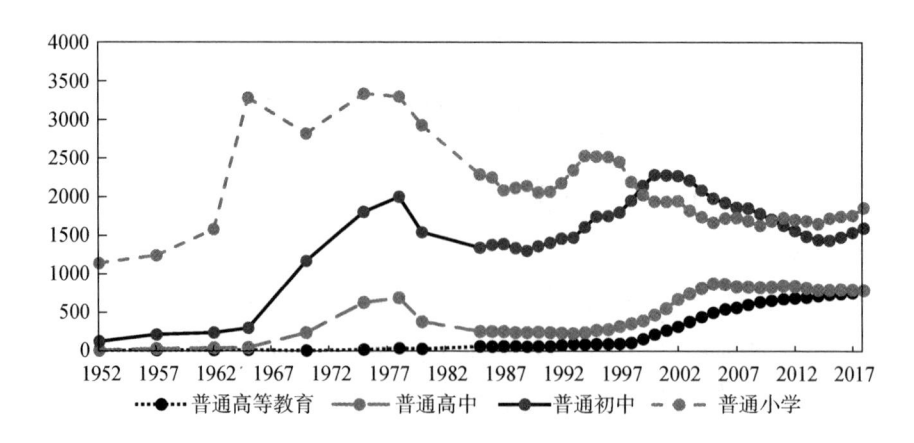

图1—2 新中国成立70年各类学校招生人数变化趋势(单位:万人)

---

① 数据来源:2004年《中国统计年鉴》表4—4。1964年的文盲人口为13岁及13岁以上不识字人口,1982、1990、2000年文盲人口为15岁及以上不识字或识字很少人口。

1952年，全国普通小学招生人数就达到了1149.3万人。但普通初中招生人数仅仅为124.2万人，普通高中招生人数仅为14.1万人，普通高校招生人数勉强达到7.9万人。因为建国之初存在的收入差距及高校招生基本格局，在高校接受教育的生源基本是城市或县城比较富裕家庭的子女。1957年社会主义改造完成之后，全国普通小学的招生人数上升到1249万人，普通初中的招生人数上升到217万人，普通高中招生人数上升到32.3万人，普通高校招生人数上升到10.6万人。可以看出，当时初中以上教育阶段的招生人数还十分有限。进入20世纪60年代，伴随50年代中期及前期"人口爆炸"出生人口达到入学年龄，中国普通小学的招生人数迅速增长，到1965年，普通小学招生人数达到了3296万人，1975年达到3352万人，此后缓慢下降。由于节制生育与计划生育的影响，学龄儿童的数字开始走低，小学招生人数也开始下降。但普通初中的招生人数却有了长足增长，在1975年达到1810万人，普通高中的招生人数也达到了历史性的633.1万人。在"学制要缩短，教育要革命"的影响下，小学教育时间缩短到5年，初中为2年，高中为2年。而且高中结合地方的特点，设计了很多与就业相配套的专业，比如农机班、木工班、铸造班等。但由于历史原因，高等教育停止招生，1966年之后，在校人数开始下滑，1970年只招收了4.2万工农兵生源。

改革开放之后，一方面是家庭联产承包责任制的实施，另外一方面是公社或乡政府对生产大队的控制有所放松，再加上农村家庭和乡镇企业对劳动力的需求，普通初中招生人数和普通高中招生人数出现萎缩趋势。1978年招生人数达到2006万人之后，1980年下降到1550.9万人，1985年下降到1349.4万人，1989年下降到1309.4万人。普通高中招生人数也随之下降，1978年达到692.9万人之后，1980年下降到383.4万人，1985年只招收了257.5万人，1993年仅仅招收了228.3万人。

"文革"结束后，1977年恢复了高考制度，① 高等教育招生人数开始平缓上升。因为高中招生人数较少，出现了初中考高中难于高中考大学的局面。总体而言，从恢复高考开始到1997年，高等学校招生人数一直上升，但普通高中招生人数则迅速下滑。比如说，1993年高等学校招生人数达到了92.4万人，但当年普通高中招生人数却仅为228.3万人。② 1989年，高中升高等教育的升学率为24.6%，1997年上升到45.1%，2003年上升到83.4%。但2003年的初中升高中的升学率却仅仅为60.2%。

改革开放之后城乡差距的拉大，逐渐使农村基础教育趋于薄弱。1982年宪法明确规定国家要普及义务教育。1985年《中共中央关于教育体制改革的决定》强调要实施九年义务制教育。1986年经第六届全国人民代表大会审议通过，于当年7月1日施行《中华人民共和国义务教育法》，采取强制措施保障学龄儿童的受教育权。中国自此走上了依法治教之路。1992年，国家教育委员会发布了《中华人民共和国义务教育法实施细则》，强化了小学阶段和初中阶段的教育工作。在这以后，初中招生规模和高中招生规模逐渐回升。初中招生人数在1995年达到1752.3万人，到2000年达到2295.6万人。高中招生人数在1995年达到273.6万人，到2000年达到472.7万人。

---

① 1977年10月国务院批转教育部《关于1977年高等学校招生工作的意见》，规定凡工人、农民、上山下乡和回城知识青年、复员军人和应届毕业生，符合条件均可参加高考，这里的条件放宽到1966年和1967年的高中毕业生，所以生源年龄差距较大。当年冬天即在各地举行考试，招生27万多人。因为有些人错过了高考机会，于是1978年7月又举行了一次考试，录取40.2万人。77级1978年春天入学，78级则在1978年秋天入学。但这并不是说"文革"期间一直没有招生。事实上，1971年即开始恢复招生，采取"自愿报名、群众推荐、领导批准、学校复审"的办法，废除了"修正主义的招生考试制度"，主要招收的是"家庭出身"较好的工农兵大学生。因为生源需具备3年及以上"实践经验"、不受文化程度限制推荐免试入学且给予19.5元伙食费和津贴费，所以"走后门"现象突出，学习成绩很不理想，但很多高校和技校在此时期有所恢复和新建。

② 这一时期普通初中、普通高中的合并降低了教育资源的可及性。住校费、学费和书本费的增加，也使一部分收入较低家庭难以为其子女提供必要的学习费用。这从另外一方面降低了普通初中、普通高中的入学率。当然，因为外出打工提供了就业途径，有些家庭还是选择安排子女辍学就业了。

当然，这一时期初中和高中阶段教育的招生人数的提升，还与各级政府对教育投入的增长、与农村人均可支配收入的增长，与计划生育使子女数减少之后父母集中投资生育子女入学等因素有密切关系。而且后者的支持力度可能要大于其他因素的影响，中国家庭高度重视子女教育。改革开放以来，国民经济的高速增长为中国人提供了更多向上流动机会，这也鼓励了家庭积极投资子女接受现代教育。

20世纪90年代中期以后小学招生人数和初中招生人数的变化，基本与计划生育政策的变化高度吻合。80年代中后期出生率回升过程中出生的人口，在拉高90年代前期小学招生人数之后，又相继拉高了90年代中后期初中的招生人数。表现在图1—2中就是初中招生人数之曲线超过小学招生人数之曲线，直到2011年小学招生人数再次超过初中招生人数，这是80年代中后期生育率回升过程中出生的同期群体在2005年之后进入婚育旺盛期的结果。

但大学的扩招却拉动了普通高中招生人数的增长。自1990年到1997年，中国高等教育招生人数从60.9万人增加到100万人，仅仅增加了不到40万人。但1999年就在1998年招生108.4万人的基础上增加到159.7万人——一年净增51.3万人。2000年又比1999年增加了60.9万人，达到220.6万人的规模。为缓解劳动力市场的就业压力，提升全民素质，2002年招生超过320万人，2004年超过447万人，2006年达到546万人，2008年达到607万人，2014年超过721万人，2018年达到791万人。因为高中招生人数的增速赶不上高等教育招生人数的增速，这使2018年的高中招生人数与大学招生人数极其相近，仅仅为793万人。在计划生育使小学招生人数下降的过程中，初中招生人数也下降了。随后必然出现高中招生人数的下降结果。

各级教育的发展，迅速提升了中国的人力资本。从表1—1可以看出，在1964年，在每10万人口中，"大专及以上"人口只有416人，在1982年第三次人口普查时上升到615人，到2000年第五次人口普查时上升到3611人，到2010年第六次人口普查时上升到8930人。但扩张最迅速的是"高中（中专）"阶段文化程度的人口。1964年第二次人口普查时，该文化程度的人口每10万人中只有1319人，在1982年第三次人口普查时上升到6779人，到1990年第四次人口普查时上升到8039人，到2010年第六次人口普查时上升到14032人。就劳动力人口而言，其素质也有很大提高。从2006年到2016年，全国劳动力人口的平均受教育程度从6.1年上升到了10.0年，城镇劳动力人口的平均受教育程度从7.8年上升到了11.2年，乡村从5.6年上升到了8.5年。2017年，根据中国社会科学院GSS全国抽样调查得到的数据，在1990—2000年出生的人口中，获得"大专及以上"文化程度教育的人数所占百分比已经达到47.1%。这就是说，在1990年之后出生的人口中，获得大学文凭的人口所占百分比已经接近50%。

表1—1　　　　第二次到第六次人口普查每10万人口中不同文化程度的人口

单位：人

	1964年	1982年	1990年	2000年	2010年
大专及以上	416	615	1422	3611	8930
高中（中专）	1319	6779	8039	11146	14032
初中	4680	17892	23344	33961	38788
小学	28330	35237	37057	35701	26779

注：第一次人口普查相关数据缺失。其他数据来源于2012年《中国统计年鉴》表3—6。

表1—2　　　　不同出生年龄段人口的文化程度

单位：%

出生年龄段	初中及以下	高中（中专）	大专及以上	总计
1949—1959	82.10	14.20	3.70	100.00
1960—1969	74.60	19.30	6.10	100.00
1970—1979	69.70	16.50	13.80	100.00
1980—1989	52.20	19.50	28.30	100.00
1990—2000	26.20	26.70	47.10	100.00

数据来源：2017年中国社会科学院社会学研究所GSS全国抽样调查。

2018年，中国高等教育毛入学率已经达到48.1%，高于中高收入国家平均水平。经过新中国70多年来的发展，中国已经从精英教育阶段转变到大众教育阶段。未来的改革趋势，就是将九年义务制教育向下扩展到幼儿园阶段，向上扩展到高中阶段。① 如果将免费教育能够向下和向上拓展三年，并免除学费和杂费，那么，未来中国人口的平均受教育水平将得到更快提升。

三　快速城镇化与就业结构的改善

新中国成立初期，城市经济恢复之后需要一定劳动力的支持，所以出现了一波比较快速的城镇化浪潮。1949年城镇人口占总人口的比重仅仅为10.64%，但在1960年即达到了19.75%，几乎达到每年1%的增长速度。改革开放之后，商品经济的启动、农业生产技术的进步、农村剩余劳动力向城镇大规模流动，加速了中国的城镇化步伐，以常住人口统计的城镇化水平连年上升，1980年达到19.39%，1990年达到26.41%，2000年达到了36.2%，2010年达到49.95%。党的十八大以来，中国的城镇化水平稳步推进，每年年均提高1.2%以上。这使8000多万农业转移人口成为城镇居民，将中国这个世界第一人口大国的城镇化率提升到新水平，在2018年达到了59.6%左右。

户籍制度在不同城市进行了大幅度改革。在因城施策、分类推进的政策配置中，除超大城市和特大城市外，其他城市已放开了落户限制。但农民对农村土地的热爱，以及市场经济与农村社会建设的完善，却逐步淡化了城市户籍的吸引力。实践证明，只要城镇化过程能够坚持基本公共服务的均等化原则，只要乡村振兴能够坚持以农民为中心的理念，农民就不会看重非农户口的价值。现在，反倒是非农户口的

---

① 2006年修订的义务教育法明确规定，实施义务教育，不收学费、杂费。当年即免除农村义务教育阶段学生的学费和杂费，2007年免除了教科书费。2008年免除了城市义务教育阶段的学费和杂费，免除享受城市居民最低生活保障家庭义务教育阶段学生的教科书费。

人很难将自己的户口再转变为农业户口。从这里可以看出，改革开放已经给中国社会带来了天翻地覆的变化。

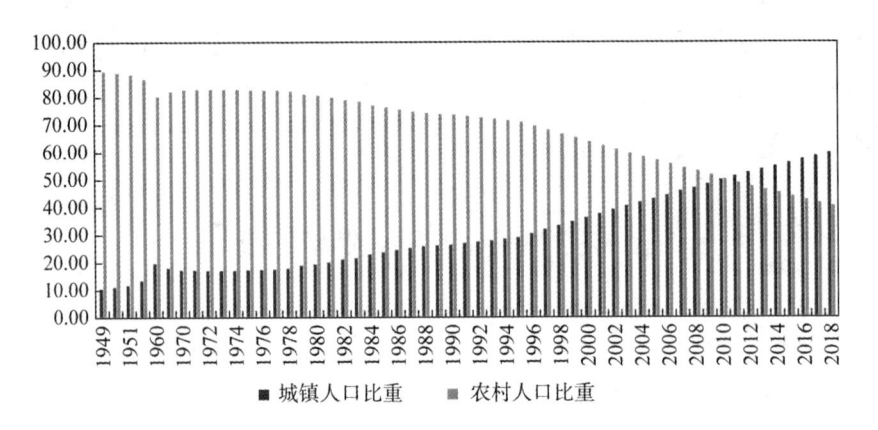

图1—3 新中国成立70年城镇化趋势（单位:%）

城镇化的有力推进，将中国迅速从村落社会转型为都市社会，从定居生活转型为迁居生活，从自给半自给社会转型为市场社会，从传统社会转变为现代社会。这是继文艺复兴之后对人类最有进步影响意义的大事件。城镇化不仅意味着农村人口向城市的转移过程，而且还深刻体现着城市生产方式与生活方式对农村的积极影响过程。中国的城镇化，不但比较顺利解决了农村转移人口的就业问题，使1亿多离土不离乡的农民工就近就地就业，使1.8亿离土又离乡的农民工在城市就业，而且还顺利解决了随迁子女的入学问题。尽管在超大城市和特大城市这一问题解决得还不够理想，但在"两为主"（教育经费以财政投入为主，上学学位以公立学校为主）的制度规约下，绝大多数流动人口的子女有学可上。

可携带可转移的社会保险政策，也使农民工获得了与城市劳动力一样的权利，能够在流入地参加城镇企业职工社会保险。按照当前的发展速度，中国常住人口的城镇化率，会在2035年超过75%，在2050年达到80%。在全面建成现代化强国、实现中华民族伟大复兴的同时，将中国绝大多数人口转化为城镇人口，不仅极大提升了中国人民的日常生活质量,提升了中国人民生活的获得感、幸福感、安全感,同时也为世界人口的城镇化做出了重大贡献。

以农民工为主的城镇化浪潮,同时也迅速改变了中国人的就业结构,使劳动力人口首先从以农业为主的第一产业流动到第二产业,然后再向第三产业转变。在新中国成立之初,第一产业从业人员所占比重高达83.5%,第二产业从业人员仅仅占7.4%,第三产业从业人员只占9.1%。重工业优先发展战略的实施和中国从农业国向工业国的转变,迅速提升了第二产业从业人员的比重。到1978年改革开放时,第一产业从业人员降低到70.5%,第二产业从业人员增加到17.3%,第三产业从业人员增加到12.2%。

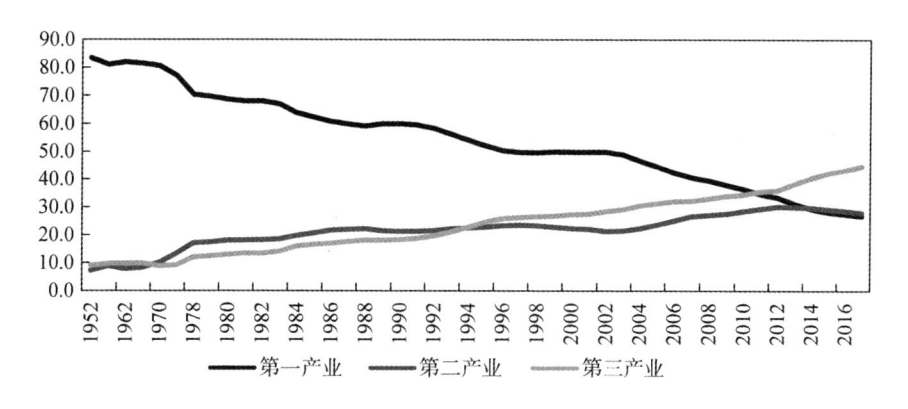

图1—4 新中国成立70年按三次产业分的就业人员数(单位:%)

尽管如此,农业从业人员的比重还是特别大。但1990年温饱型小康实现时,第一产业从业人员的比重就降低到60.1%,第二产业从业人员的比重就上升到21.4%,第三产业从业人员的比重上升到18.5%。所以,在20世纪60年代中期以前,第三产业从业人员所占比重高于第二产业。但在60年代中期以后到1994年,第二产业从业人员所占比重才又一次超过了第三产业人员所占比重。1994年,第三产业从业人员占比达到23%,再一次超过第二产业从业人员的占比。此后,在经济快速发展的拉动下,第三产业从业人员占比增速长期快于第二产业，加强了后工业化的特征。这是新中国成立70多年来发生的最重大的就业结构变迁。在市场经济与社会发展的要求下，服务业的需求开始越来越大，中国在转变为制造业大国之后，开始向服务业大国转型。

另外，农业现代化程度的进一步加强，土地流转与化肥的使用，使第一产业从业人员逐步减少。如果说第一代农民工主要以男性为主的话，那么，第二代农民工中女性的需求量大增。这强化了城市对农村年轻劳动力的拉力。所以，在中国粮食产量不断上升的过程中，第一产业从业人员直线下降。2000年，第一产业从业人员降低到50%左右，第二产业从业人员占比达到22.5%，第三产业从业人员占比上升到27.5%。2010年，第一产业从业人员占比降低到36.7%，第二产业从业人员占比上升到28.7%，第三产业从业人员占比达到34.6%。

2011年，中国三次产业结构中从业人员占比发生第二次根本性的转变——第一产业从业人员占比降低到第二位；第二产业从业人员占比上升；第三产业从业人员占比达到35.7%，成为吸纳劳动力最多的部门。这是第三产业从业人员占比对第一产业的完美超越。

2015年，中国劳动力从业人员占比的结构又发生了第三次划时代意义的转变——第一产业从业人员占比第一次低于第二产业，降低到28.3%，第三产业从业人员占比上升到42.4%。2018年第一产业从业人员的比重继续降低到26.1%，第二产业从业人员占比降低到27.6%，而第三产业从业人员占比却上升到46.3%。在第三次转型中，继第一产业从业人员的下降后，第二产业从业人员也开始显著下降。

未来，伴随农业科学技术的进步、农业机器人和农业机械化水平的提升，第一产业从业人员的比重还会逐步降低。当最后一代传统农业告别历史，现代农业的特征还将进一步强化。在这一趋势的稳定演化中，在第二产业从业人员保持一定比重的同时，未来最大的变化，将是第三产业从业人员占比与数量的继续攀升。后工业化浪潮将最终把这个社会带入到机器与人结合的"人机社会"。"人机社会"的最大特征，就是人的劳动时间的缩短、劳动强度的减轻，但同时也是人的闲暇和消费时间的延长。因此，"人机社会"对服务业的需求还会大大拓展。

四　阶层结构优化与消费结构升级

自有文字记载历史以来，中国长期呈现为典型的农业社会特征。不管是北方还是南方，不管是东部还是中西部，农业就业人口中的绝大多数依靠土地进行生产和再生产并借此取得生活资料，甚至在基本依靠畜力与人力的结合并在靠天吃饭的气候约束中生存繁衍。在整个社会中，农民阶层是主要社会阶层。

新中国成立 70 多年来，中国完成了初期工业化和中期工业化。不管是在工业化初期还是工业化中期，从事工业劳动的人总能够比从事农业劳动的人获得更多的收入。由收入结构决定的消费结构激励农民力图"跳出农门"以改变生活方式。

改革开放之后，以人民公社、生产大队、生产队三级所有制为基础的经济与组织方式，被乡镇、行政村和自然村所代替，家庭联产承包责任制也广泛推广。为解决收入问题，农民先是在农闲时节外出打工，接着便驻扎在进入的城市长期务工成为农民工，社会流动的渠道逐渐被打开。农民在通过自己进城务工经商将自己转变为工人阶层的同时，也通过教育子女参加高考将其转变为"国家干部""非体力劳动者"或"白领劳动者"。这使改革开放之后中国农民的社会流动在工人化和中产化两条道路上并行，并在 2000 年前后成为名正言顺的"产业工人"。中国的社会流动与阶层结构转型，与西方相比具有重大区别，西方是先迎来工业化并形成庞大的工人阶层，然后在第二次世界大战之后才迎来后工业化，并将工人阶层转变为"中产阶层"。作为第一人口大国的中国，在大城市后工业化的同时，也在很多省会城市（即"二线"城市）延续着工业化——表现为同一时空中的工业化与后工业化，也表现为同一时空中大规模的、并行不悖的工人化和中产化。

正因为存在并行不悖的双重社会转型特征，中国才比较好地解决了社会转型中存在的不均衡发展问题，并在一定程度上化解了转型过程带来的社会风险，维持了社会的长期稳定与和谐发展。具有渐进改革特征的制度变迁，通过增量改革造就了体制外的经济与社会，形成了庞大的个体企业和乡镇企业，形成对农村剩余劳动力的吸纳态势，以价格双轨制为体制内和体制外建构不同的改革逻辑，最后完成市场经济的一体化改造。尽管国有企业的改革还没有完成，但民营企业却以市场化的草根性增长成功占有了重要份额，成为解决劳动力就业的主战场。现在，民营经济贡献了50%的税收、创造了60%以上的GDP、占有了技术创新和新产品70%的比重、解决了80%以上的城镇就业，对新增就业的贡献也超过90%。

中国经济的多元发展格局，顺利完成了各个历史时期提出的现代化任务。1990年实现了温饱型小康目标，2000年实现了总体性小康目标。在不断发展中，提出了"建设小康社会"的宏伟目标。后来将"建设小康社会"调整为"全面建设小康社会"，现在又继续设计为"全面建成小康社会"，并努力在经济、政治、文化、社会和生态文明等方面持续发力，使民生建设登上了一个又一个台阶。

中国社会的工业化和后工业化过程，迅速提升了城乡居民的人均可支配收入。1978年全国居民人均年可支配收入为171.2元，其中城镇居民为343.4元、农村居民为133.6元。2000年全国居民年人均可支配收入为3721.3元，其中城镇居民为6255.7元，农村居民为2282.1元。2010年全国居民人均年可支配收入为12519.5元，其中城镇居民为18779.1元，农村居民为6272.4元。到2018年，全国居民人均可支配收入增长到28228元，其中城镇居民为39251元，农村居民为14617元。

全国居民人均可支配收入的提升，为贫困人口的脱贫创造了条件，使贫困人口的数量迅速下降。在改革开放之初，依照2010年2300元不变价格确定的贫困线,则1978年农村贫困人口占农村总人口的比重高达97.5%,但到2000年就下降到49.8%,到2010年下降到17.2%,到2018年下降到1.7%。而农村中的贫困人口也下降到差不多只有1660万人。按照联合国2%的贫困发生率标准,可以说在2010年2300元不变价格的基础上,已经消除了绝对贫困现象。

精准扶贫工作的重大成功,缩小了社会阶层中的贫困人口规模,支持了社会阶层的优化过程。[①] 这使中国的阶级阶层结构发生了重大变化。2017年,根据中国社会科学院GSS的抽样调查,在劳动力人口中,雇主阶层所占比重为4.93%,老中产阶层所占比重为12.83%,新中产阶层所占比重为23.22%,工人阶层所占比重为31.28%,农民阶层所占比重为27.74%。从这里可以看出,中国不再是一个以农民阶层为主的国家了。中国传统产业工人阶层的队伍,也开始在后工业化过程中收缩。自改革开放以来,中国中产阶层的规模一直处于持续性扩大之中。在国内与国际形势影响下,中国加速了"去工业化"的步伐,这使一部分本应在工人阶层的就业人员,进入了中产阶层的队伍。

表1—3　　　　　中国阶级阶层结构的变化趋势　　　　　单位:%

年份	雇主阶层	老中产阶层	新中产阶层	工人阶层	农民阶层
2001	2.78	10.61	6.79	28.21	51.61
2006	3.15	11.51	7.77	30.61	46.96
2010	3.66	11.03	12.68	36.21	36.52
2013	4.62	13.85	15.74	35.46	30.32
2015	5.06	14.92	18.91	32.79	28.32
2017	4.93	12.83	23.22	31.28	27.74

数据来源:2017年中国社会科学院GSS调查。

---

① 李强、杨艳文:《"十二五"期间我国社会发展、社会建设与社会学研究的创新之路》,《社会学研究》2016年第2期。

中国阶层结构的变化,使中国从以农民阶层为主的国家向以中产阶层为主的国家转变。在这个转变过程中,消费结构也随之迅速升级。[①]

在传统农业社会,农民阶层主要以粮食作物为生,而且经常处于饥饿威胁之中。即使在新中国成立很长时间之后,由于农业部门的低效率,加上农业生产过程中科学技术水平与机械化程度低下,粮食单产量长期低迷。

改革只有率先在农村取得重大突破,提升粮食产量,增加市场供给,满足全国人民生活之所需,票据制度才能伴随市场商品的丰富而走出历史舞台。家庭联产承包责任制实施之后,调动了农民生产的积极性,粮食产量连年提高,由此也解决了中国长期"吃不饱"的问题。因为农民余粮增多,市场供给增加,城市市场上计划外面粉供应充足。经济特区深圳率先闯关,取消粮票限制,利用价格机制调控粮油分配,形成了市场需求制。1991年广东省和海南省实行粮食购销同价改革,1992年推行到全国,同年10月在党的十四大确立了社会主义市场经济体制,全国放开粮油及副食品价格,以市场机制调配供给,粮票逐渐退出历史,停止使用。自此开始,中国的消费品市场逐渐从短缺阶段过渡到充足供应阶段。

经过70年的发展,中产阶层占比迅速提高之后,中国人的消费结构也发生了重大变化。从恩格尔系数上来说,在1949年,中国城市高达60.2%,农村会更高。1956年完成了农业、手工业和资本主义工商业的社会主义改造。1957年城市的恩格尔系数为58.4%,但农村仍然高达65.7%。1979年城市为57.5%,农村为64.0%。2000年,城市下降到39.2%,农村下降到49.1%。到2010年,城市为37.5%,农村为41.1%。进入新时代,中国人的生活水平迅速提升,在所有家庭消费中,用于食品方面开支所占的比重越来越低,全国的恩格尔系数

---

① 张翼:《社会新常态:后工业化社会和中产化社会的来临》,《江苏社会科学》2016年第1期。

已经降低到28.4%，这说明中国人已经将主要的消费转移到教育、卫生保健、旅游、住房改善等方面。中国人的消费方式，也已经从模仿型排浪式向个性化和多样化、定制化转变。

从食品消费结构来说，对农村居民而言，1978年改革开放之初的粮食消费量较高，为家庭人均247.8公斤，1980年增长到257.2公斤，1990年增长到262公斤。在此之后开始下降，到1998年下降到249.3公斤。但对猪肉、羊肉的消费量却逐步增加，1978年农村家庭平均每人的年消费量为5.7公斤，1990年增长到11.3公斤，1998年增长到13.2公斤。进入新时代之后，2013年农村居民家庭年人均粮食消费量降低到178.5公斤，2017年又降低到154.6公斤。与此同时，农村居民家庭人均年肉类消费量在2013年增加到22.4公斤（包括猪肉、羊肉和牛肉），2017年增长到23.6公斤。

同样在食品消费中，对于城镇居民家庭来说，年粮食人均消费量迅速下降，比如说，其在1985年人均粮食消费量为134.7公斤，1990年下降到130.7公斤。但对猪肉的消费量却呈现先增长后降低的态势，1985年家庭人均消费量为16.7公斤，到1990年增长到18.5公斤，到1998年降低到15.9公斤。牛羊肉的人均年消费量，在1985年仅仅为2公斤左右，到1998年增长到3.34公斤。肉类年人均消费量持续增长，2013年增长到28.5公斤，2017年增长到29.2公斤。

从耐用消费品上来说，不管是在农村还是在城镇，在2000年之前国家统计局的统计中，仍然将"呢大衣""毛毯""大衣柜""沙发""自行车""缝纫机"等作为家庭耐用消费品。比如说，在农村家庭中，每百户家庭的自行车拥有量，1978年仅30.1辆，1998年上升到137.2辆；每百户的缝纫机拥有量，1978年为19.8台，到1998年增长到65.8台；每百户的手表拥有量，1978年为27.4只，1998年增长到154.6只。在城镇每百户家庭中，1998年的呢大衣拥有量为191.1件，毛毯拥有量为142.1条，大衣柜为84.0台，沙发为207.6个，自行车为182.1辆，缝纫机为56台。进入新时代之后，不管是在农村地区还是在城镇地区，自行车、缝纫机和手表等所谓的"老三大件"都已经充分满足了需要，已经很难将这些消费品当作耐用消费品了。对于"新三大件"，即家用汽车、移动电话和计算机来说，在农村每百户家庭中，2013年家用汽车拥有量为9.9辆，到2017年增长到19.3辆；2013年移动电话拥有量为199.5部，到2017年增长到246.1部；2013年计算机拥有量为20台，2017年增长到29.2台。在城镇每百户家庭中，2013年家用汽车拥有量为22.3辆，到2017年增长到37.5辆；2013年移动电话拥有量为206.1部，到2017年增长到235.4部；2013年计算机拥有量为71.5台，到2017年增长到80.8台。

从家庭住房面积上来说，1978年中国农村人均住房面积仅8.1平方米，到1990年增长到17.8平方米，到1998年增长到23.7平方米。城镇人均住房面积，1978年仅为3.6平方米，到1990年增长到6.7平方米，到1998年增长到9.3平方米。2016年，农村居民人均住房面积已经达到45.8平方米，城镇居民人均住房面积达到36.6平方米。到2018年，城镇居民人均住房建筑面积达到39平方米，农村人均住房建筑面积达到47.3平方米。[①]

中产阶层的扩大与消费市场的扩展，提升了整个社会的生活水平，改善了营养条件，减轻了劳动强度，提升了人均预期寿命。中国的发展模式，也从投资驱动阶段过渡到消费牵引阶段。中国有史以来第一次进入中产化社会，中国有史以来第一次进入网络社会，中国也有史以来第一次进入汽车社会。这些变迁，将对中国未来的社会发展造成极其强烈的影响。

中国的发展，将在未来不可避免地进入到人口负债阶段。老龄化水平开始迅速提高。2018年年底，60岁及以上老年人口占总人口的比重已经达到17.9%，65岁及以上老年人口占总人口的比重已经提高到11.9%。中国在经历"十三五时期"较缓的老龄化速度之后会进入到"十四五时期"的快速老龄化阶段。青年的结婚率开始降低，离婚率

---

① 2000年之后中国房地产以建筑面积计算。2018年数据来自于国家统计局发布的《建筑业持续快速发展、城乡面貌显著改善——新中国成立70周年经济社会发展成就系列报告之十》。

仍然在上升。初婚年龄连年推迟，降低了人口出生率。现在，只有将人口大国转变为人力资源强国，才能缓解劳动力老化的影响。依靠廉价劳动力、廉价土地、充足供应的资本以及以牺牲环境为代价的、以劳动密集型产业为基础的发展模式已经式微。在进入中高收入阶段之后，唯有迅速发展科技、开发自动化设备与人工智能、加强机器人的生产与再生产，才能最终解决未来劳动力的短缺问题。中国仍然是教育招生大国，但却不是教育强国。只有继续加大教育体制和科研体制改革，调动教师和科研人员的积极性，才能促进生产力发展，尽快形成创新力量。另外，中国在进入后工业化阶段之后，原有工业基地开始衰落，北方老工业基地很难形成新产能，地区发展差距似有继续拉大之势，这在一定程度上延缓了新旧动能的更替。城镇化率在日益增长，可城镇化质量还需进一步改善。[①]

参考文献

[1] 张翼：《社会新常态：后工业化社会与中产化社会的来临》，《江苏社会科学》2016年第1期。

[2] 李强、杨艳文：《"十二五"期间我国社会发展、社会建设与社会学研究的创新之路》，《社会学研究》2016年第2期。

[3] 徐延辉、龚紫钰：《社会质量与农民工的市民化》，《经济学家》2019年第7期。

[4] 王元、孔伟艳：《未来30年中国社会发展趋势及促进共享发展的建议》，《宏观经济研究》2019年第5期。

---

① 徐延辉、龚紫钰：《社会质量与农民工的市民化》，《经济学家》2019年第7期。

第二章

中国经济结构分析与预测

娄 峰

中国社会科学院数量经济与技术经济研究所研究员

本文在分析中国经济潜在增长主要影响因素及其传导机制的基础上,构建一个中国宏观经济系统模型,对中国未来17年的经济规模及其结构进行了预测分析。研究结果表明：基准情景中,在2016—2020年、2021—2025年、2025—2030年和2031—2035年期间,中国国内生产总值（GDP）平均增长率将分别达到6.5%、5.6%、4.9%和4.5%。2035年,中国GDP规模将比2000年增长10.06倍,比2010年增长3.99倍,比2020年增长2.02倍,未来17年,投资拉动型经济增长将逐步向消费需求拉动转变。面对国际发达国家经济发展长期低迷和国内劳动力红利逐步消失的情况,中国需要加强研究和教育投资,依靠科技创新,提高全要素生产率,促进技术进步和制造业转型升级,同时需要加快税收体制改革,减税降费,切实降低企业宏观税负,促进社会经济和谐发展。

一 引言

改革开放以来,中国经济经历了年均10%左右的高速增长,取得了巨大的成功。然而国际金融危机后,在发达经济体低速增长的国际环境和国内新增劳动力减少、资源环境约束日益突出的背景下，中国经济未来的增长潜力如何？

从文献上看，不少中外学者对中国经济中长期的发展趋势进行了预测，既有2009年之前进行的预测，也有国际金融危机发生后进行的预测。

Jianwu He和Louis Kuijs（2007）采用DRC-CGE模型，对2045年的中国经济的增长趋势进行了预测，研究结果表明，中国GDP年均增长率在2005—2015年、2015—2025年、2025—2035年及2035—2045年间分别为8.3%、6.7%、5.6%和4.6%。Louis Kuijs（2009）认为尽管资本深化的规模依然可观，但由于劳动力人口和全要素生产率的增速将会放慢，因此未来十年潜在GDP的增长速度可能会放缓，并利用柯布—道格拉斯生产函数计算出中国经济2015年增速为7.7%、2020年为6.7%。李善同和刘云中等（2011）利用DRC-CGE模型，分别按照基准情景、发展方式转变较快情景以及风险情景等三种方案对2030年中国经济发展的前景进行了预测，在基准情景的各项设定下，该研究预计"十二五"期间中国经济年均增长7.9%，2016—2020年期间年均增长7.0%，2021—2030年期间年均增长6.2%。

Goldman Sachs（2009）通过计算，认为中国的GDP增长率在2011—2020年、2021—2030年、2031—2040年和2041—2050年间预计分别在7.9%、5.7%、4.4%和3.6%左右。

HSBC（2012）基于调整了的巴罗增长模型（Barro's growth model），预测中国经济未来四十年可以保持大于5%的年均增长率，其中2010—2020年间GDP年均增长率约为6.7%，2020—2030年间约为5.5%，2030—2040年间约为4.4%，2040—2050年间约为4.1%。该报告预计2010—2020年间中国的经济增长在全世界基本是最快的，但自2020年以后，亚洲不少国家增长率会开始陆续超过中国。

PwC（2008）基于包括资本存量、劳动力、人力资本和技术进步四个要素的增长模型，预计2007—2050年基于美元市场汇率中国经济年平均增长率在6.8%左右；按购买力平价则在4.7%左右，并且指出由于受到人口快速老龄化等因素的影响，尽管中国在接下来的几年中是金砖国家（BRICS）中经济增长速度最快的经济体，但其增长率很可能在2015年就会被印度超越，2025年被巴西超越。

Dwight H. Perkins 和 Thomas G. Rawski（2008）认为，2005—2025年间中国经济仍能保持快速的增长，预计实际GDP的年均增长率大约在6%—8%之间，其中2005—2015年要实现这一速度的经济增长是比较符合现实的，但2015—2020年间要达到这个增长速度的上限几乎是不太可能的。

胡鞍钢（2008）认为，中国GDP在2006年至2020年期间的年均增长率在7.5%—8.5%之间，未来经济的增长率主要取决于全要素生产率的增长率，如果全要素生产率能够保持过去30年的增长速度，那么中国GDP增长率可能会超过8.5%。胡鞍钢、鄢一龙、魏星（2011）进一步给出了对中国在2010—2030年间经济增长趋势的估计：中国GDP潜在增长率区间为5.9%—9.2%，在考虑这些生态变化约束以及中国政府不再追求高速增长而是追求增长质量的变化时，2011—2030年间的适度增长率为7.5%，其中2011—2020年约为8.0%，2020—2030年约为7.0%。

王小鲁、樊纲、刘鹏（2018）利用一个扩展的卢卡斯式增长模型，对经济增长率按贡献因素进行了分解，预测在"基于各贡献要素当前变动趋势的延伸"情景下，2008—2020年间中国经济平均增长率约为6.7%；在"做了三个乐观但可能性很大的假设"（包括未来的政治体制改革抑制了政府管理成本的膨胀，教育条件的改善提高了人力资本的增长率以及通过一系列政策抑制了消费率下降的趋势）的情景下，2008—2020年间的中国经济增长仍能继续保持在9.3%左右。

Ping Zhang 和 Hongmiao Wang（2011）在综合考虑能源和环境等自然约束以及城市化和技术进步这两个驱动中国经济发展的主要因素之后，基于中国总量生产函数对2010—2030年间中国的经济增长进行了预测，结果显示，2010—2015年间中国经济的潜在年平均增长率在9.5%左右，2016—2020年间在7.3%左右，2020—2030年间在5.8%

左右。

从以上的文献中可以看出，国际金融危机发生之后进行预测的不少学者和机构趋于谨慎，认为未来15年中国经济年均增速将低于8%，例如HSBC（2012）预测2010—2020年间中国经济增长率约为6.7%，2020—2030年间约为5.5%。但也有部分学者表达了对中国未来经济发展的乐观态度，认为中国未来几十年的增长速度仍能保持在8%左右。诺贝尔经济学奖获得者Robert W. Fogel（2007）认为受未来30年产业间人口转移以及教育对劳动力素质提高等因素的影响，预计中国在2000—2040年间GDP的年均增长率为8.4%左右，高于美国、欧盟、日本、印度等经济体。同为诺贝尔经济学奖获得者的Robert A. Mundell（来自《证券时报》）在2008年第四届东北亚经济合作论坛上发表讲话时指出，中国GDP年均增长率在未来15年到20年间应该不会低于8%，到2030年也仍会实现较快增长，到2050年将成为世界第一大经济体。林毅夫于2011年11月在旧金山发表讲话时表明，中国经济有潜力在未来的20年仍保持8%的增长速度。林毅夫表示中国大陆2008年的水平相当于1951年时的日本、1977年的韩国以及1975年的台湾地区，而日韩以及中国台湾地区在之后20年分别维持了9.2%、7.6%和8.3%的高速增长。同时林毅夫也表示要实现经济高速增长这一目标，中国也面临着解决经济和社会失衡等问题的挑战。姚洋（2012）在为英国《金融时报》的撰稿中也表示，通过与其他国家的横向比较，综合考虑中国青年受教育水平的提高、研发投入的加大等因素，2020年前中国经济增长维持在8%水平上的可能性较大。

综上所述，不同学者和机构对中国经济中长期发展趋势的预测结果差别较大，尚未在中国中长期潜在经济增长率上达成共识。本文考虑多种影响潜在产出的因素及其传导机制，运用中国宏观经济计量模型（2018版），基于较新的数据，对中国经济中长期的经济增长进行进一步的研究，并与国际主要发达经济体及其他金砖国家未来的经济增长进行对比，以期能够为勾勒出未来中国经济增长的路径提供参考。

二 1979—2018 年中国经济增长的分解

根据索洛经济增长模型对 1979—2018 年期间我国经济增长的动力进行分解（见表 2—1）可以看出：如果将资本、劳动力和全要素生产率作为经济增长的主要投入要素，过去 39 年时间里我国的经济增长主要依靠投资驱动（平均贡献率为 61.8%）；劳动力对经济增长的贡献率从 1979—1985 年的 12.30% 下降至 2011—2018 年的 1.29%；全要素生产率对经济增长的贡献率从 1979—1985 年的 39.70% 上升至 2001—2005 年的 60.40%，然后逐步下滑到 2011—2018 年的 45.50%。

表 2—1　　　　　　　　1979—2018 年中国经济增长分解

年份	GDP增速	实际利用的资本存量			劳动力			全要素生产率		
		增长率	贡献率	贡献度	增长率	贡献率	贡献度	增长率	贡献率	贡献度
1979—1985	10.20	8.92	48.00	4.90	3.29	12.30	1.25	4.22	39.70	4.05
1986—1995	10.00	9.48	47.60	4.76	3.21	12.20	1.22	3.74	40.20	4.02
1996—2000	8.60	10.23	58.80	5.06	2.18	9.60	0.83	2.32	31.60	2.72
2001—2005	9.80	8.61	37.30	3.66	0.73	2.30	0.23	5.16	60.40	5.92
2006—2010	11.20	12.07	47.40	5.31	0.42	0.80	0.09	4.53	51.80	5.80
2011—2018	7.80	9.18	53.20	4.15	0.37	1.29	0.10	2.94	45.50	3.55
1979—2018	9.70	10.02	48.70	4.72	1.78	6.40	0.62	3.78	44.90	4.36

从表 2—1 可以看出，我国三大生产要素的一个基本发展趋势是实际利用的资本存量基本上保持在一个较高的增长水平之上。我国的劳动力增长率逐步下降，这与我国劳动年龄人口份额下降、人口抚养比上升相关。技术进步被认为是长期经济增长的重要源泉之一，可以看到，我国的全要素生产率（TFP）增长率在 1979—1985 年期间总体处于相对较高水平；在 2001—2005 年期间我国的 TFP 增长率达到最高水平，对经济增长的贡献度为 5.92 个百分点；2006 年以后我国的 TFP 增长率总体呈现下降趋势。其中主要的原因是我国产能过剩加剧，与

国际技术前沿面的差距正在缩小，利用外资势头趋缓，通过吸收引进国际先进技术所带来的边际收益正在不断降低。

为明确全要素生产率的内部驱动要素，我们依据相关理论，构建模型把全要素生产率进一步细分为以下六个子要素：

1. 城镇化与劳动力转移

由于中国第一产业的劳动生产率远低于第二产业和第三产业的劳动生产率，随着城镇化比率的不断提高，越来越多的农村人口会不断转移到城镇，从第一产业转向第三产业或第二产业，这样，总的劳动生产率将趋向于继续提高。从表2—2可以看出，1995—2018年间，城镇化与劳动力转移对全要素生产率增长率的贡献度平均高达1.44个百分点，在六个子要素中贡献度最大。

表2—2　　　　各项因素对TFP增长率的贡献度（百分点）

年份	全要素生产率	城镇化与劳动力转移	国外技术溢出效应	科技进步	人力资本提高	市场化进程	其他影响因素
1995—2000	2.75	0.63	0.42	0.42	0.32	0.36	0.60
2001—2005	5.92	1.83	1.71	1.09	0.95	0.50	-0.16
2006—2010	5.80	1.74	1.39	1.28	1.20	0.53	-0.34
2011—2018	3.55	1.57	0.95	1.54	1.36	0.32	-2.19
1995—2018	4.36	1.44	1.12	1.08	0.96	0.43	-0.67

注：由于表中部分指标在1994年以前没有统计数据，因此从1995年开始计算。

2. 国外技术溢出效应

一般来说，外商直接投资在给东道国提供资金的同时，也会从管理和技术两个途径对东道国产生正向技术溢出效应，从而提高东道国的全要素生产率，外商直接投资占比越大，这种正向溢出效应往往越强。本报告用该变量来反映国外资本技术对中国全要素生产率的影响。从表2—2可以看出，1995—2018年期间，国外技术溢出效应对全要素生产率的平均贡献度为1.12个百分点，在六个子要素中贡献度居第二位。从不同阶段看，国外技术溢出效应对全要素生产率的平均贡献度呈现先升后降的发展趋势，其中加入世贸组织效应显著的2001—2005年间，其贡献度达到1.71个百分点的最高峰。但由于我国与国际技术前沿的差距在不断缩小，通过学习、模仿和吸收国际先进技术和管理所带来的边际收益正在逐步降低。2011—2018年国外技术溢出效应对全要素生产率的贡献度已经下降到0.95个百分点，比2001—2005年大幅下降了0.76个百分点。

3. 科技进步

该变量用研究与开发（R&D）经费实际增长率进行衡量，根据经济学理论，研发投入是提高全要素生产率的有效途径，是影响全要素生产率的显著因素。表2—2显示，科技进步对全要素生产率的贡献率总体呈现不断上升的趋势，尤其是最近几年上升幅度有所增加，这可能与我国近几年来加强研发投入和自主创新财税政策激励有关。1995—2018年期间，科技进步对全要素生产率的贡献度平均为1.08个百分点。

4. 人力资本提高

根据人力资本理论，教育是提高劳动者素质、增加人力资本的有效途径，一个国家的教育经费在GDP中的比重往往可以衡量该国的人力资本的强弱，而人力资本是影响生产率的显著因素。由于中国缺乏家庭教育经费的可靠数据，因此，本文用财政性教育经费在GDP中的比重来衡量教育对全要素生产率的影响。表2—2显示，人力资本提高对全要素生产率的贡献度呈现不断增强的趋势，尤其是2011年以来，贡献度有所加大。这与我国近几年大幅提高教育经费投入有关。

5. 市场化进程

根据经济学理论，一般来说，市场化程度越高，越能促进市场竞争，从而加快提高技术进步和企业管理水平，这有利于全要素生产率的提高和发展。本报告采用樊纲、王小鲁、朱恒鹏著的《中国市场化指数：各地区市场化相对进程2018年报告》中的中国分省市场化指数数据，并估算得到全国市场化总指数。其指标主要包括政府与市场的关系、非国有经济发展、产品市场发育、要素市场发育、中介组织发育和法律 5 个子指数,用于衡量各省、自治区、直辖市市场化改革的深度和广度,基本概括了市场化进程的各个主要方面。从表 2—2 可以看出,1995—2018 年期间,随着市场化改革红利的逐渐减弱,市场化进程对全要素生产率的贡献度逐渐走低,平均贡献度约为 0.43 个百分点。

6. 其他影响因素

其他影响因素是除了上述五种子要素以外的其他影响因素,比如规模经济效应、管理经营能力、国外专利使用和技术购买、资源约束等因素。表 2—2 显示,其他影响因素对我国全要素生产率的贡献度时正时负。值得注意的是,近几年其他影响因素对我国全要素生产率的贡献度负向影响较大,这可能与我国产能过剩严重导致规模经济效应下降、生产要素成本过高导致企业经营盈利能力减弱、投资回报率显著下降等因素有关。

三 影响潜在产出的因素及其传导机制

本文在中国社会科学院数量经济与技术经济研究所中国宏观经济年度模型(2018 年版)基础上,对模型进行更新和补充,新版年度模型(2018 年版)有如下特点:(1)运用协整理论,对各方程进行协整性检验,并引入误差修正模型,使得模型不仅包含经济理论中隐含的长期均衡关系,而且能反映变量短期波动之间的关系;(2)以"LS – LM 模型 + 菲利浦斯曲线"为理论核心,依次估计了中国消费需求函数、投资需求函数、净出口需求函数和货币需求函数,建立中国的 LS – LM 模型,并通过拟合附加预期的菲利普斯曲线建立了卢卡斯函数形式的中国 AS 函数模型,同时引入中国税收政策规则和货币供应规则,从而将总供给和总需求有效地联系起来;(3)纳入了更多金融变量,加入反映中央银行和商业银行的行为方程,加强了金融模块,有助于对货币政策的作用与效果进行分析;(4)适当减少了虚拟变量,尽量避免方程拟合过程中自由度的损失。

新版年度模型（2018年版）分为产出、价格、收入和消费、政府税收、金融、贸易、人口和就业、投资及储蓄共九大模块，包括253个变量、216个方程、37个外生变量。

为了对2035年的中国经济进行预测，我们对一些重要经济变量如全要素生产率（TFP）、城镇化、国际经济环境等因素对潜在经济增长影响的传导机制设定如下。

1. 全要素生产率与潜在经济增长

本文首先应用道格拉斯生产函数估计中国GDP方程，该方程为生产函数的长期均衡方程：

$$ECMGDPC = LOG（GDPC/LTOT）- TFP - 0.71518 * LOG（TKC/LTOT）$$

其中，GDPC为中国国内生产总值（1980年不变价），LTOT为就业总人数，TKC为资本存量（1980年不变价），ECMGDPC为协整误差调整项。

根据经济学理论，以GDP历史值减去GDP长期均衡估计方程中非常数项部分，即可得到全要素生产率（TFP）的时间序列，然后以此序列为被解释变量，构造出全要素生产率方程：

$$TFP = -2.4691 + 0.0042 * RUB + 0.0654 * RRD + 0.0081 * RFDI + 0.1028 * RFEDUGDP$$
$$（-15.9705）（2.6312）（1.5816）（2.5680）（4.0532）$$

$$（R^2 = 0.9036，AIC = -3.5121，DW = 1.7392）$$

其中，TFP为全要素生产率，RUB为城镇化率，即城镇人口与总人口的比值，该解释变量的经济内涵在于：根据中国实际情况，第一产业的单位劳动生产率低于第二产业和第三产业的单位劳动生产率，因此，随着城镇化比率的不断提高，越来越多的农村人口会不断转移到城镇，从第一产业转向第二产业和第三产业，这样，总的劳动生产率将会提高；RRD为研究与试验发展（R&D）经费实际增长率，根据经济学理论，研发投入是提高全要素生产率的有效途径，是影响全要素生产率的显著因素；RFDI为外商直接投资在总投资中的比重，一般说来，外商直接投资在给东道国提供资金的同时，也会从管理和技术两个途径对东道国产生"正向溢出"效应，从而提高东道国的全要素生产率,外商直接投资占比越大,这种"正向溢出"往往越强,因此,本文用该变量反映国外资本技术对中国全要素生产率的影响;RFEDUGDP 为财政性教育经费在 GDP 中的比重,根据人力资本理论,教育是提高劳动者素质、增加人力资本的有效途径,一个国家的教育经费在 GDP 中的比重往往可以衡量该国的人力资本的强弱,而人力资本是影响生产率的显著因素。由于中国缺乏家庭教育经费的可靠数据,因此,本文用财政性教育经费在 GDP 中的比重来衡量教育对全要素生产率的影响。

应用协整理论,构造出生产函数的短期波动方程,也即生产函数的协整方程:

D(LOG(GDPC/LTOT)) = 0.4849 * D(LOG(GDPC(-1)/LTOT(-1))) - 0.1594 * D(LOG(GDPC(-2)/LTOT(-2)))

(5.1153)　　　　　　　　　　　　　　(-2.9506)

+1.0112 * D(LOG(TKC/LTOT)) - 0.5649 * D(LOG(TKC(-1)/LTOT(-1))) - 0.1203 * ECMGDPC(-1)

(18.6228)　　　　　　　(-5.9477)　　　　　　　　　　(-2.2069)

(R^2 = 0.9279, AIC = -5.8249, DW = 1.9787)

2. 城镇化、国际经济环境对投资、资本存量及潜在产出的影响机制

国内城镇化进程将对中国未来的基础设施投资产生重要影响,国际经济变化将首先影响中国的出口进而影响中国制造业的投资。综合起来看,国内城镇化进程与国际经济变化都将影响中国的投资、资本形成与资本存量,进而影响中国的中长期潜在经济增长。我们将投资方程设定如下:

LOG(INVC) = 1.1752 * LOG(INVC(-1)) - 0.6273 * LOG(INVC(-2)) + 0.2332 * LOG(LOANTT)

(7.5230)　　　　　　(-3.9399)　　　　　　(1.9983)

+ 0.0277 * RUB + 0.0816 * LOG(WGDPC)

(2.7722)　　(1.9445)

(R^2 = 0.9958, AIC = -2.1841, DW = 2.1049)

其中,INVC 为固定资产投资(1980 年不变价),INVC(-1) 和 INVC(-2) 分别为固定资产投资的滞后一期和滞后二期,反映固定资产投资的惯性。RUB 是城镇化率，由于近年来和今后相当一段时期，中国的城镇化率将不断提高，而城镇化的推进，势必需要道路、交通、房地产等设施的大量投资和建设，城镇化水平将直接影响未来中国固定资产投资。另外，随着全球经济一体化的快速进展，世界经济对中国经济的影响越来越显著，世界经济通过影响中国的出口，从而影响中国制造业的投资，投资方程中加入世界 GDP 变量（WGDPC，1980 年不变价）以反映这种国际因素对中国投资影响的传导机制。国内城镇化、国际经济状况通过影响投资从而影响资本存量，并影响长期潜在经济增长。LOANTT 为贷款总额，是国内城镇化、国际经济状况之外影响投资的变量。

四　中国经济预测和分析

1. 2019—2035 年中国经济总量预测和分析

假定 2019 年至 2035 年期间，国际环境和国内社会、经济和政治保持稳定，不发生重大技术革命，在此前提下，运用上述经济增长机制和中国经济年度模型（2018 版），中国宏观经济预测主要结果如下：

（1）2019—2035 年我国国内生产总值（GDP）年均增长 5.4%（详见表 2—3），这期间经济增长总趋势是逐渐缓慢下降。其中，2016—2020 年，GDP 平均增长率仍将保持在 6.5% 左右，到 2020 年，我国 GDP 总量将达到 82.2 万亿元（2010 年价），人均达到 5.9 万元（2010 年价）。经过 20 世纪 80 年代、90 年代以及 21 世纪的前 20 年总共 40 年的高速增长，我国经济实力已经得到大大加强，庞大的经济规模将成为影响世界经济发展的重要力量。因此，2016—2020 年这一时期既是我国未来经济发展的黄金时期，也是我国经济发展进行量的积累的完成时期。

（2）2021—2035 年，GDP 平均增长率将保持 5.0% 左右（其中 2021—2025 年平均为 5.6%，2026—2030 年平均为 4.9%，2031—2035

年平均为4.5%）。这一时期是我国经济总量的积累到质的改善的重要转折时期，注重经济发展的高技术成分，注重经济和环境的相互协调发展，注重社会经济生活的质量等等，将成为衡量和判别经济发展的新标准，到2035年，GDP总量将超过290万亿元（现价），人均接近12.2万元（2010年价）。该阶段突出特点是经济的质的调整，大量采用高新技术，提高经济发展的质量是本阶段的主要目标和动力。

表2—3　　　　　　2019—2035年中国经济总量预测

区间	GDP平均增长率（%）	期末GDP总量（万亿元，2010年不变价）	期末人均GDP（万元/人，2010年不变价）	期末人均GDP（美元，当年价）
"十三五"2016—2020年	6.5	1054977	59047	10177
"十四五"2021—2025年	5.6	1528683	76967	13742
2026—2030年	4.9	2146049	97670	18557
2031—2035年	4.5	2940260	122095	24771
2016—2035年	5.4			

2. 2019—2035年期间我国经济结构变化预测分析

（1）三次产业结构变化的预测和分析

在2019—2035年间，国民经济的增长不仅表现在总量的迅速增加，而且也将使得经济结构发生重大改变，这是由于三次产业的增长速度不同，经长期积累从量变到质变的结果。未来三次产业变化趋势大致说明如下（表2—4所示）：①从增速上看，三次产业的增长速度均呈现逐年下降的发展趋势，第三产业的增长率最高，第一产业的增长率最低，第二产业的增长率居中；②三次产业的结构将随着三次产业增长速度的不同而出现根本性的变化。2012年第一、第二、第三产业占GDP的比重分别为10.1%、45.3%和44.6%,第二产业在国民经济中占比最高,略微超过第三产业占比;自从2015年开始,第三产业将以50.2%的份额首次超过经济总量的一半,成为我国国民经济的第一大产业,到2035年左右,其份额已经超过62.8%,在国民经济中处于绝对支配的地位。2031—2035年期间,三次产业的平均比重分别为4.3%、32.9%和62.8%。

表2—4　　　　2016—2035年三次产业增长速度与结构变化情况

区间	三次产业增加值增长率（%）			三次产业产业结构期末值（%）		
	第一产业	第二产业	第三产业	第一产业	第二产业	第三产业
2016—2020年	3.0	5.8	7.2	7.3	37.4	55.3
2021—2025年	2.7	5.4	6.5	6.0	35.3	58.7
2026—2030年	2.5	5.0	5.6	5.0	34.0	61.0
2031—2035年	2.4	4.5	4.9	4.3	32.9	62.8

（2）经济结构（投资、消费、净出口）变化的分析和预测

在市场经济条件下,消费结构对经济的发展和产业结构的变化起着举足轻重的作用。根据预测,2019—2035年我国城镇居民消费比重将逐渐增加,而农村居民消费和政府消费比重将逐渐减少,农村居民消费比重减少的主要原因在于2019—2035年内,随着城镇化的大力发展,大量农村居民会逐渐转变成城镇居民,农村总人数会逐渐减少;政府消费比重下降的主要原因在于其消费增长率小于城镇居民消费增长率,其相对占比逐渐下降,详见表2—5。

表2—5　　　　2019—2035年我国消费及其结构变化表

年份	农村居民消费（亿元,当年价）	城镇居民消费（亿元,当年价）	政府消费（亿元,当年价）	农村居民消费在总消费中的占比,%	城镇居民消费在总消费中的占比,%	政府消费在总消费中的占比,%
2019	65914	295365	113872	13.9	62.2	24.0

续表

年份	农村居民消费（亿元，当年价）	城镇居民消费（亿元，当年价）	政府消费（亿元，当年价）	农村居民消费在总消费中的占比,%	城镇居民消费在总消费中的占比,%	政府消费在总消费中的占比,%
2020	69550	321477	124160	13.5	62.4	24.1
2025	90472	497984	184811	11.7	64.4	23.9
2030	125012	744389	267071	11	65.5	23.5
2035	172847	1096343	376971	10.5	66.6	22.9

显然，2019—2035年内，以投资拉动型为主的经济增长将逐步发生改变，以市场需求为导向的消费增长，尤其是居民消费增长将成为未来我国经济增长和发展的主要动力；投资增长将更多地取决于市场需求，取决于经济发展状况，这无疑有利于改善投资结构，有利于提高投资效率，详见表2—6。

表2—6　　　2019—2035年期间经济增长动力及其结构变化表

年份	最终消费（亿元，当年价）	资本形成（亿元，当年价）	净出口（亿元，当年价）	最终消费在GDP中的占比,%	资本形成在GDP中的占比,%	净出口在GDP中的占比,%
2019	523487	412662	24781	54.8	42.9	2.6
2020	566651	446810	23222	54.7	43.1	2.2
2025	881314	639762	16814	57.3	41.6	1.1
2030	1322359	887252	2987	59.8	40.1	0.1
2035	1932198	1202254	-19804	62.0	38.6	-0.6

注：资本形成指投入产出表中的"固定资产投资"项+"存货增加"；净出口为货物和服务净出口，不包括投入产出表中的"误差调整项"；支出法GDP=资本形成投资+最终消费+净出口。

根据预测，2020年中国不变价GDP规模将为2000年的5.0倍、2010年的2.0倍；2035年中国不变价GDP规模将为2020年的3.6倍、2030年的2.1倍；2035年第三产业增加值在GDP中的比重将上升到

62.8%，第三产业在国民经济中处于绝对主体地位。

世界银行从 1987 年开始，按人均国民总收入（与人均 GDP 大致相当）对世界各国经济发展水平进行分组。通常把世界各国分成四组，即低收入国家、中等偏下收入国家、中等偏上收入国家和高收入国家。按世界银行公布的数据，2012 年的国际最新收入分组标准为：人均国民收入低于 1035 美元为低收入国家，1035—4086 美元之间为中等偏下收入国家，4086—12615 美元之间为中等偏上收入国家，高于 12615 美元为高收入国家。但以上标准不是固定不变的，而是随着经济的发展不断进行调整，高收入国家门槛年均上调幅度为 200—300 美元左右。

如果 2019—2035 年期间改革开放能够取得预期的决定性进展，预计中国将于 2030—2035 年迈出中等国家陷阱，并进入高收入国家行列。

预计 2019—2035 年期间，人民币兑美元基本保持稳定，但总体趋势呈现缓慢贬值的发展趋势。假定 2019—2035 年间人民币兑美元年均贬值幅度按照 1.5% 匡算，即 2035 年 1 美元兑换人民币 10.4 元，则 2035 年中国人均 GDP 将达到 2.47 万美元，将显著高于全球人均 GDP 水平，达到高收入国家中的非 OECD 成员国的人均 GDP 水平。

五　不断开辟发展新境界

世界经济的历史发展证明，当一个经济体迅速发展并达到一定水平时，经济增长速度就会减慢，然后才进入逐步下降的阶段。中国仍然是一个发展中国家，其技术进步和创新仍有改进的余地，消费和投资不断增长的市场需求依然巨大。

第一，深化行政体制改革，积极转变政府职能。推进供给侧结构性改革和鼓励企业发展的关键是改善政府与市场的关系。由于传统的生产供给侧因素（如资本和劳动力）已呈现出规模回报率下降的趋势，未来的可持续发展必须依靠新的因素，如 TFP（如信息技术、创新、管理等），以及这些新的生产、培育、发展和增长因素。因此，政府应深化行政体制改革，通过建立合法的"权力清单"和"负面清单"，确定政府和市场的合理界限，最大限度地减少政府对微观市场交易的干预，提高政府的决策水平。这也有助于加大进一步开放市场的力度，激发市场活力，让市场在资源配置中发挥决定性作用，建立价格形成机制，以及成本和投资回报的传导机制。市场发展应通过"广泛的创业和创新"来促进私人资本市场的发展，防止将市场置于权力的笼中。

第二，打破垄断，改革国有企业制度，创造一个全面公平的市场竞争环境。历史证明，垄断不仅引起了市场矛盾的激化、阻碍了产业转型升级，而且制约了技术和管理水平的创新，导致了社会冲突，阻碍了资源配置效率和社会财富效率的公平分配。目前，严重阻碍我国企业研发主动性的因素有两个，即企业的短期行为和企业的垄断。由于研发需要大量的资金和人力进行长期投资（虽然回报不是很明显），追求企业的短期利益对研发没有优势，另外，当一些企业从政府给予的特殊垄断地位中受益时，他们没有足够的动力进行再创新、搜索和开发。这种追求短期利益、过度依赖政府垄断和补贴的做法，是我国大多数国有企业普遍存在的问题。但是，由于我国仍有一些垄断和产业政策，电信等服务领域对民营资本开放程度不高，民营资本难以进入竞争领域。这既不利于资源的有效配置，也不利于私人资本的发展。不公平的制度严重阻碍了生产者的技术创新和激励机制。因此，我国应改革国有企业，改变干部任用制度，消除垄断，引入竞争，消除短期行为，进一步放开高端制造业和现代服务业的市场准入，这对我国国有企业的发展具有重要意义。无论中国能否通过自主研发摆脱中等收入陷阱，成为创新型经济体，一个关键因素是国有企业的改革和推进。因此，在社会管理方面，中国政府应通过引入相关法律法规，完善和加快建立统一、开放、竞争、有序的市场体系，创造公平竞争的市场环境，打破地域分割和行业垄断，从而更好地促进公平竞争。

第三，增强自主创新能力，促进科技创新。核心技术是现代企业竞争的基础。只有注重科学研究和技术创新，才能建设自己的核心技术，提高自己的长期生存和发展能力。当前，我国经济发展正处于产业结构调整升级的关键时期，迫切需要加强和依靠科技创新。一方面，以"供给侧结构性改革"为发展契机，制定和完善相关规划和产业政策，促进企业自主创新、自主能力和自主意愿。另一方面，中国政府应建立和完善风险投资机制创新，促进风险投资机构的发展，确保企业科技研发管理制度的改革和优化，鼓励和引导企业加强研发投资，提高企业的创新意识。加强知识产权保护，完善科技成果和产业支持体系、技术服务体系、技术产权交易体系，建立企业知识产权外部环境保护体系，确保企业知识产权的可持续发展。

第四，中国应以质量和效率代替数量，提高资本利用率和劳动生产率。在加大科技创新力度，努力提高全要素生产率的同时，"供给侧结构性改革"也需要提高传统生产资源的供给效率和供给质量。我国人口短期增长趋势不会改变，要适应现代经济发展的需要，就必须加大人力资本投资，促进人口红利对人员变动的影响，提高劳动力素质，以抵消负面影响。通过构建统一的劳动力市场，中国需要优化劳动力配置，降低劳动力成本，促进城乡、企业、大学、科研机构、技术性体育之间的劳动力有序流动。最后，中国应加快实施金融部门改革，提高资本使用效率，改变金融企业垄断谋利现象，加快构建与实体经济相协调的多层次金融体系、组织体系多元化和立体化服务体系。有效整合多种金融资源，加快金融市场改革，有效降低成本。

参考文献

[1] Chow, Gregory C. (2005), *China's Economic Transformation*, Beijing: China Renmin University Press (in Chinese).

[2] Coopers, Price Waterhouse (2008), *The World in* 2050——*Be-*

yond the BRICs: a broader look at emerging market growth prospects*, Pricewaterhouse Coopers LLP economics group.

[3] Fogel, Robert W. (2007), *Capitalism and Democracy in 2040: Forecasts and Speculations*, NBER Working Paper.

[4] HSBC (2012), *The World in 2050*, HSBC Global Research.

[5] Hu, Angang (2008), "The Quantitative evaluation and Prospects of China's Economic Power (1980—2020)", *Journal of Literature, History and Philosophy*, No. 1 (in Chinese).

[6] Hu, Angang, Yan, Yilong & Wei, Xing (2011), *China 2030: to Common Wealth*, Beijing: China Renmin University Press (in Chinese).

[7] Kuijs, Louis (2009), *China through 2020——A Macroeconomic Scenario*, World Bank China Office Research Working Paper, No. 9.

[8] Li, Shantong & Liu, Yunzhong (2011), *Chinese Economy 2030*, Beijing: Economic Science Press (in Chinese).

[9] Lin, Justin Yifu (Dec. 30, 2011), China to maintain 8% growth rate for over 20 years, *China Business Network*, Retrieved July 26, 2012, from the World Wide Web: http://www.yicai.com/news/2011/11/1236989.html (in Chinese).

[10] Perkins, Dwight H. and Rawski, Thomas G. (2008), "Forecasting China's Economic Growth to 2025", *China Business Review*, 35, No. 6, 34 - 9, 45 N/D.

[11] Research Group of Input - Output Table of China 2007 (2011), China's Economic Prospect for the 12th Five - Year Plan Period and 2030, *Statistical Research*, Vol. 28, No. 1 (in Chinese).

[12] Robert A. Mundell (Sept. 4, 2008), "Chinese Economy Can Grow Fast to 2030", *Securities Times* (in Chinese).

[13] Sachs, Goldman (2009), "The Long-Term Outlook for the BRICs and N - 11 Post Crisis", *Global Economics Paper*, No 192.

[14] The World Bank, DRC of the State Council the PRC (2012), China 2030, Building a Modern, Harmonious, and Creative High – Income Society, the World Bank.

[15] Wang, Xiaolu, Fan, Gang & Liu, Peng (2018), "Transformation of Growth Pattern and Growth Sustainability in China", *Economic Research Journal*, No. 1 (in Chinese).

[16] Yao, Yang (July 4, 2012), "Why I'm still Bullish on China's Growth", *FT Chinese*, Retrieved July 24, 2012, from the World Wide Web: http://www.ftchinese.com/story/001045324 (in Chinese).

[17] Zhang, Ping & Wang, Hongmiao (2011), "China's Economic Outlook into 2030: Transformation, Simulation and Policy Suggestions", *China Economist*, Vol. 6, No. 4.

[18] Zhang, Jun, Wu, Guiying, & Zhang, Jipeng (2016), "The Estimation of China's Provincial Capital Stock: 1952—2000", *Economic Research Journal*, No. 10 (in Chinese).

第二篇

格鲁吉亚经济社会发展

第三章

格鲁吉亚经济发展与前景

欧阳向英

中国社会科学院世界经济与政治研究所研究员

格鲁吉亚地处欧亚接合部，素有"欧亚十字路口"的美誉，是欧亚历史、文化融合和经贸往来的交汇处，更是古代丝绸之路和现代欧亚交通走廊必经之地，地理位置和战略地位重要。发展中格关系，以"一带一路"推动两国发展战略对接，促进民心相通，实现共同繁荣，符合两国长期利益和根本利益。

一 格鲁吉亚基本情况和中格关系

格鲁吉亚是个经济发展综合条件不错的国家，营商环境综合得分在前苏联地区居于前列。2000年，格鲁吉亚加入世界贸易组织（WTO）。当前，格鲁吉亚是世界贸易政策最自由的国家之一，包括自由的对外贸易制度和通关程序、较低的进口关税及较少的非关税管制措施。格鲁吉亚也是世界上税种最少的单一税制国家之一，总税赋水平16.5%，在美国《福布斯》杂志评选的全球税赋指数中排名第四。根据世界银行发布的《2017年营商环境报告》，格鲁吉亚在全球190个国家中综合排名第16位。

中国是最早承认格鲁吉亚独立并与之建交的国家之一。自1992年建交以来，中格各领域合作富有成果，先后签订了中格经济贸易协定、关于鼓励和相互保护投资的协定等一系列合作协定。2017年，中格签署自由贸易协定，并于2018年1月1日正式生效。根据《协定》，双方对绝大多数货物贸易产品相互取消了关税，对众多服务部门相互作出了高质量的市场开放承诺，并完善了知识产权、环境保护、电子商务和竞争等规则。签署《协定》的目的是为两国企业营造更加开放、便利和稳定的营商环境，全面提升两国务实合作水平，为实现共同繁荣打下基础。那么，我们就来审视一下，协定签署后的效果如何，以及未来应该努力的方向。

二 中格自由贸易协定的初步效果评估

中格自由贸易协定的签署对发展两国经贸关系是一件大事。协定内容十分详细，关税清单覆盖的商品种类非常之多。格鲁吉亚对中国96.5%的产品实施零关税，所覆盖的商品贸易额约占格鲁吉亚自中国进口总额的99.6%；中国对格鲁吉亚93.9%的产品实现零关税，所覆盖的商品贸易额约占中国自格鲁吉亚进口总额的93.8%。中国对格鲁吉亚的减让表共含7000多项，绝大多数商品为A类，即自协定生效之日起取消关税并约束为0，格鲁吉亚对中国的减让表分类更细一些，同样也是绝大多数商品取消关税并约束为0。

中格自由贸易协定签署后，中格经济联系得到进一步加强。目前，中国是格鲁吉亚第五大贸易伙伴、第三大出口市场、第二大葡萄酒出口市场及主要的投资来源国。格鲁吉亚主要出口商品为汽车、铁合金、铜矿砂等，主要进口商品为石油产品、汽车、药品等。2018年，格鲁吉亚对中国出口总额约2亿美元，自中国进口约8.3亿美元。双边贸易额首次超过了10亿美元，中格追赶格土、格俄的步伐在加快。

然而，我们也应看到，2018年是中格自贸协定生效的第一年。相比2017年中格双边贸易额9.34亿美元，2018年有所增长，但增长的数额却并不多。2019年1—7月格鲁吉亚对中国出口总额与2018年同期相比下降37%，从中国进口额也有微弱下降，约2%。对比中国与周边国家的贸易额，如2018年中越贸易额超过1000亿美元，2018年中哈贸易额为100多亿美元（受国际原材料价格下跌的影响而缩水，2013年已超过200亿美元），2019年上半年中国与阿塞拜疆双边贸易额就已达到去年全年总额，约13亿美元，2018年中国与吉尔吉斯斯坦双边贸易额也有15亿美元。从两国长远利益出发，应该查找制约双边贸易发展的主要因素，并逐一化解，推动中格"一带一路"的深入对接。

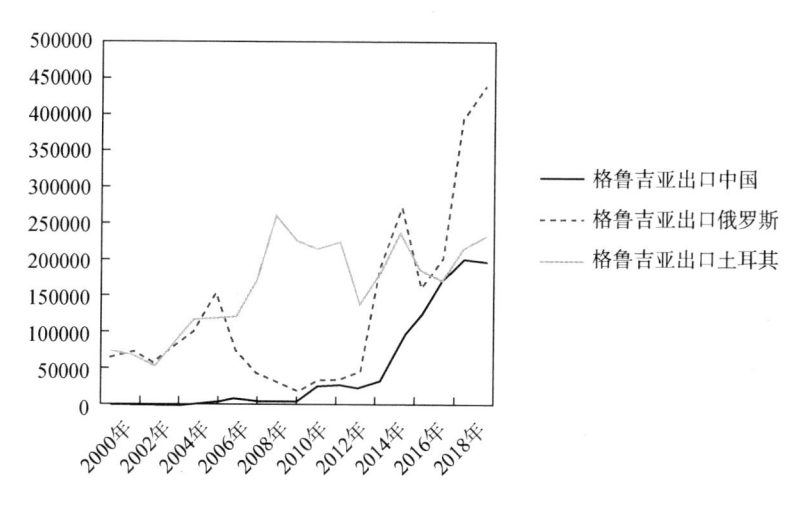

图3—1 格鲁吉亚对主要贸易伙伴的出口额（2000—2018），单位：千美元

数据来源：格鲁吉亚统计局。作者自制。

表3—1　　　　　2017—2019年格对主要国家出口　　　　单位：千美元

	格出口中	格出口俄	格出口土
2017年	201701.71	396672.04	216673.60
2018年	198034.35	437303.54	232714.29
2019年（截止7月）	66493.72	303813.42	135103.65

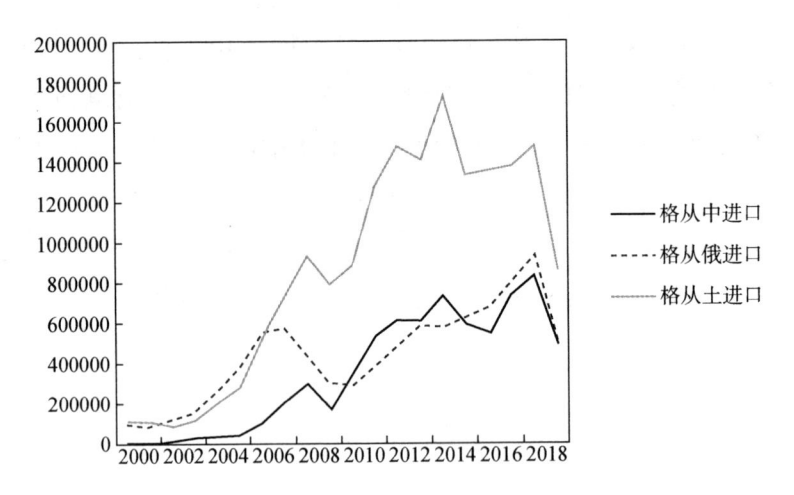

图3—2　格鲁吉亚从主要贸易伙伴的进口额（2000—2019），单位：千美元

数据来源：格鲁吉亚统计局。2019年数据为1—7月。作者自制。

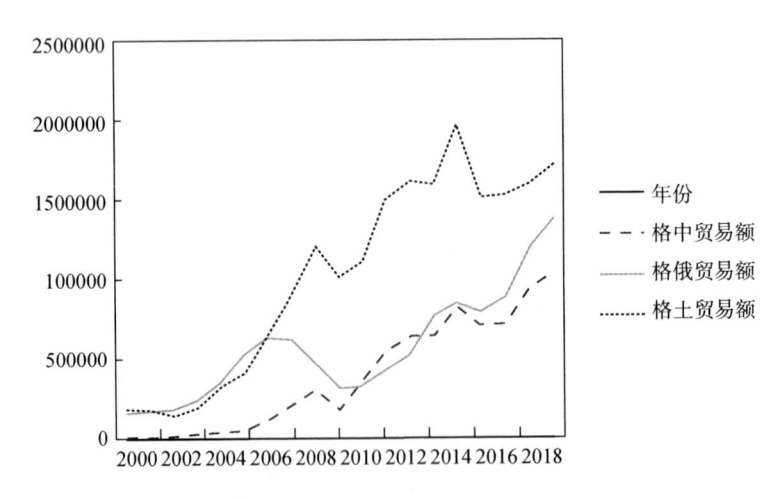

图3—3　格鲁吉亚和主要贸易伙伴的双边贸易额（2000—2018），单位：千美元

数据来源：格鲁吉亚统计局。作者自制。

表3—2　　格鲁吉亚和主要贸易伙伴双边贸易额（2016—2018）单位：百万美元

年份	格中贸易额	格俄贸易额	格土贸易额
2016	721	882	1527
2017	934	1184	1590
2018	1032	1373	1706

数据来源：格鲁吉亚统计局。作者自制。

三　主要制约因素

制约中格经贸关系进一步发展的因素是多重的，其中客观原因居多，有待两国市场进一步培育和完善。

首先，和平稳定的大环境至关重要。近年来，格鲁吉亚奉行务实外交和平衡外交，充分发挥经济外交的作用，着力恢复发展与欧亚国家的关系，包括坚持对俄务实政策，积极发展与欧盟的关系。对华关系也是格鲁吉亚重点发展的方向之一，中格经贸增长也受益于此。然而，受前些年俄格战争和周边地区局部冲突的影响，一些企业界人士对到格鲁吉亚投资和经商持谨慎态度。尽管中华人民共和国商务部在2016年就发布，格鲁吉亚已成为继新加坡和韩国后世界上最安全的三个国家之一，但这主要指的是国内治安情况。坦率地说，格鲁吉亚是否会卷入大国地缘政治冲突，还是一些大公司担心的问题。

其次，受经济体量和人口总数的制约。2016年，格GDP为143亿美元，同比增长2.7%，人均GDP为3853美元。2017年，格GDP为151.6亿美元，同比增长5%。截至2019年1月，格鲁吉亚人口总数为372万。372万是个什么概念呢？对比一下中国城市的人口数量：北京常住人口是2000多万，天津常住人口1500多万，济南常住人口800多万，大同常住人口300多万。所以，372万人口大约是中国一个地级市的人口规模。人均GDP在5000美元以下，反映出格鲁吉亚的经济结构仍以低附加值产品为主，而人口数量则与消费需求和消费能力密切相关。格鲁吉亚是个非常美丽的国家，号称"上帝的后花园"，加速工业化和实行生育鼓励政策有可能改变这一面貌。促进发展关键在于改变格鲁吉亚的经济结构，将格鲁吉亚纳入到依靠高新技术实现快速发展的轨道上来，但这是非常不容易的一件事情。

再次，缺乏名牌产品的带动效应。中格间大量的商品相互免税，照理说双边贸易额应该很快增长，然而实际上并没有。中国人熟悉的格鲁吉亚产品还是红酒，而格鲁吉亚知道中国的产品应该是华为手机。缺乏名牌产品的带动效应，会直接影响双边贸易额。其实，中国早已成为世界上种类最齐全的制造业大国，机械电子、成套设备、通信和汽车等各个产业都有物美价廉的好产品。格鲁吉亚的矿泉水和手工制品也很不错，需进一步加大品牌运营和推广高度。

最后，格鲁吉亚应更加重视中国市场。中国是世界上最大的市场，无论对高端机器设备，还是对普通农产品，消化能力都很强。格鲁吉亚应高度重视对中国市场的开发，同时对中国企业加大开放力度，让自由贸易协定真正结出硕果。

四 未来发展与合作方向

未来，双方应在以下领域重点开展合作：

一是基础设施建设。近年来，中国在基础设施建设上取得的成就举世瞩目。中国的道路、桥梁、隧道、通信、供水、供电等项目遍地开花，出口到全世界多个国家。为什么中国能够输出基础设施建设？是因为中国的基础设施建设有几个特点，一是建设速度快，二是完成质量好，三是报价较低，四是经验丰富。改革开放以来，中国的基础设施已经不仅在大中城市实现了现代化，就连在小城市和小乡镇也实现了换代升级。格鲁吉亚中部克维什赫季的9号隧道全长超过8.3公里，是格鲁吉亚有史以来建设的最长铁路隧道，也是格鲁吉亚铁路现代化项目的咽喉工程。从2011年开始，中铁二十三局建设者群策群力，大胆采用了数十项国际先进施工工艺，克服了围岩沉降、可燃气体释放、岩层破碎等工程技术难题,确保了隧道按时高标准贯通。同样的事情也发生在塔吉克斯坦、巴基斯坦、乌克兰、白俄罗斯、马尔代夫、匈牙利等多个国家。这些项目顺利完工,交付使用,得到当地政府和人民的好评。克维什赫季隧道也成为海外基础设施建设的示范性窗口,并推动中格在基础设施领域的进一步合作。

二是发展数字经济。格鲁吉亚是比较重视发展数字经济的,2016年在全球创新指数排名中居于第64位。近年来,中国的数字经济快速发展,经济规模、专利申请、技术运用等综合实力居于世界第二位,仅次于美国。所以,数字经济也是这几年欧盟、俄罗斯和中亚等国与中国的发展重点。格鲁吉亚也应加入到这一进程中,用互联网和移动通信技术改造原有工业企业和农产品销售系统,为本国经济发展服务。

三是推进金融合作。中格在金融合作领域已有一定成果。2017年9月21日,中国出口信用保险公司(以下简称"中国信保")与格鲁吉亚伙伴基金签署《中国出口信用保险公司与格鲁吉亚伙伴基金框架合作协议》。根据协议,双方将在基础设施、能源、机械、物流、电力、大型成套设备等领域建立融资保险合作平台。金融助力加实业对接,将成为中格合作的有效模式。

四是大力发展旅游业。格鲁吉亚有较为丰富的旅游资源,而中国国内有旺盛的旅游需求。2018年内地公民出境游人次近1.5亿。中国人均出游(包括国内游)每年五次,这种发展速度是非常快的。对于中国游客而言,尽管格鲁吉亚不是传统的热门旅游目的地,但2018年上半年却强势上榜,热度涨幅达到216%。这不是单一现象,同期塞尔维亚和土耳其的新增游客量涨幅分别达到383%和265%,摩洛哥、俄罗斯和冰岛紧随其后。游客在欧洲和大洋洲的人均花费明显高于亚洲国家,约为10000元。旅游业绿色、可持续、门槛低,格鲁吉亚可开发文化节和美食节等特色旅游项目,吸引更多中国游客的到来。

随着"一带一路"项目总体顺利推进,中格有待在更高水平上实现战略对接,真正做到"我中有你,你中有我",促进两国共同繁荣,造福两国人民。

第四章

格鲁吉亚社会发展：现状与展望

马 峰

中国社会科学院社会发展战略研究院副研究员

格鲁吉亚是"一带一路"沿线重要国家，也是"一带"与"一路"的重要交汇地。格鲁吉亚是欧亚地区目前唯一与中国签署自贸协定的国家，中格两国和两国人民携手共建"一带一路"，不但为两国和两国人民带来了发展的新契机，也使得两国人民从古丝绸之路时代缔造的友谊得以传承。自格鲁吉亚独立以来，格鲁吉亚社会发展事业实现了历史性转变，由高度集中的计划经济体制向市场经济体制转轨。我国提出的"一带一路"倡议为格鲁吉亚扭转经济颓势提供了宝贵的机遇，格鲁吉亚亦视丝绸之路经济带为其实现战略发展目标的重要依托。目前格鲁吉亚的社会形势相对稳定，与周边国家关系良好。虽然格鲁吉亚仍将不可避免地受到西方与俄罗斯对峙以及政党纷争影响，但这些不利因素不足以动摇格参与丝绸之路建设的决心。[①]

从国家基本概况经济方面来看，近年来格鲁吉亚经济社会发展稳定，"格鲁吉亚梦想"联盟于 2012 年 10 月在格举行议会选举，为

---

① 吕萍：《格鲁吉亚与丝绸之路经济带倡议：态度、意义与前景》，《俄罗斯学刊》2016 年第 5 期，第 75 页。

格鲁吉亚的稳定发展提供了重要的政治前提。"2018年6月,克维里卡什维利宣布辞职,巴赫塔泽接任总理。目前,'格鲁吉亚梦想—民主格鲁吉亚'党掌控格议会、政府与地方,保持一定控局能力。"① 这为格鲁吉亚社会发展提供了较为有利的政治条件。格鲁吉亚社会发展的现实与前景,对于我们更深入了解处于不同发展阶段的"一带一路"沿线国家和地区的社会发展阶段和社会发展政策具有重要的意义,有利于我们更深入地聚焦双边合作,让成果惠及两国人民。

一 中国与格鲁吉亚:"一带一路"倡议促进社会发展的新纽带

格鲁吉亚是较早支持和参与"一带一路"倡议的国家,并将涉及国家发展的经济、社会领域发展与倡议对接。"我国提出'一带一路'倡议后,多数沿线国家予以响应和支持,格鲁吉亚的态度尤其积极。相较一些国家的纠结、疑虑和质疑,格鲁吉亚则是张开怀抱对这一倡议表示了热烈的欢迎。格鲁吉亚领导人在不同场合多次明确强调丝绸之路经济带的重要性及其对格国家经济发展的意义,表达了强烈的参与意愿,并为推动其发展采取了各种具体措施,以实际行动表明了对丝绸之路经济带建设的坚定支持。"② 2019年5月24日,格鲁吉亚总统祖拉比什维利在第比利斯总统府会见国务委员兼外交部长王毅时指出:"近年来,格方致力于实现国家稳定,经济发展,同邻国改善发展关系,取得了积极进展。格方愿继续积极参与共建'一带一路',以此为契机推进同中方在各领域的合作,促进地区互联互通,助力格加快国家发展建设,成为连接欧亚大陆的通道

---

① 《格鲁吉亚国家概况》(更新时间:2019年1月),外交部:https://www.fmprc.gov.cn/web/gjhdq_676201/gj_676203/yz_676205/1206_676476/1206x0_676478/。

② 吕萍:《格鲁吉亚与丝绸之路经济带倡议:态度、意义与前景》,《俄罗斯学刊》2016年第5期,第76页。

和走廊"。① 同日，时任格鲁吉亚总理巴赫塔泽在第比利斯会见国务委员兼外交部长王毅时表示："格方是最早支持'一带一路'倡议的国家之一"，"格方愿通过共建'一带一路'加强同中方在经贸、投资、交通、基础设施建设、高新科技等领域的合作，促进格中及地区各国的互联互通和民心相通。"② 此外，2019年7月1日，在来华参加夏季达沃斯论坛之际，时任格鲁吉亚总理巴赫塔泽与国务院总理李克强会见时，进一步表示："格中高层交往密切，政治互信牢固。格方积极支持共建'一带一路'，欢迎中方企业扩大对格投资，愿同中方扩大双边贸易规模，密切人文等领域合作，实现互利共赢"。③ 李克强总理表示："格鲁吉亚是欧亚地区首个同中国建立自贸安排的国家。中方愿将双方发展战略更好相衔接，充分发挥格鲁吉亚地理区位优势，共商共建共享开展'一带一路'合作。"④

两国自贸协议的签订，有力促进了双边经贸关系的发展，"据格国家统计局数据，2019年1—3月中格双边贸易额为2.57亿美元，同比增长26.8%，其中格对华出口3525.52万美元，同比增长72.6%；自华进口2.22亿美元，同比增长21.6%。中国是格第二大进口来源国，格自华进口占全部进口额的11.2%"⑤。而且，作为格鲁吉亚重要出口产品的葡萄酒，其对华出口量也呈现上升趋势（见表4—1、表4—2），客观上有助于格鲁吉亚相关行业的发展和葡萄种植农的收入的增加。

---

① 《格鲁吉亚总统祖拉比什维利会见王毅》，外交部：https://www.fmprc.gov.cn/web/wjbzhd/t1666381.shtml。
② 《格鲁吉亚总理巴赫塔泽会见王毅》，外交部：https://www.fmprc.gov.cn/web/wjbzhd/t1666386.shtml。
③ 《李克强会见格鲁吉亚总理巴赫塔泽》，中国政府网：http://www.gov.cn/premier/2019-07/01/content_5405027.htm。
④ 《李克强会见格鲁吉亚总理巴赫塔泽》，中国政府网：http://www.gov.cn/premier/2019-07/01/content_5405027.htm。
⑤ 《2019年1—3月中格贸易额同比增长26.8%》，驻格鲁吉亚经商参处：http://ge.mofcom.gov.cn/article/jmxw/201905/20190502862441.shtml。

表 4—1　　　　2017—2019 年格鲁吉亚葡萄酒出口统计①

年度	出口国家、数量（单位：万瓶）						
	中国	波兰	美国	白俄罗斯	俄罗斯	乌克兰	哈萨克斯坦
2019 年 1—4 月	219	117	22	60	—	—	—
2019 年 1—2 月	60	63	—	—	869	98	35
2019 年 1 月	28	27	—	—	460	55	15
2018 年	695	351	—	—	5368	1069	360
2017 年	760	—	—	—	4780	850	—

表 4—2　　　　2017—2019 年格鲁吉亚葡萄酒对华出口量趋势

年度	趋势—同比增长（单位:%）	
	中国	总趋势
2019 年 1—4 月	22	4
2019 年 1—2 月	12	13
2019 年 1 月	12	24
2018 年	—	13
2017 年	43	54

中格两国的政治、经济、社会、民间关系随着自贸协定的签订和"一带一路"倡议的实施，变得更加紧密，有力地推动了双方互利共赢的发展。格鲁吉亚总统在接受新任中国驻格鲁吉亚大使递交国书时表示："当前格中关系发展势头良好。格方高度重视对华关系，愿同中方不断加强交往，推动各领域合作取得更多丰

---

① 表 4—1、表 4—2 为自制表格，数据来源为中国驻格鲁吉亚大使馆经商处转发格鲁吉亚有关政府部门统计数据，具体来源为："2019 年 1—4 月格葡萄酒出口量同比增长 4%"，http：//ge.mofcom.gov.cn/article/jmxw/201905/20190502862442.shtml；"2019 年 1—2 月格葡萄酒出口量同比增长 13%"，http：//ge.mofcom.gov.cn/article/jmxw/201904/20190402853365.shtml；"2019 年 1 月格葡萄酒出口量同比增长 13%"，http：//ge.mofcom.gov.cn/article/jmxw/201904/20190402853359.shtml；"2018 年格葡萄酒出口量同比增长 13%"，http：//ge.mofcom.gov.cn/article/jmxw/201904/20190402853345.shtml；"格鲁吉亚 2017 年葡萄酒出口量同比增长 54%"，http：//ge.mofcom.gov.cn/article/jmxw/201801/20180102703055.shtml。

硕成果。"① 在丝绸之路经济带建设框架内与中国合作有利于格经济快速发展和改善民生，符合格国家利益。②

"一带一路"的合作，给格鲁吉亚带来了来自中国的投资，为格鲁吉亚的优势出口项目，提供了广阔的出口市场，对于促进格鲁吉亚就业，改善民生，促进格鲁吉亚社会发展，发挥了积极作用。例如："目前中国在格鲁吉亚有30多家企业，涉及投资、工程承包、通信、物流、农业、金融、贸易、服务等行业。中国企业和公司为格鲁吉亚的社会经济发展做出了很大贡献。如中国铁建二十三局集团，在承建格现代化铁路改造项目过程中雇用了300多名当地工作人员，为当地民众提供了更多的工作岗位。"③

两国从高层到民间的互动，从经贸到人文等多领域的合作，为两国关系的发展奠定了坚实的基础，提供了广阔的发展平台。"一带一路"倡议正成为两国合作与促进社会发展的新纽带。

二 格鲁吉亚发展现状及前景

格鲁吉亚自独立二十多年以来，经历了复杂的发展过程。政治体制过渡到资本主义多党竞争、西式民主选举的格局，经济体制从高度集中的计划经济体制过渡到资本主义市场经济体制，两个体制的转换推动格鲁吉亚社会发展发生深刻变革。此外，地缘政治、大国博弈的因素也深刻影响着格鲁吉亚政治进程、经济发展和社会发展。格与俄罗斯、西方的关系在这个方面发挥着重要作用，甚至是决定性作用。独立以来的格鲁吉亚，其社会发展现状与民生改善的国家治理能力也在发展中演化。

---

① 《新任驻格鲁吉亚大使李岩向格总统递交国书》，中国驻格鲁吉亚大使馆：https：//www.fmprc.gov.cn/ce/cege/chn/xwdt/t1682540.htm。
② 吕萍：《格鲁吉亚与丝绸之路经济带倡议：态度、意义与前景》，《俄罗斯学刊》2016年第5期，第76页。
③ 吕萍：《格鲁吉亚与丝绸之路经济带倡议：态度、意义与前景》，《俄罗斯学刊》2016年第5期，第77页。

（一）格鲁吉亚的经济成长

格鲁吉亚独立后，经济成长经历了明显的起伏变化。独立之初的格鲁吉亚，经历了一段时间的经济和国民收入的大幅下降，这种下降是苏联骤然解体的结果。在从高度集中的计划经济体制向市场经济过渡过程中，造成了国民经济的大滑坡，GDP 增长率、人均 GDP 增长率在 1992 年甚至为 -44.9% 和 -45.325%。自 1995 年起，格鲁吉亚有关经济数据才恢复正增长。格鲁吉亚 1990 年的人均 GDP 为 1614.64 美元，此后持续下降，1994 年达到独立后的最低点为 519.816 美元。2005 年人均 GDP 为 1642.775 美元，恢复到 1990 年的水平，这一过程用了约 15 年的时间。总体上看，从 1990 年到 2018 年，格鲁吉亚各项经济指标呈现增长态势，无论经济增长率，还是人均 GDP 与独立之初相比，都实现了跨越式发展。截至 2018 年，格鲁吉亚 GDP（现价美元）达到 162.1 亿美元，GDP 增长率达到 4.717%，人均 GDP 增长率达到 4.633%，人均 GDP（现价美元）达到 4344.634 美元，以上数据均创独立以来的高值，这与近两年来格政局稳定，努力发展经济有着密切的联系。表 4—3 详细汇聚了自 1990 年到 2018 年格鲁吉亚经济发展综合统计数据。

表 4—3　　　　　　　1990—2018 年格鲁吉亚经济发展综合统计

年份	GDP（现价美元）单位：十亿	GDP 增长率（年百分比,%）	人均 GDP 增长（年增长率,%）	人均 GDP（现价美元）
1990	7.754	-14.788	-14.765	1614.64
1991	6.358	-21.1	-21.653	1314.671
1992	3.69	-44.9	-45.325	757.224
1993	2.701	-29.3	-29.841	550.016
1994	2.514	-10.4	-9.01	519.816
1995	2.694	2.6	6.529	578.337
1996	3.095	11.2	15.31	689.017
1997	3.51	10.519	14.121	807.015

续表

年份	GDP（现价美元）单位：十亿	GDP 增长率（年百分比,%）	人均 GDP 增长（年增长率,%）	人均 GDP（现价美元）
1998	3.613	3.105	5.688	851.516
1999	2.8	2.869	5.008	673.526
2000	3.057	1.838	3.838	749.896
2001	3.219	4.805	6.444	801.99
2002	3.396	5.474	6.424	853.528
2003	3.991	11.059	11.811	1010.008
2004	5.125	5.794	6.452	1305.047
2005	6.411	9.59	10.288	1642.775
2006	7.745	9.42	10.044	1996.057
2007	10.173	12.579	13.168	2635.354
2008	12.795	2.419	2.73	3324.736
2009	10.767	−3.651	−2.791	2822.652
2010	11.639	6.249	7.027	3073.525
2011	14.435	7.222	8.085	3842.618
2012	15.846	6.351	7.137	4249.67
2013	16.14	3.387	3.698	4341.435
2014	16.509	4.624	4.574	4438.687
2015	13.994	2.881	2.719	3756.384
2016	14.378	2.847	2.785	3857.282
2017	15.081	4.833	4.819	4045.417
2018	16.21	4.717	4.633	4344.634

资料来源：世界银行。① 表格为作者自制。

---

① 表格中数据来源为世界银行公开数据，数据检索时间为 2019 年 8 月 20 日—9 月 5 日。具体来源为：GDP（现价美元），https：//data.worldbank.org.cn/indicator/NY.GDP.MKTP.CD?locations = GE；GDP 增长率（年百分比），https：//data.worldbank.org.cn/indicator/NY.GDP.MKTP.KD.ZG? end = 2018&locations = GE&start = 1990；人均 GDP 增长（年增长率），https：//data.worldbank.org.cn/indicator/NY.GDP.PCAP.KD.ZG? end = 2018&locations = GE&start = 1990；人均 GDP（现价美元），https：//data.worldbank.org.cn/indicator/NY.GDP.PCAP.CD? end = 2018&locations = GE&start = 1990。

2008年国际金融危机的爆发，给世界各国经济发展造成了负面影响。2009年格鲁吉亚经济和国民收入又出现了负增长，但是幅度总体不大，2010年即恢复正增长。2010年、2011年、2012年三年保持了6%以上的增长率，人均GDP和GDP总量也处在持续增加的状态。2013年、2014年、2015年、2016年四年，经济增长和国民收入进入一个增速减缓的区间，这与这个时期的政治纷扰有一定关系。

2017年、2018年这两年，经济和国民收入再次进入一个增速上升区间，且发展成果明显，政局的稳定对经济的增长和国民收入的增加具有决定性的意义。格鲁吉亚独立之初及独立后所面对的两次经济和国民收入负增长的状态，既有内部因素，也有外部因素。

（二）格鲁吉亚的社会发展

1. 人口发展

表4—4从人口总数、劳动力总数、抚养比、65岁及以上的人口占总人口的百分比、15—64岁的人口占总人口的百分比等指标，清晰展示了格鲁吉亚自1990年以来的人口变化情况，可以看到，格鲁吉亚人口的变化情况与国家发展状况有着密切的联系。

表4—4　　　　1990—2018年格鲁吉亚社会发展综合统计（人口）

年份	人口总数单位：万人	劳动力总数单位：万人	女性人口（占总人口的百分比）	抚养比（占劳动年龄人口的百分比）	65岁及以上的人口（占总人口的百分比）	15—64岁的人口（占总人口的百分比）
1990	480.2	239.2170	52.459	51.907	9.31	65.83
1991	483.59	242.4362	52.442	52.73	9.71	65.475
1992	487.35	246.0919	52.443	53.683	10.181	65.069
1993	491.11	250.0268	52.457	54.647	10.668	64.664
1994	483.6076	248.4436	52.478	55.429	11.084	64.338
1995	465.7722	238.5030	52.498	55.897	11.379	64.145
1996	449.1699	228.3032	52.515	55.889	11.701	64.148
1997	434.9913	219.6503	52.53	55.578	11.896	64.227
1998	424.3607	214.3245	52.545	55.046	12.024	64.497

续表

年份	人口总数 单位：万人	劳动力总数 单位：万人	女性人口（占总人口的百分比）	抚养比（占劳动年龄人口的百分比）	65岁及以上的人口（占总人口的百分比）	15—64岁的人口（占总人口的百分比）
1999	415.7139	210.1786	52.566	54.452	12.178	64.745
2000	407.7131	200.3899	52.595	53.891	12.409	64.981
2001	401.4373	206.1536	52.634	53.443	12.82	65.171
2002	397.8515	199.2008	52.68	53.089	13.296	65.321
2003	395.1736	203.4586	52.724	52.676	13.773	65.498
2004	392.7340	199.6802	52.753	52.022	14.145	65.78
2005	390.2469	199.1946	52.76	51.07	14.349	66.194
2006	388.0347	199.1317	52.738	50.426	14.506	66.478
2007	386.0158	199.2318	52.693	49.609	14.524	66.841
2008	384.8449	199.7277	52.63	48.779	14.451	67.214
2009	381.4419	198.8971	52.562	48.136	14.364	67.505
2010	378.6695	201.3146	52.498	47.776	14.312	67.67
2011	375.6441	202.9544	52.44	47.923	14.292	67.603
2012	372.8874	205.0357	52.386	48.205	14.315	67.474
2013	371.7668	202.4016	52.339	48.635	14.383	67.279
2014	371.9414	203.4761	52.301	49.225	14.487	67.013
2015	372.5276	206.2766	52.273	49.991	14.615	66.671
2016	372.7505	203.9265	52.258	50.78	14.73	66.322
2017	372.8004	203.2153	52.255	51.622	14.864	65.953
2018	373.1	203.1381	52.261	52.506	15.012	65.571

资料来源：世界银行。[1] 表格为作者自制。

---

[1] 表格中数据来源为世界银行公开数据，数据检索时间为2019年8月25日—9月10日。具体来源为：人口总数，https://data.worldbank.org.cn/indicator/SP.POP.TOTL? end =2018&locations = GE&start =1990；劳动力总数，https://data.worldbank.org.cn/indicator/SL.TLF.TOTL.IN；女性人口（占总人口的百分比），https://data.worldbank.org.cn/indicator/SP.POP.TOTL.FE.ZS? end =2018&locations = GE&start =1990；抚养比（占劳动年龄人口的百分比），https://data.worldbank.org.cn/indicator/SP.POP.DPND? end =2018&locations = GE&start =1990；65岁及以上的人口（占总人口的百分比），https://data.worldbank.org.cn/indicator/SP.POP.65UP.TO.ZS? end =2018&locations = GE&start =1990；15—64岁的人口（占总人口的百分比），https://data.worldbank.org.cn/indicator/SP.POP.1564.TO.ZS? end =2018&locations = GE&start =1990。

格鲁吉亚的人口总数和劳动力总数自 1990 年以来总体上呈现下降趋势，人口总数的下降趋势是一个持续的过程，中间年份很少有上涨的区间，而劳动力总数自 2000 年后基本稳定，没有明显的大起大落。相对于人口总数的变化，劳动力总数的变化 2000 年后较具有稳定性。自 2000 年后人口总数与劳动力总数的契合性较高，两者偏离不大。

自 1990 年以来女性人口占总人口的百分比，呈现了一个先上升后下降的趋势，1990—2008 年女性人口占比是一个稳步增长的态势，但是自 2008 年起，女性人口的占比持续下降，与 2008 年之前稳步上升的态势相比，下降的幅度较大，自 2015 年起，基本趋势相对稳定，没有较大的起伏。从抚养比来看，自 1990 年以来，经历了一个上升后长期下降又上升的过程。期间从 2005 年到 2015 年的十年间，抚养比持续下降。

格鲁吉亚 65 岁及以上的人口占总人口的比例自 1990 年起呈现一个上升的态势，65 岁及以上老年人口持续增加，也是一个稳步变化的过程。尽管总趋势上是一直上涨的，但是过程也有变化。1990 年到 2003 年是一个上涨比较快的过程，自 2003 年以后，发展趋势比较稳定，占比没有明显的起伏变化。总体上看，自进入 21 世纪以来，格鲁吉亚 65 岁及以上老年人口的占比保持了一定的稳定性和连续性。在 15—64 岁的人口占比方面，自 1990 年以来的起伏变化非常明显，经历了一个先降后升又下降的过程，拐点与发展变化比较明显，具有鲜明的时代发展特征。总体上看，2018 年格鲁吉亚 15—64 岁的人口比为 65.571%，这一占比已经与 1990 年和 2003 年的 65.83%、65.498% 大致持平。从 2005 年到 2018 年的十三年间，格鲁吉亚 15—64 岁的人口占比经历增长到下降，又回到 2003 年的水平，且与 20 世纪 90 年代初持平，变化是显著的，也折射社会发展对人口发展的深刻影响。

2. 教育发展

教育发展体现一个社会基本的起点公平，它是社会成员成长，并能够进入社会的第一步，也是推进社会化进程的关键一步。教育在社会发展中，占据举足轻重的地位，可以说教育与医疗、住房、养老、就业构成了人在社会发展中贯穿一生的刚性需求，这些也是基本社会保障的重要内容。表4—5从小学入学率、高等院校入学率、教育公共开支总额总数（占GDP的比例）、公共教育支出总数（占政府支出的比例）四个方面清晰展示了格鲁吉亚自1991年以来教育发展在社会发展中的状态。

表4—5　　1991—2018年格鲁吉亚社会发展综合统计（教育）

年份	小学入学率（占总人数的百分比）	高等院校入学率（占总人数的百分比）	教育公共开支总额（占GDP的比例）	公共教育支出总数（占政府支出的比例）
1991	97.291	36.189		
1992	95.475			
1993	86.339			
1994	85.003		6.916	
1995	82.688	44.596		
1996	82.512	42.068		
1997	84.895	45.012		
1998	88.982		2.109	10.851
1999	92.408	36.379	2.155	10.605
2000	95.181	38.325	2.181	12.541
2001	92.782	39.206	2.138	12.362
2002	89.47	41.271	2.235	13.604
2003	88.671	42.51	2.066	12.493
2004	90.71	41.723	2.914	15.037
2005	89.758	45.923	2.484	11.181
2006	93.018	37.434	3.004	12.895
2007	98.36	36.635	2.697	9.487
2008	100.868	34.183	2.92	8.938
2009	101.644	25.723	3.222	8.998
2010	101.77	29.199		
2011	102.845	31.433	2.696	9.269
2012	105.5	29.694	1.983	6.708

续表

年份	小学入学率 （占总人数的百分比）	高等院校入学率 （占总人数的百分比）	教育公共开支总额 （占GDP的比例）	公共教育支出总数 （占政府支出的比例）
2013	106.371	35.647		
2014	105.077	40.623		
2015	104.319	45.614		
2016	102.598	51.883	3.785	12.666
2017	102.774	57.528	3.83	12.953
2018	98.631	60.334	3.521	12.951

资料来源：世界银行。[1] 表格为作者自制。

小学教育是基础教育，也是人立足社会后续发展的基础和重要前提。1990年到2017年格鲁吉亚小学入学率变化起起伏伏，从长周期上看，是稳步增长的，但是每到一个阶段总是会有一个下降与调整的时期，但即使在历史低点的1996年，小学入学率也为82.512%，保持了一个较高的水平。"格鲁吉亚独立后，教育和科技发展受到政治经济局势的严重干扰，处于非常困难的境地，但改革的进程仍比较快。"[2]

高等院校入学率方面，由于缺失部分数据，无法清晰展现格鲁吉亚独立以来高等教育发展的情况，但是从既有的数据来看，格鲁吉亚高等院校的入学率平均在50%以下，高等院校入学率占总人数的比重是偏低的，而且有的年份的入学率甚至低于30%，较低的年份是2009年、2010年和2012年，分别为25.723%、29.199%、29.694%，这三年也是2008年金融危机发生后，对格鲁吉亚经济影响较大的三年，

---

[1] 表格中数据来源为世界银行公开数据，数据检索时间2019年8月25日—9月10日。具体来源为：小学入学率（占总人数的百分比），https://data.worldbank.org.cn/indicator/SE.PRM.ENRR?end=2017&locations=GE&start=1990；高等院校入学率（占总人数的百分比），https://data.worldbank.org.cn/indicator/SE.TER.ENRR；教育公共开支总额（占GDP的比例），https://data.worldbank.org.cn/indicator/SE.XPD.TOTL.GD.ZS?locations=GE；公共教育支出总数（占政府支出的比例），https://data.worldbank.org.cn/indicator/SE.XPD.TOTL.GB.ZS?locations=GE。

[2] 杨恕：《格鲁吉亚教育科技现状》，《东欧中亚研究》1997年第5期，第94页。

2012年后，随着危机后续影响逐步缓解，格鲁吉亚出现了一个高等院校入学率直线上升的过程，截止到2017年，这一趋势没有改变，这或许与危机中与危机后，劳动者为了提高自身在就业市场的竞争力，而主动提高自身素质的需求，具有一定关联。2017年格鲁吉亚高等院校入学率达到57.528%，进入高等教育普及化阶段，为格鲁吉亚发展带来新的契机。高等教育是人才资源的主要培训场所，入学率代表一个国家整体的人口素质的质量与水平。在今天新工业革命兴起的情况下，大力发展高等教育，提高高等院校入学率，并根据社会发展的能力和未来发展的需求，调整专业、开设新的专业，以培养人才，拓展人才红利，有助于提高国家整体的综合竞争力。

从既有数据来看，格鲁吉亚教育公共开支总额（占GDP的比例）在3%以下的年份比较多，开支总额占比最高的年份是2016年和2017年，分别为3.785%和3.83%，最低值出现在2012年，为1.983%，教育公共开支一个比较稳定的区间是1998年到2009年，这一区间的统计数据连续不间断，而且稳定性较好，在2000年后，基本呈现了一个上升的态势，教育公共开支是稳定的，持续性较好。整体上看，这一指标的变化折射了格鲁吉亚整体的经济发展的变化与经济增长的态势，与GDP的增长密切相关。这意味着国家在发展的过程中，有多少资源或者是新增资源可以投入到教育中。但是，"由于预算欠款不断增加，格鲁吉亚不得不降低开支水平，因此妨碍了国家宏观经济环境健康化的发展，降低了行政管理效率，削弱鼓励经营活动的发展力度"。[①]

从既有数据来看，格鲁吉亚公共教育支出占政府总支出的比例，起伏变化是比较明显的。公共教育支出占政府总支出的比例都在10%左右，最低点出现在2012年为6.708%，这也是目前看到的自格鲁吉亚独立以来的最低点。格鲁吉亚政府财政在公共教育的支出比例的变化，折射出政府财政整体收入水平的变化。公共教育属于民生支出，

[①] 小舟：《格鲁吉亚经济发展起伏不定》，《俄罗斯中亚东欧市场》2003年第6期，第29页。

这是刚性支出,且这一支出的比例和需求在一定时期以内具有一定的固定性,但是这一支出也与政府的财力、国家的经济实力有着密切的关系。"相较于发达国家的教育经费占 GDP 的比例(如经合组织国家的平均水平为 11.3%,欧盟的平均比例为 9.9%),格鲁吉亚国家教育经费投入仍处于较低水平,且高等教育支出占政府教育支出的比例呈下降趋势。"[①] 整体上看,这一支出在格鲁吉亚政府的总支出中的比例是相对稳定的,尽管个别年份会有下降,或者会有一个下降区间,但是也会在之后迅速反弹,在 2016 年、2017 年这一比例又获得了大幅提升,由 2012 年的 6.708%,上升到 2016 年和 2017 年的 12.666% 和 12.953%,这一时期也是格政局发展稳定的阶段,这一趋势一直延续到今天。

3. 就业发展

表 4—6 从农业、工业、服务业三大产业的就业结构关系,以及总失业人数、15—24 岁年轻群体总失业人数等方面揭示了 1991 年到 2018 年从就业结构分布到总体就业和青年群体就业的情况。

表 4—6　　　　1991—2018 年格鲁吉亚社会发展综合统计(就业)

年份	农业就业人员(占就业总数的百分比)	工业就业人员(占就业总数的百分比)	服务业就业人员(占就业总数的百分比)	总失业人数(占劳动力总数的比例)	年轻群体总失业人数(占 15—24 岁所有劳动力数量的比例)
1991	49.757	10.385	39.858	2.7	5.461
1992	49.65	10.244	40.105	5.4	10.216
1993	49.543	10.103	40.354	5.4	10.223
1994	49.36	10.097	40.544	8.4	15.352
1995	49.165	10.111	40.725	7.6	13.889
1996	48.964	10.134	40.903	11.5	20.317
1997	48.755	10.171	41.074	11.5	20.369
1998	48.553	10.193	41.254	14.53	25.519
1999	52.252	9.449	38.298	13.8	24.24

---

① 刘进、王艺蒙:《"一带一路"沿线国家的高等教育现状与发展趋势研究(十七)——以格鲁吉亚为例》,《世界教育信息》2018 年第 23 期,第 38 页。

续表

年份	农业就业人员（占就业总数的百分比）	工业就业人员（占就业总数的百分比）	服务业就业人员（占就业总数的百分比）	总失业人数（占劳动力总数的比例）	年轻群体总失业人数（占15—24岁所有劳动力数量的比例）
2000	52.173	9.804	38.023	10.82	20.865
2001	52.792	9.227	37.93	11.16	19.869
2002	53.77	8.22	38.01	12.59	27.489
2003	54.897	8.354	36.748	11.51	24.521
2004	54.002	8.835	37.162	12.62	27.832
2005	54.341	9.292	36.367	13.81	27.979
2006	55.304	9.049	35.646	13.57	29.455
2007	53.431	10.372	36.197	13.28	30.737
2008	52.92	10.461	36.62	17.87	37.174
2009	52.392	10.579	37.029	18.3	40.092
2010	51.843	10.736	37.42	17.41	37.318
2011	51.269	10.94	37.791	17.34	39.252
2012	50.609	11.181	38.21	17.22	35.795
2013	49.695	11.394	38.911	16.94	38.949
2014	48.738	11.675	39.587	14.62	34.564
2015	47.78	11.969	40.251	14.08	33.381
2016	46.824	12.254	40.921	13.97	32.781
2017	43.124	13.171	43.704	13.93	29.103
2018	42.897	13.222	43.881	14.106	30.441

资料来源：世界银行。[1] 表格为作者自制。

---

[1] 表格中数据来源为世界银行公开数据，数据检索时间为2019年8月25日—9月10日。具体来源为：农业就业人员（占就业总数的百分比），https：//data.worldbank.org.cn/indicator/SL.AGR.EMPL.ZS? locations = GE；工业就业人员（占就业总数的百分比），https：//data.worldbank.org.cn/indicator/SL.IND.EMPL.ZS? locations = GE；服务业就业人员（占就业总数的百分比），https：//data.worldbank.org.cn/indicator/SL.SRV.EMPL.ZS? locations = GE；总失业人数（占劳动力总数的比例），https：//data.worldbank.org.cn/indicator/SL.UEM.TOTL.ZS? locations = GE；年轻群体总失业人数（占15—24岁所有劳动力数量的比例），https：//data.worldbank.org.cn/indicator/SL.UEM.1524.ZS? locations = GE。

农业是格鲁吉亚的重要支柱产业，葡萄酒是格鲁吉亚重要的出口创汇项目，格鲁吉亚工业发展相对滞后，这从工业领域就业人数的比例关系就可以看出。服务业在格鲁吉亚就业中占有重要的位置，近年来，特别是2016年以来，其就业人数的占比已经与农业就业人数占比持平，2017年、2018年格鲁吉亚农业就业人员占比为43.124%和42.897%，服务业就业人员占比为43.704%、43.881%。

分项来看，农业就业人员占比自1990年以来，整体呈现一个下降趋势，而且2000年以后下降明显，且这一趋势直至2018年都没有发生根本性的扭转。这一趋势在近三十年间，经历了一个曲折的变化过程：1991—1998年是一个稳步的下降趋势，但是波动幅度不大，自1999年到2006年经历了一个非常快速的上升和发展过程，例如1998年占比为48.553%，1999年为52.252%，增幅接近4%，这是自格鲁吉亚独立以来到1999年为止未曾出现的高增长数字。此后，经历了农业就业人数占比高增长时期。自2007年始，格鲁吉亚农业就业人数占比开始持续下降，到2018年占比跌至42.897%，比1991年独立之初时的49.757%还要低。农业是格鲁吉亚的支柱产业，就业人数占比的持续减少，与进入21世纪后全球经济发展大环境和格鲁吉亚经济发展小环境有着密切的关系。工业和服务业就业人员的占比关系也经历了起伏变化，总体上也是经历了下降与上升的过程，农业就业人口占比的减少也与就业人员向工业和服务业转移有一定的关系，但是格鲁吉亚农业就业人员占就业总数的百分比，自1991年至2018年一直维持在40%以上，其依然是格鲁吉亚重要的劳动力就业领域与部分，农业依然是经济发展的重要支撑和社会发展物质积累的基础。

在工业领域就业人数的占比经历了一个从降低再到上升的过程，从1991年到2003年，工业部分就业人数占比从10.385%降低到8.354%，经历了持续十多年的下降过程，反映了工业部门发展的不足，特别是在吸纳就业方面。自2004年开始，工业领域就业占比开始上升，从8.835%，上升到2018年的13.222%，为独立以来的历史最高值，特别是2012年之后增长逐步加快，这与格鲁吉亚参与"一带一路"建设,中国企业投资格鲁吉亚工业领域有着较为密切的关系,有力地促进了格鲁吉亚经济的发展、就业的提高和民生的改善。在工业就业占比提高的同时,农业就业人数占比有所下降,两者一增一减,具有一定的互补性,但是总体上,格鲁吉亚工业领域就业人数占比还是比较低的,不到15%,未来可能会有大的发展,特别是在格鲁吉亚政局稳定,且积极对接"一带一路"倡议的情况下。

格鲁吉亚服务业就业人员的占比,自1991年以来,经历了一个微幅上涨后近似直线急速下跌,然后又逐步下跌的过程。自2007年开始,就业人员占比开始回升,此后持续增长,特别是自2015年增幅加快,2018年服务业就业人员就业比例达到独立以来的最高值43.881%。服务业超过农业成为格鲁吉亚就业人员占比最高的部门,这是经济活力逐步恢复的表现,这与格鲁吉亚作为旅游资源丰富的国家有着密切的关系。"为此格鲁吉亚制定了'巴库—苏普萨''巴库—第比利斯—杰伊汉'这样一些运输项目,制定了'丝绸之路'贸易运输纲要,通过世界旅游组织和联合国教科文组织参加了'丝绸之路'项目范围内的旅游基础设施发展纲要。无疑这些都会推动格鲁吉亚的运输业、贸易和旅游业的发展。"①

可以看到,独立近三十年来,在格鲁吉亚农业就业人员占比降低的同时,其工业和服务业部门就业人员占比在增长。从总趋势来看,格鲁吉亚工业和服务业吸纳就业人数的占比,在进入21世纪特别是2012年以后发展迅速,这一段时间也是格鲁吉亚摆脱政治动荡,走向政局稳定和经济稳定发展的阶段。农业、服务业在经济结构构成中占比较大,而且到2017年服务业首次超过农业成为最大的就业部门,占比分别为43.704%和43.124%,虽然幅度较小但是后期发展趋势值得关注,2018年,这一比例变为43.881%和42.897%,服务业占比比农业高0.984%。

自1991年到2018年格鲁吉亚的总失业人数和年轻群体总失业人

---

① 小舟:《格鲁吉亚经济发展起伏不定》,《俄罗斯中亚东欧市场》2003年第6期,第29页。

数的变化趋势具有一定的一致性和契合性，都是从1991年以来呈现一个逐步上升的趋势，大致自2009年以来开始有所下降，但是仍然没有降低到独立之初的水平。1991年格鲁吉亚独立之初，总失业人数和年轻群体总失业人数分别为2.7%和5.461%，为历史低点。2008年总失业人数达到历史高点为17.87%，2009年年轻群体总失业人数达到历史高点为40.092%。自2008年以后，格鲁吉亚总失业人数和年轻群体总失业人数两项指标分别平均保持在15%和30%左右，15—24岁之间年轻群体的失业情况比较严重，自1996年格鲁吉亚年轻群体总失业人数达到20.317%至2018年止，这一数字没有低于20%，且大部分年份在30%以上。2008年爆发的国际金融危机也影响了格鲁吉亚的经济，就业市场的反应非常明显，对年轻群体就业的影响也是显而易见的。

  总体上看，格鲁吉亚独立以来就业结构的变化是明显的，主要国民经济构成部分，通过就业结构的变化也可以清晰地勾勒出来。农业、工业、服务业的分布在格鲁吉亚的国民经济的构成中具有鲜明的特征和占比。农业长期在国民经济中占有重要的地位，且长期是吸纳就业的第一大产业，自服务业就业人数占比超过农业后，服务业与农业构成了格鲁吉亚国民经济中的重要部门。工业在吸纳就业上有明显的增加，但是在占比中相对还是较小的。格鲁吉亚总失业人数和年轻群体总失业人数占比自独立以来处于持续上涨区间，近年来虽有所下降，但是也没有达到独立之初的状态。年轻群体的失业情况值得高度关注，特别是2008年金融危机以来的时间段，30%左右的15—24岁的年轻群体的总失业人数占比是较高的，"统计数据表明，格鲁吉亚公民的生活水平很低。即使按照官方数据报道，生活在贫困线下的人口占比也超过了20%——此处将平均消费（即家庭的平均消费）的60%作为相对贫困标准。另据专家评估，格鲁吉亚人中遭遇严重困难的社会困难者高达86%"[1]。可见，青年的发展需要稳定的环境，为经济发展提

---

  [1] ［格鲁吉亚］Vladimer. Papava：《格鲁吉亚在后革命时代的经济成就：误区与现实》，王凡妹、邱建梅、张雪童、王子轩等译，《北京科技大学学报》（社会科学版）2017年第6期，第64页。

供可持续的保障,促进就业、促进青年成长。

4. 健康事业发展

"格鲁吉亚政府认为,人民健康是国家经济发展和国防的基础。政府通过调查和评估,制定了到2010年国家卫生发展规划,提出保护和提高居民健康的重点工作,包括:改善母亲和儿童的健康,减少心血管疾病的发病率和死亡率,加强对肿瘤的预防、研究和治疗,减少意外伤害,减少传染病和有社会危险的疾病,加强精神卫生,确定健康的生活方式,解决环境对人体健康的影响问题。"[①]

表4—7　　1990—2017年格鲁吉亚社会发展综合统计(健康)

年份	出生时的预期寿命,总体(岁)	粗死亡率(每千人,%)
1990	70.386	9.352
1991	70.29	9.51
1992	70.156	9.723
1993	70.003	9.98
1994	69.849	10.27
1995	69.718	10.574
1996	69.635	10.868
1997	69.613	11.132
1998	69.654	11.357
1999	69.756	11.537
2000	69.902	11.68
2001	70.065	11.801
2002	70.22	11.921
2003	70.349	12.054
2004	70.451	12.204
2005	70.538	12.369

---

① 卫Ⅷ项目考察团,《1989—2001年格鲁吉亚的卫生改革及对中国的启示——经济转型国家卫生改革经验报告(一)》,《中国卫生经济》2005年第6期,第73页。

续表

年份	出生时的预期寿命,总体(岁)	粗死亡率(每千人,%)
2006	70.635	12.542
2007	70.765	12.711
2008	70.946	12.863
2009	71.18	12.922
2010	71.46	13.088
2011	71.773	13.146
2012	72.097	13.168
2013	72.412	13.158
2014	72.707	13.121
2015	72.973	13.062
2016	73.207	12.992
2017	73.414	12.918

资料来源：世界银行。[①] 表格为作者自制。

实际上，自独立以来，格鲁吉亚人的预期寿命是持续增长的，尽管中间有的年份有所下降，但是总趋势上是增加的，而且这一趋势在2008年后尤为明显，平均预期寿命在70岁以上，最低预期水平出现在1995年为69.718岁，最高预期寿命出现在2017年为73.414岁。独立之初的1990年为70.386岁，此后所有下降。1994年到2003年间，预期寿命低于独立之初1990年的水平，直到2004年达到70.451岁，再次超过1990年的预期寿命。

在粗死亡率上看，自1990年到2017年是一个稳步上升的过程，但是在2013年后呈现一个下降的趋势，1990年粗死亡率为9.352%，也是1990年来的历史低点。最高点出现在2012年为13.168%，每千

[①] 表格中数据来源为世界银行公开数据，数据检索时间为2019年8月25日—9月10日。具体来源为：出生时的预期寿命，总体（岁），https://data.worldbank.org.cn/indicator/SP.DYN.LE00.IN?end=2017&locations=GE&start=1990；粗死亡率（每千人,%），https://data.worldbank.org.cn/indicator/SP.DYN.CDRT.IN?end=2017&locations=GE&start=1990。

人的粗死亡率自1994年以来，一直保持在10%以上，这一比例是相对比较高的，需要高度关注国民健康水平，提高国民健康水平能力建设。自2013年开始的下降趋势，具有积极意义，这是自1990年开始二十多年来的首次下降。2017年降至12.918%，基本达到2004年的水平，2004年为12.204%，这一逐步下降的趋势是否具有可持续性，需要进一步观察。

三 结语

无论从地理上还是从历史上看，格鲁吉亚千年来都是人类文明交流的重要通道和汇集之地。格鲁吉亚的经济社会发展既受到其国内政治发展环境的影响，也受到外部经济局势及大国关系的深刻影响。

格鲁吉亚经济与可持续发展部前部长、格鲁吉亚国际问题和战略研究基金会高级研究员、第比利斯国立大学经济学教授弗拉基米尔·帕帕（Vladimer Papava），在《处于地缘十字路口的格鲁吉亚及其战略选择》一文中，对格鲁吉亚所处的位置有着清晰的认识，对格鲁吉亚在地缘十字路口的战略选择有着清晰的表述。作为格鲁吉亚精英阶层的一员，他认为："从比较的角度看，欧盟无论在成立的目的、经济现状方面，还是在成员国的清廉程度方面，都好于欧亚经济联盟，而且长期以来，格鲁吉亚倾向于选择欧洲和欧洲—大西洋机制，并加入了欧盟的'欧洲睦邻政策'和'东部伙伴关系计划'合作机制。而俄罗斯主导的欧亚经济联盟，尽管在入盟难度上相对较小，但是其将油气资源收益的再分配机制作为基础，以俄罗斯向其他成员国让渡部分收益为手段，以此维持和增强俄罗斯的政治影响力。这导致欧亚经济联盟的脆弱性和不稳定性，因此使其与欧盟相比不具有优势。中国提出的'一带一路'倡议为世界经济发展创造了新的机遇。中国与格鲁吉亚在世界贸易组织框架下已经开展了一些合作，并奠定了合作基础。丝绸之路经济带规划中的中国—中亚—西亚经济走廊建设或将成为格鲁吉亚经济发展的新机遇。"① 中国的"一带一路"倡议无疑为沿线国家提供了发展的新契机,这一和平的、繁荣的、互利的倡议,一经提出即受到沿线国家的广泛欢迎,它没有地缘政治的算计,而是为后危机时代世界发展提供的解决问题的中国方案。

近年来,格鲁吉亚政局稳定,经济社会恢复发展,给格鲁吉亚民生改善、国家建设提供了独立以来难得的发展契机,格鲁吉亚营商环境的持续改善、腐败的有效遏制,以及积极构建联通欧亚的过境通道建设,成为格鲁吉亚再发展的重要前提。农业、工业、服务业,既是格鲁吉亚发展的优势,也是发展的短板。格鲁吉亚前总理巴赫塔泽认为:"格现行经济中存在诸多问题,包括经济结构不合理,工业正在衰退,国家经济发展主要靠服务业和旅游业,就业形势严峻致使大批青年人纷纷到俄罗斯和欧盟寻找工作等等。"②

格鲁吉亚现政府进行的全方位经济社会改革,将进一步优化投资环境,发挥格鲁吉亚在全球市场中的比较优势,发挥优质旅游资源带来的发展优势,成为格鲁吉亚经济发展的新亮点和吸纳就业的新方向。就业是民生之本,青年的就业是社会发展之本。从格鲁吉亚教育、就业两个指标的分析来看,在涉及青年发展的教育和就业领域,还有进一步发展和提升的空间,这样可以为经济和社会长远发展奠定基础,拓展格鲁吉亚经济社会发展新空间。

---

① [格鲁吉亚]弗拉基米尔·帕帕瓦:《处于地缘十字路口的格鲁吉亚及其战略选择》,《国际展望》2018 年第 2 期,第 1 页。

② Россия—враг? Грузия перетряхнула правительство, https://www.gazeta.ru/politics/2018/06/20_ a_ 11808697. shtml? updated.

第三篇

中国与格鲁吉亚的交流与合作

第五章

"一带一路"倡议框架下中格旅游合作前景与展望

张艳璐

中国社会科学院俄罗斯东欧中亚研究所副研究员

在当今世界经济中,旅游业是发展最快的产业之一。旅游合作正在成为国家间双边及地区多边合作的重要方向。有"上帝后花园"之称的格鲁吉亚拥有丰富的旅游资源,旅游业是格鲁吉亚政府提振本国经济的重要手段之一。尽管自独立以来受国内外冲突以及世界经济危机等因素的影响,格鲁吉亚的旅游业不复当年盛景,但仍具备较好的发展基础。对于中格旅游合作,虽然还存在着阻碍,但在资源、政策、市场等方面已具备较好的合作条件,中格旅游合作的发展前景较为广阔。如果能够采取第三方市场联合开发、区域旅游集群建设、消费支付手段便利化等促进措施予以推动,未来中格旅游合作有潜力成为两国务实合作的一大亮点以及"一带一路"合作的典范。

近几十年来,世界旅游业持续快速发展,特别是国际游客的数量保持着逐年递增的态势。截至2017年,旅游业已成为世界经济发展最快的产业之一。根据联合国世界旅游组织(UNWTO)的评估,2018年全球国际游客的出游量增长了6%,已达14亿人次。旅游业及围绕其所形成的经济体系已成为世界经济增长的重要动力,对全球GDP的贡献率超过了10%。作为公认的资源消耗低、创造就业岗位多、综合效益高的产业，旅游业被许多国家确定为产业结构调整的重点方向以及增强国家综合竞争力的重要途径，在国民经济中的占比日益增加。与此同时，旅游已不再仅局限于一种表示游客关系集合的经济学概念，还演变成了一种当代国家（地区）间关系中的社会现象，是一种不同国家人民间积极的文化合作方式以及加强国家（地区）间相互关系总体趋势的自然结果，在人文交流、文化传播上扮演着重要的角色。旅游合作正在日益成为国家间双边以及地区多边合作的重要方向。

一　中格旅游合作的条件与基础

位于太平洋西岸、亚洲东部的中国与地处南高加索中西部、黑海沿岸的格鲁吉亚，尽管相距遥远，自然风貌与风土人情存在巨大差异，但两国间的旅游合作却已具备了一定的基础和较为广阔的发展前景。

首先，稳定、紧密的中格双边关系为两国间的旅游产业合作及相关的人文交流营造了良好的政治环境基础。

国家间的旅游产业合作需要以友好的双边关系为基础。中国与格鲁吉亚于1992年6月9日建交。此后，两国关系始终保持良好发展的势头，各项合作发展顺利，合作领域不断扩大。中格双方在联合国等国际组织中保持着良好的沟通与协调。2018年，中格贸易额首次超过10亿美元。目前，中国是格鲁吉亚第四大贸易伙伴、第三大葡萄酒出口市场和主要投资来源国。而格鲁吉亚则是欧亚地区首个与中国建立自贸安排的国家。

其次，中国和格鲁吉亚政府都重视本国旅游业的发展，并为此制定并实施了相关的发展规划和政策，且取得了阶段性成效。这为两国间的旅游合作奠定了较为坚实的物质基础。

发展旅游业被包括格鲁吉亚在内的外高加索国家视为是2030年前实现可持续发展目标的重要方向之一。格鲁吉亚经济和稳定发展部前部长德米特里·库姆西什维利（Dmitry Kumsishvili）指出："（格鲁吉亚政府）计划努力促进旅游业的发展，这其中包括投资旅游基础设施建设，资助旨在提高格鲁吉亚知名度的项目等。格鲁吉亚政府致力于逐步实现旅游市场的多元化，提高国家的知名度，协助私营部门创造质优价廉的旅游产品，改善服务质量并刺激国内旅游市场的进一步发展。"[1] 格鲁吉亚经济与稳定发展部部长乔治·科布里亚（George Kobulia）则表示："我们（格鲁吉亚政府）一直都知道旅游业将是一个非常强大的行业，能实现迅速发展，但事实上现实远超出期望。"[2]

为切实推动旅游业的发展，格鲁吉亚经济和稳定发展部会同国家旅游局在世界银行的财政和技术支持下于 2015 年制定并开始实施《格鲁吉亚旅游业发展战略 2025》。该战略旨在提升到访游客的满意度和发展格鲁吉亚旅游产业，创造新的工作岗位和消除贫困，并预计实现八大战略目标，即：

（1）尊重生态规律实现可持续发展，重建和保存格鲁吉亚的文化和自然遗产；

（2）在熟悉自然和文化遗产的基础上，营造独特、真实的游客体验；

（3）通过为游客提供世界一流的服务来提高行业竞争力；

（4）通过扩大和提高旅游服务市场营销和推广的有效性，吸引消费能力强的国际游客；

---

[1] Манана Девидзе, Развитие туризма в Грузии: в интересах экономики и на благо граждан. https：//www.ictsd.org/bridges – news/%D0%BC%D0%BE%D1%81%D1%82%D1%8B/news/%D1%80%D0%B0%D0%B7%D0%B2%D0%B8%D1%82%D0%B8%D0%B5 – %D1%82%D1%83%D1%80%D0%B8%D0%B7%D0%BC%D0%B0 – %D0%B2 – %D0%B3%D1%80%D1%83%D0%B7%D0%B8%D0%B8 – %D0%B2 – %D0%B8%D0%BD%D1%82%D0%B5%D1%80%D0%B5%D1%81%D0%B0%D1%85 – %D1%8D%D0%BA%D0%BE%D0%BD%D0%BE%D0%BC%D0%B8%D0%BA%D0%B8 – %D0%B8 – %D0%BD%D0%B0 – %D0%B1%D0%BB%D0%B0%D0%B3%D0%BE – %D0%B3%D1%80%D0%B0%D0%B6%D0%B4%D0%B0%D0%BD.

[2] George Kobulia, The tourism development rate exceeded our expectations, http：//www.economy.ge/? page = news&nw = 995&s = giorgi – qobulia – turizmis – seqtoris – swrafma – ganvitarebam – molodins – gadaacharba.

（5）扩大和发展收集、分析旅游活动数据以及评估旅游业效率的能力；

（6）增加对旅游部门的国家和个人投资；

（7）改善经营环境，以增加国内外投资额；

（8）在政府、旅游业、非政府组织以及公众之间构建实现上述目标所必需的伙伴关系。

根据《格鲁吉亚旅游业发展战略2025》，截至2025年，格鲁吉亚的旅游业收入将从18亿拉里（约合6.7亿美元）大幅提升到55亿拉里（约合20亿美元），而到访格鲁吉亚的外国游客数量将增长至1100万人次。此外，为吸引外国游客，格鲁吉亚实行较为宽松的签证政策。目前，格鲁吉亚对来自94个国家的公民实施免签政策，并对拥有包括美国、阿拉伯联合酋长国、欧盟各成员国和以色列等50个国家永久居留权的人实施免签政策。[1]

为进一步落实《格鲁吉亚旅游业发展战略2025》，格鲁吉亚于2019年4月签署《筹建国际旅游学院备忘录》。该学院致力于培养酒店管理、餐饮服务以及烹饪等方面的专业人才。学院课程采取格鲁吉亚语和英语双语授课，并且课程设置遵从欧美标准，所颁发的毕业证书获国际认可。格鲁吉亚成立该学院的目标是希望将职业培训和员工再培训打造成格鲁吉亚经济发展战略的新重点。[2]

---

[1] 以上参见：Манана Девидзе，Развитие туризма в Грузии：в интересах экономики и на благо граждан. https：//www. ictsd. org/bridges – news/% D0% BC% D0% BE% D1% 81% D1% 82% D1% 8B/news/% D1% 80% D0% B0% D0% B7% D0% B2% D0% B8% D1% 82% D0% B8% D0% B5 –% D1% 82% D1% 83% D1% 80% D0% B8% D0% B7% D0% BC% D0% B0 –% D0% B2 –% D0% B3% D1% 80% D1% 83% D0% B7% D0% B8% D0% B8 –% D0% B2 –% D0% B8% D0% BD% D1% 82% D0% B5% D1% 80% D0% B5% D1% 81% D0% B0% D1% 85 –% D1% 8D% D0% BA% D0% BE% D0% BD% D0% BE% D0% BC% D0% B8% D0% BA% D0% B8 –% D0% B8 –% D0% BD% D0% B0 –% D0% B1% D0% BB% D0% B0% D0% B3% D0% BE –% D0% B3% D1% 80% D0% B0% D0% B6% D0% B4% D0% B0% D0% BD。

[2] Memorandum on Establishing International College of Tourism Signed. http：//www. economy. ge/? page = news&nw = 1118&s = turizmis – saertashoriso – kolejis – gaxsnstan – dakavshirebit – memorandumi – gaformda&lang = en.

此外，格鲁吉亚经济与稳定发展部与国家旅游局自 2015 年起联合举办"欢迎来到格鲁吉亚！"国家旅游奖评选活动，以鼓励格鲁吉亚旅游业和酒店业的发展，提升对格鲁吉亚旅游业务和品牌的认识，并在全世界树立格鲁吉亚旅游的良好形象。①

与格鲁吉亚相似，中国政府也非常重视旅游业的发展。中国政府于 2009 年 12 月 1 日出台《国务院关于加快发展旅游业的意见》，提出要把旅游业培育成为国民经济战略性支柱产业和人民群众更加满意的现代服务业的目标。此后，中华人民共和国国务院又于 2011 年进一步将 5 月 19 日确定为"中国旅游日"。根据国家旅游局数据中心发布的最新统计数据，中国国内旅游增速超过预期，出入境旅游实现稳步增长。截至 2018 年上半年，中国的入境旅游人数达 6923 万人次。其中，入境外籍游客 1482 万人次，增长 4%。国际旅游收入达 618 亿美元，比上年同期增长 2.8%。与此同时，中国公民出境旅游人数为 7131 万人次，比上年同期增长 15%。② 此外，据《2018 年旅游市场基本情况》，2018 年文旅融合开局顺利，按照"宜融则融、能融尽融；以文促旅、以旅彰文"的工作思路，以文化拓展旅游经济发展空间，以供给侧改革促进品质旅游发展，不断增强民众对旅游的获得感。国内旅游市场持续高速增长，入境旅游市场稳步进入缓慢回升通道，出境旅游市场平稳发展。国内旅游人数 55.39 亿人次，同比增长 10.8%；出入境旅游总人数 2.91 亿人次，同比增长 7.8%；全年实现旅游业总收入 5.97 万亿元，同比增长 10.5%。全年全国旅游业对 GDP 的综合贡献为 9.94 万亿元，占 GDP 总量的 11.04%。旅游直接就业人数达 2826 万，旅游直接和间接就业 7991 万人，占全国就业总人口的 10.29%。在出境旅游方面，中国公民出

---

① George Kobulia, The tourism development rate exceeded our expectations, http：//www. economy. ge/？ page = news&nw = 995&s = giorgi - qobulia - turizmis - seqtoris - swrafma - ganvitarebam - molodins - gadaacharba.

② 《2018 年上半年旅游统计数据报告》，中华人民共和国文化和旅游部官网，2018 年 8 月 22 日，http：//zwgk. mct. gov. cn/ceshi/lysj/201808/t20180822_ 834337. html？ keywords =.

境人数达14972万人次，比上年同期增长14.7%。[①] 中国已经成为全球第一大出境旅游市场，并愿意同包括格鲁吉亚在内的其他国家一起推动旅游领域合作，分享旅游市场红利。[②] 蓬勃发展中的中国和格鲁吉亚旅游行业以及所取得的成果为两国之间的旅游合作奠定了坚实的物质基础。

最后，中国和格鲁吉亚的旅游资源各具特色，彼此之间存在较大的差异，为两国的旅游合作提供了空间与潜力。

中国与格鲁吉亚都拥有丰富的旅游资源，并且两者所具备的旅游资源在种类、类型、功能上存在着较大的差异。在自然资源方面，素有"上帝后花园"之称的格鲁吉亚以多样性的动植物资源见长；中国的自然旅游资源则因辽阔的地域以及大纬度的跨度而以雄奇多变的地理风景和气候奇景为特色。在人文资源方面，格鲁吉亚的相关旅游资源带有鲜明的高加索文化特色；而中国则是东亚文明圈的中心，其相关旅游资源带有儒家文化的鲜明特点。此外，从功能角度看，格鲁吉亚兼具山海风光，气候温润、冬暖夏凉，使其在开发生态休闲旅游上具有优势；而中国则得益于旅游资源的全面性而适合开发各种现代旅游产品。正是旅游资源的差异性使得中国和格鲁吉亚在旅游业发展过程中彼此之间的竞争较低，并能实现优势互补，从而为两国间开展旅游合作提供了较为广阔的空间。

二 深化中格旅游合作

中国与格鲁吉亚间的文化旅游合作拥有较好的基础，并取得了一些进展。例如，双方签署了旅游合作协定、文化合作议定书等文件，为双方相关领域合作奠定了基础。此外，格鲁吉亚优秀艺术家和团体

---

① 《2018年旅游市场基本情况》，中华人民共和国文化和旅游部官网，2019年2月12日，http://zwgk.mct.gov.cn/auto255/201902/t20190212_837271.html?keywords=。
② 《格鲁吉亚新任大使拜会中国文化和旅游部》，中国文化网，2019年2月14日，http://dy.163.com/v2/article/detail/E80CHDF60514A015.html。

于 2019 年 5 月参加了在北京举办的亚洲文明对话框架下的系列活动，而格鲁吉亚的优秀青年汉学家还参与了"青年汉学家研修计划"项目。中格旅游合作，还推动中格旅游合作高度发展，但是深化还要关注以下几点：

第一，尽管格鲁吉亚是世界上旅游业增长最快的国家之一，但中格两国的旅游市场仍有较大差异，发展水平存在一定差距。

据统计，2009—2013 年间到访格鲁吉亚的游客总数的增长超过了 300%，从 150 万人次激增至 540 万人次。格鲁吉亚同期的旅游总收入从 4.75 亿美元增长到 18 亿美元，超过全球平均水平 20 多倍。但目前，每位游客在格鲁吉亚的平均费用却仅为每天 74 美元，低于世界平均水平。另据统计，2016 年访问格鲁吉亚的国际游客人数超过 630 万人，比 2015 年增加了 45%。在 2016 年的 11 个月中，国际游客通过外国支付卡进行的支付交易额约为 150 万拉里（约合 53.6 万美元），比 2015 年同期增长 10.1%。2016 年，格鲁吉亚首次从国际旅游中获得了 20 亿美元的收入，比 2015 年增长了 19%。根据此后的数据，在 2017 年 1 月至 5 月期间，超过 230 万外国游客访问了格鲁吉亚，比 2016 年同期增长了 9.7%。[①]

虽然格鲁吉亚旅游业近十年来实现了长足的发展，但是与中国旅游业相比仍存在一定的差距。根据世界经济论坛 2017 年所公布的《旅游业竞争报告》，中国旅游业竞争力的综合评分为 4.72，世界排名第 15 位，在亚太地区则位列第 4 位。而格鲁吉亚旅游业竞争力的

---

① МананаДевидзе，Развитие туризма в Грузии：в интересах экономики и на благо граждан. https：//www.ictsd.org/bridges-news/%D0%BC%D0%BE%D1%81%D1%82%D1%8B/news/%D1%80%D0%B0%D0%B7%D0%B2%D0%B8%D1%82%D0%B8%D0%B5-%D1%82%D1%83%D1%80%D0%B8%D0%B7%D0%BC%D0%B0-%D0%B2-%D0%B3%D1%80%D1%83%D0%B7%D0%B8%D0%B8-%D0%B2-%D0%B8%D0%BD%D1%82%D0%B5%D1%80%D0%B5%D1%81%D0%B0%D1%85-%D1%8D%D0%BA%D0%BE%D0%BD%D0%BE%D0%BC%D0%B8%D0%BA%D0%B8-%D0%B8-%D0%BD%D0%B0-%D0%B1%D0%BB%D0%B0%D0%B3%D0%BE-%D0%B3%D1%80%D0%B0%D0%B6%D0%B4%D0%B0%D0%BD.

综合评分为3.7，世界排名第70位，在欧亚地区仅次于俄罗斯，排名第2位。尽管格鲁吉亚在商业环境、安全和卫生条件、环境可持续性等旅游业发展影响因素上的评分较大幅度优于中国，但是在基础设施、自然和文化资源等影响旅游业发展的决定性因素上的评分则与中国存在较大的差距。而这将在一定程度上对两国的旅游业合作发展产生消极影响。

表5—1　　　　　　中格旅游业竞争力各指标对照表[①]

		中国	格鲁吉亚
	综合评分	4.72	3.7
排名	世界总排名	15	70
	地区排名	4（亚太地区）	2（欧亚地区）
环境条件	商业环境	4.2	5.3
	安全条件	5.0	6.0
	健康卫生条件	5.4	6.1
	人力资源	5.2	4.8
	信息技术准备度	4.6	4.5
政策条件	旅游业发展优先性	4.8	4.9
	国际开放度	3.0	3.1
	价格竞争力	5.3	4.9
	环境可持续性	3.2	4.4
基础设施	机场	4.3	2.2
	地面和港口基础设施	4.0	3.3
	旅游服务基础设施	3.2	4.0
自然和文化资源	自然资源	5.3	2.4
	文化资源和商务旅行	6.9	1.6

第二，格鲁吉亚与周边国家旅游资源存在同质化问题。同时，中国游客对格鲁吉亚旅游资源的认知度较低。

[①] 根据世界经济论坛的《旅游业竞争力报告—2017》（《The Travel & Tourism Competitiveness Report 2017》）自行编制。

格鲁吉亚与其邻国阿塞拜疆和亚美尼亚，在地理地貌上存在相似之处，并拥有较多的历史共同点。因此，三国在旅游产业发展过程中在自然和文化旅游资源上存在同质化的问题。这在一定程度上降低了格鲁吉亚旅游产品的独特性，削弱了其在国际旅游市场上的竞争力。

此外，中国和格鲁吉亚不是彼此主要的客源市场和旅游目的地。据统计，格鲁吉亚 2016 年前三大国际游客来源国分别是阿塞拜疆（152.3 万人次）、亚美尼亚（149.6 万人次）、土耳其（120 万人次）。值得关注的是，到访格鲁吉亚的俄罗斯游客在 2016 年首次超过了 100 万人次，达 103 万人次。同时，来自欧盟成员国的游客数量继续呈快速增长趋势。同年，来自拉脱维亚、立陶宛、捷克、保加利亚和德国的国际游客数量继续保持较快的增长，相较 2015 年同期分别增长 24%、16%、15%、12% 和 11%。尽管得益于较为宽松的签证制度，中国到访格鲁吉亚的游客数量实现了 116% 的较大幅度增长，正在逐渐成为格鲁吉亚新的国际旅客来源地，[①] 但对于中国游客而言，格鲁吉亚旅游产品仍缺乏吸引力。根据国家旅游局公布的数据，格鲁吉亚并未进入 2017 年中国 17 大旅游客源市场国的名单。[②]

第三，持续紧张的国内局势和频繁发生的抗议示威活动在一定程度上损害了格鲁吉亚的国家旅游形象，妨碍了中格两国间的旅游交往合作。

[①] Манана Девидзе, Развитие туризма в Грузии: в интересах экономики и на благо граждан. https：//www.ictsd.org/bridges‑news/%D0%BC%D0%BE%D1%81%D1%82%D1%8B/news/%D1%80%D0%B0%D0%B7%D0%B2%D0%B8%D1%82%D0%B8%D0%B5‑%D1%82%D1%83%D1%80%D0%B8%D0%B7%D0%BC%D0%B0‑%D0%B2‑%D0%B3%D1%80%D1%83%D0%B7%D0%B8%D0%B8‑%D0%B2‑%D0%B8%D0%BD%D1%82%D0%B5%D1%80%D0%B5%D1%81%D0%B0%D1%85‑%D1%8D%D0%BA%D0%BE%D0%BD%D0%BE%D0%BC%D0%B8%D0%BA%D0%B8‑%D0%B8‑%D0%BD%D0%B0‑%D0%B1%D0%BB%D0%B0%D0%B3%D0%BE‑%D0%B3%D1%80%D0%B0%D0%B6%D0%B4%D0%B0%D0%BD.

[②] 《国家旅游局：2017 年全国旅游收入 5.40 万亿元》，新华网，2018 年 2 月 6 日，http：//www.xinhuanet.com/travel/2018‑02/06/c_1122376586.htm.

安全问题是游客选择旅游产品时的关键考量因素之一。但自2003年爆发"玫瑰花革命"后，格鲁吉亚国内局势始终动荡，2008年俄格武装冲突对其国家旅游形象造成了负面影响，持续动荡的国内外局势损害了格鲁吉亚的国家旅游形象，对其旅游产业的发展和对外旅游合作造成了不利影响。

三　中格旅游合作策略的初步思考

在中格旅游合作具备较好的发展基础但又存在诸多问题与阻碍的情况下，需要根据具体情况采取有针对性的措施，以将潜力转化为成果，切实推动两国在旅游领域的务实合作发展。

首先，在"一带一路"框架下推动中格两国联合开发国际旅游的第三方市场。

市场是影响中格旅游合作的关键因素之一，但市场动能的缺乏以及未来盈利能力偏低的预期直接导致了中格旅游合作项目的投资吸引力偏弱。在此情况下，可依托"一带一路"倡议加强中格两国针对国际旅游产品第三方市场的联合开发，以拓宽中格旅游合作的市场渠道、增加合作项目的投资吸引力。

其次，利用格鲁吉亚的地缘特点，推动跨境（区域）旅游合作的发展，构建独具特色的区域旅游集群。

格鲁吉亚与阿塞拜疆、亚美尼亚等邻国存在共同开发区域旅游集群的条件与可能性。通过跨境、跨地区的旅游项目开发不仅可以部分抵消格鲁吉亚与邻国之间的旅游资源同质化问题，还可以减少同类项目的重复建设。这在一定程度上降低国际旅游成本、提升旅游产品性价比的同时，还将减少甚至避免不必要的恶性竞争，并进而推动地区经济合作的深化。

再次，引入第三方支付平台、推广互联网支付，实现旅游消费支付的便利化。

旅游是一个集食、住、行、娱乐于一体的综合性经济活动，其中最重要的一个环节就是消费支付。要开发中国出境游市场就要懂得中国旅游市场，并为中国游客打造符合其消费习惯的旅游产品和服务。随着手机支付在中国的普及，中国游客已经习惯了无纸币的消费方式。因此，在中格开展旅游合作时需要加强金融支付方面的协作，加强推广更为便利的移动支付方式，从而间接激发游客的消费力。

最后，注重市场推广，采取新媒体以及热门电视秀等新途径推介彼此的旅游产品。

当下，世界进入5G时代，生活与网络紧密连接，可以尝试更多地采用互联网、手机应用软件等新媒体对彼此的旅游产品进行推介。同时，还可以利用热门综艺秀、影视剧来让中格两国潜在旅游产品消费者对彼此的文化、景点有一个初步的了解，从而带动旅游产品消费。

综上所述，在中格旅游产业务实合作的问题上，尽管在推进过程中还存在一定不利因素，但在政治环境、政策支持以及资源互补等方面已经具备了较好基础，未来前景较为广阔。在具体的合作实施策略上，可根据产业特点以及所具备的合作条件与阻碍，采取共同开发第三方市场、发展区域旅游集群、加强消费支付的便利化和产品推介的多样化等措施来推动中格在旅游行业的合作，将其打造为中格间务实合作的一大亮点和"一带一路"合作的典范。

第六章

中格两国文学在"一带一路"语境下的交流和研究

王玉欢

格鲁吉亚第比利斯开放教育大学孔子学院

中国与格鲁吉亚有着悠久的文化交流史。格鲁吉亚文学在中国的传播和研究随着苏联解体等特定历史时期的转变而发生变化；中国文学在格鲁吉亚同样受国家政策层面的影响，存在机遇与挑战。"一带一路"倡议提出后，两国文化教育往来日益密切，本文旨在梳理两国之间文学传播和研究概况，总结格鲁吉亚文化市场特点，分析在"一带一路"背景下，两国文学交流发展的应对策略。

一 引言

民心相通是"一带一路"建设的"五通"之一，能增进中国与对象国的相互了解、信任和友谊，是"一带一路"倡议的根本归宿。正如习近平主席在多个外交场合所强调的，国之交在于民相亲。多年来，中格两国始终注重发掘对方深厚的历史人文积淀，不断扩大两国文化教育等方面的交流合作，促进两国文化交融和民心相通。可以说，正是历久弥新的中格人文交流，增进了两国人民的彼此了解，促进了两国间的文化交融与民心相通，为确定两国间未来合作发展方向提供了坚实支撑。

文学，作为重要的人文学科，在中格两国人文交流中也占据举足轻重的地位。文学是生活的载体，能反映出一个国家的国民性格、社会发展、风俗习惯、审美情趣等，可以说是了解一个国家最便捷的管道和理解一个民族心灵最直接的窗口。中国与格鲁吉亚历史悠久，文化灿烂，都保有浩如烟海的文学作品。这些文学作品犹如文化交流的使者，可以让两国人民相互了解沟通，促进双方文化传播交流，进一步实现两国民心相通。

格鲁吉亚拥有3000多年的悠久历史，地处欧亚接合部，素有"欧亚十字路口"的美誉。对中国人来说，格鲁吉亚虽是外高加索的一个小国，但却不陌生，令人最为熟知的是——格鲁吉亚是原苏联领导人斯大林的故乡。我国著名作家茅盾先生曾撰写《第比利斯地下印刷所》一文，记述了青年时期斯大林在格从事革命活动的故事。文章曾经收录于我国中学教材，广为流传。可以说文学作品令一代代中国人对格鲁吉亚充满憧憬之情。

1992年6月9日，中格正式建立外交关系，中国成为世界上最早承认格独立并与之建交的国家之一，受到格方高度评价。1993年6月3日两国签署了《中华人民共和国政府和格鲁吉亚政府文化合作协定》，提出双方鼓励和支持两国文学、戏剧、音乐、美术、文物保护以及图书馆、博物馆组织和机构之间的信息和人员交流。建交28年来，中格两国政治互信不断增强，文化教育等各领域合作日益深化。

2013年，"一带一路"倡议的提出为两国文化交流带来新机遇，格鲁吉亚人民对中国的了解需求日益强烈，两国的文学艺术团体走动更加频繁，官方或民间的交流活动日益增多。其中，当地的两所孔子学院——第比利斯开放大学孔子学院和第比利斯自由大学孔子学院为中格两国文化教育发展牵线搭桥，促成了双方文化互访、作家专题讲座、专家学者采风、文化艺术展等活动，也为两国文学交流作出了一定的贡献。

二 格鲁吉亚文学在中国的传播和研究

格鲁吉亚文学起源于公元 5 世纪，经历了漫长的历史发展进程，以每个历史时期的进步思想为其主导思想，以历史和现实的生活为基础，凭借作家们的真情实感，描绘出格鲁吉亚各个历史时期的社会风貌，大千世界的生活图景，全面呈现了国家的发展情况，对于研究者深入了解格鲁吉亚社会历史和民族文化极具参考价值。20 世纪以来，格鲁吉亚经历了诸多历史巨变，1922 年加入苏联，1991 年苏联解体，2008 年俄罗斯格鲁吉亚战争爆发……这些历史事件给格鲁吉亚带来诸多变化，文学作品也呈现出全新的思潮和大众心理。

1. 格鲁吉亚文学概览[①]

格鲁吉亚文学历史十分悠久。从古代开始，歌谣、故事、神话、英雄传说等就在民间流传。随着封建社会的发展和基督教的传入，5 世纪出现教会文学。12 世纪肖·鲁斯塔维里的长篇叙事诗《虎皮武士》富于爱国精神，影响深远。

外来势力的入侵长时期阻碍了格鲁吉亚文学的发展，至 17 世纪才得以渐趋复兴。17—18 世纪，摆脱奴役，争取解放，成为格鲁吉亚文学的主题。达·古拉米什维里（1705—1792）的长诗《格鲁吉亚的灾祸》描绘 18 世纪前半期格鲁吉亚发生的悲惨事件。苏·奥尔别里安尼和维·加巴什维里（1750—1791）的作品则反映了格鲁吉亚要求挣脱波斯、土耳其统治的愿望。

1801 年，格鲁吉亚被并入沙皇俄国。大俄罗斯主义的民族压迫引起格鲁吉亚人民的不满。19 世纪 30—40 年代占据主导地位的浪漫主义流派反映了这种社会情绪。它的奠基者阿·恰夫恰瓦泽（1786—1846）的诗作浸透着民族自由和社会正义的思想。尼·巴拉塔什维里（1817—1845）的诗歌，把个性自由的思想与民族解放的目标联系

[①] 整理自翁义钦《格鲁吉亚文学掠影》，《苏联文学》1988 年第 3 期，第 77—78 页。

起来。

19世纪下半期，格鲁吉亚封建专制瓦解，进入资本主义时期，阶级斗争激化，现实主义流派在文学上占据优势。格·艾里斯塔维（1811—1864）的戏剧、拉·阿尔达吉阿尼（1815—1870）和达·昌卡泽（1830—1860）的小说表现了这一倾向。拉·艾里斯塔维、尼·洛莫乌里、叶·加巴什维里等人的作品描述了农民痛苦不堪的生活。批判现实主义文学奠基者伊·恰夫恰瓦泽（1837—1907）的长诗《幻影》《强盗卡科》、小说《他是人吗?》暴露社会弊端，抨击专制制度与农奴制度。阿·采烈杰里（1840—1915）的诗歌反映了格鲁吉亚人民争取自由与独立的斗争。

19世纪90年代至20世纪初，随着无产阶级革命运动的高涨，达·克尔季亚什维里（1862—1931）等作家继续反映人民大众的悲惨生活；艾·尼诺什维里（1859—1894）等作家在作品中反映出农民革命的思想；伊·叶夫多什维里（1873—1916）首次在格鲁吉亚诗歌中描写了工人遭受残酷剥削和压迫的情景，号召人民团结斗争。俄国第一次革命失败后，一些作家的作品充斥悲观绝望情绪，而像沙·达季阿尼（1874—1959）、尼·洛尔德基帕尼泽（1880—1944）等作家，则描写了格鲁吉亚人民在1905—1907年革命及其失败后的斗争。

格鲁吉亚建立苏维埃政权后，文学进入新的时期。加·塔比泽（1892—1959）的诗集《时代》（1930）、《革命的格鲁吉亚》《世界进行曲》歌颂十月革命和人民的劳动。伊·阿巴希泽、阿·米尔茨胡拉瓦、西·契柯瓦尼、桑·尚希阿什维里、捷·申盖拉雅、格·列昂尼泽、伊·莫萨什维里等作家的作品，描写了旧世界的崩溃，歌颂了新生的格鲁吉亚、社会主义建设者和人民领袖，反映了农村社会主义改造的历程。

卫国战争时期，加·塔比泽的诗篇、西·契柯瓦尼的《达维德·古拉米什维里之歌》、格·阿巴希泽的《百战百胜的高加索》、格·姆季瓦尼的《营队向西开去》都谴责了德国法西斯，抒发了爱国主义思想感情。战后，格·阿巴希泽、格·姆季瓦尼、伊·阿巴希泽、桑·尚希阿什维里等老的作家继续发表作品，同时也出现了列·贾帕里泽、诺·杜姆巴泽、安·卡兰达泽、绍·尼什尼阿尼泽、贾·查尔克维阿尼、塔·奇拉泽等后起的作家。他们在作品中描写格鲁吉亚的历史，表现卫国战争，有的则触及当代社会的问题。

20 世纪 50 年代以后，现代题材的小说占据主导地位。柯·加姆萨胡尔吉阿的长篇小说《藤花》(1956)、阿·别利阿什维里的长篇小说《鲁斯塔维》(第 1、2 部，1959—1960) 和《什维德卡沙》(1960—1961) 等，歌颂了人民战斗的和劳动的功绩。杜姆巴泽的长篇小说《白旗》(1974) 和《永恒的规律》(1980，同年获列宁奖金)，揭露社会种种弊端和不良风气，受到社会舆论的重视。

自 1991 年格鲁吉亚宣布独立至今，格鲁吉亚经历了诸多历史变故，1993 年加入独联体，2008 年 8 月 8 日爆发了俄罗斯格鲁吉亚战争，同年 8 月 14 日格鲁吉亚决定退出独联体，并于 2009 年 8 月 18 日完成手续，正式退出。本阶段文学作品侧重展现战争对格鲁吉亚人民的影响，展现了格鲁吉亚"脱亚入欧"的社会思潮。

2. 格鲁吉亚文学在中国的传播和研究情况

纵观国内学者对格鲁吉亚文学的研究情况，可以发现，在时间段上出现了明显的断层，研究兴旺期集中在 20 世纪 80 年代末，即苏联解体之前，对格鲁吉亚文学的译介和赏评频繁出现在《苏联文学》《俄罗斯文艺》等主流刊物上。但 1991 年苏联解体之后，格鲁吉亚作为一个独立的国家，中国对其文学的研究却极为稀少。值得一提的是，"一带一路"倡议提出后，格鲁吉亚掀起"汉语热"，格鲁吉亚当地两所孔子学院的教师和志愿者队伍不断壮大，他们对于格鲁吉亚文学的研究也颇有贡献。

目前，国内对于格鲁吉亚文学的研究主要体现为三种形式：

一是整体介绍，如翁义钦撰写的《格鲁吉亚文学掠影》，大致呈现格鲁吉亚文学从古至今的发展历程、代表作家、代表作。

二是翻译作品，如李佐的《格鲁吉亚当代诗选》、戈宝权的《伊利亚·恰夫恰瓦泽诗十首》、张敬铭翻译的《诺·顿巴泽：我看见了太阳》等。

三是文本分析，针对格鲁吉亚文学的文本分析研究主要集中在一部作品上，即诞生于12世纪的肖·鲁斯塔维里的长篇叙事诗《虎皮武士》，相关文献如金朝霞的《评格鲁吉亚史诗〈虎皮武士〉》。

综上，国内现有研究成果具有三个特点：一是研究时间主要集中在苏联解体之前，将格鲁吉亚文学当作苏联文学的一部分进行研究；二是格鲁吉亚现当代文学作品鲜有涉及；三是对于文本分析、社会历史、比较文学等层面的研究较为缺乏。

如果不将格鲁吉亚文学作为苏联文学的一部分，而是作为单独的国别文学来看，国外对格鲁吉亚文学的研究也并不多见，主要体现在格鲁吉亚本国学者对自身文学的研究探索上，但研究对象也主要集中在史诗、民间传说等古代文学作品上，对于现当代文学的探讨较为少见。如 Bela Mosia 的 *The Symbols of the Fire in Georgian Folklore in Comparison With Global Experience*，主要从文化符号、宗教等角度对格鲁吉亚民间传说等较为古老的文学作品进行了深入解读，对于非格鲁吉亚本国研究者来说，具有一定的参考和研究价值。

但是，随着2013年"一带一路"倡议的提出，格鲁吉亚人民学习汉语的热情愈发高涨，这也促成了格鲁吉亚地区孔子学院的发展壮大。目前，格鲁吉亚共有两所孔子学院，第比利斯开放大学孔子学院和第比利斯自由大学孔子学院，两所孔子学院的教师和志愿者通过论文等途径间接承担起研究格鲁吉亚文学的任务，如发表于2016年的《通过〈虎皮武士〉分析中国与格鲁吉亚观念文化异同》的作者胡航就是孔子学院的志愿者。同时，随着国内对于"一带一路"沿线国家文学研究日益增多，格鲁吉亚文学也日益受关注，国内部分高校和科研院所都加强了对格鲁吉亚文学的研究，如在广东外语外贸大学编纂的"一带一路国家当代文学精品译库"系列作品中就编入了格鲁吉亚著名作家古拉姆·奥季沙里亚的代表作《总统的猫》。

三 中国文学在格鲁吉亚的传播和研究

从7世纪开始，格鲁吉亚从欧洲文学中了解中国文学。格鲁吉亚人认为，中国是神奇的童话般的世界，这里的人们充满了善意。在历史上，格鲁吉亚和北高加索、蒙古、波斯、土耳其都发生过战争，但是没有和中国发生过冲突，对中国的这种友善美好的印象一直就存在于格鲁吉亚人心中，并且表现在文字当中。直到9世纪，有一本中国的书籍被译介过去，格鲁吉亚人才对中国有了一个大致的认识。格鲁吉亚了解中国文学大多是从苏联时期开始，但大多了解的都是一些主流文学，对于民间文学知之甚少。格鲁吉亚对与中国文学的研究团队固定，主要以当地华侨学者、高校汉学研究所为主，"一带一路"倡议提出后，格国民众学习汉语的需求日盛，也间接促进了中国文学在格鲁吉亚的传播和研究。

1. 格鲁吉亚汉学及中国文学研究概况

苏联解体之前格鲁吉亚第比利斯外国语学院1984年曾经加设社会教学系并进行汉语教学，但后来因各种原因停教。1991年苏联解体后，格鲁吉亚独立，中国是第一批承认格鲁吉亚独立和自主的国家之一，1992年就设立了中华人民共和国驻格鲁吉亚大使馆。在格鲁吉亚的高等学府中，第比利斯亚非国家学院（Tbilisi Institute of Asia and Africa）率先开始汉学研究和汉语教学。第比利斯亚非国家学院是格鲁吉亚东方研究所附属的高等学校，而格鲁吉亚东方研究所是世界上最有名的研究所之一。第比利斯亚非国家学院是专门进行东方语言教学和研究的中心。目前除了汉语，还进行其他东方语言和相关历史教学与研究。亚非国家学院1992年在格鲁吉亚正式设立了中文系，为格鲁吉亚大学生学习汉语提供了良好的基础。至此，格鲁吉亚的汉学研究和汉语教学才得以开启了新的一页。对中国文化和语言感兴趣的年轻人开始选择这个专业。但由于当时亚非学院初建汉学专业，所以规模较小。①

在格鲁吉亚长期居住的华侨刘光文对格鲁吉亚汉学和中国文学研究发展起到至关重要的作用，格鲁吉亚的汉学家大部分都出自她的门下。刘光文的祖父刘峻周老先生，是格鲁吉亚"刘茶"创始人。地处黑海沿岸的格鲁吉亚，之前从未有过茶叶生产，19世纪末，受到一位俄国茶商的邀请，刘峻周经过反复试种，为高加索地区培育出了优良的茶品种，他也因此被称为"高加索的中国茶王"。因为祖辈的渊源，1958年，刘光文从北京来到第比利斯留学，学习水彩画，并嫁给了当地的一名画家。刘光文现为第比利斯自由大学教授，职业画家，"格中丝绸之路文化中心"发起人、主席，旅格知名华人。1986年，刘光文率先在第比利斯东方研究所开设汉语教学，为当地人讲授汉语、中国文学史和中国历史，所培养的格鲁吉亚汉语人才已经遍布格鲁吉亚各行各业。1992年，刘光文创立"格中丝绸之路"文化中心，并任主席，现有会员50多人。1995年以来，中心成员编译了《中国古典诗歌》《孙子兵法》《时空中的中国文化》《格鲁吉亚人眼中的中国》《莫言短篇小说选》等近20部文学作品。刘光文曾将蒲松龄的《聊斋》、莫言的《蛙》等多部汉语作品译成格语。2017年，由刘光文主持编写的《丝绸之路与高加索》一书出版。

格鲁吉亚的汉学家一般都把科研与教学相结合，几乎都有个人或集体的研究课题。汉学研究课题所涉及的面较宽。例如：格鲁吉亚语和汉语成语、汉文献、《论语》辩、文化、哲学、中国宗教、中国早期封建主义的文学与评论、中国文化史、中国当代（诗歌）文学、汉格词典、唐宋诗歌（汉译格）、道德经（汉译格）、中国经济体制与改革、中国区域经济、中国国家与政治、格鲁吉亚与中国关系、中国外交关系、中国香港和澳门回归、21世纪的中国等。

近年来，随着"一带一路"倡议的提出，两国往来日益密切，中

---

① 整理自玛琳娜·吉布拉泽：《格鲁吉亚汉学发展与汉语教学》，《世界汉语教学》2004年第4期，第109—111页。

文图书在格鲁吉亚越来越受欢迎，莫言、劳马等很多中国的优秀作家作品在格鲁吉亚翻译出版，都备受热议。2015年9月，中国作家劳马的短篇小说集在格鲁吉亚出版，登上了该国最高级别杂志的封面，里面大篇幅刊登了劳马的小说。2017年，在中国与格鲁吉亚建交25周年时，格鲁吉亚国家图书馆专门建立了中国图书角，这也为中格两国文学作品互译提供了平台。

2. 中国文学走进格鲁吉亚的途径

格鲁吉亚翻译家、作家、伊利亚州立大学副教授安娜曾经表示，格鲁吉亚人很多都会俄语、德语、法语等欧洲语言，但是了解汉语的人很少，而且对于格鲁吉亚人来说，阅读中国的文学作品非常困难。格鲁吉亚读者对中国的人名、地名不太了解，对汉语隐喻的理解比较难。欧洲的文学作品多是以一个人为主线展开，而中国的文学作品多是场面很大，人物众多。因受译者翻译水平的限制，或者文化信息不对等等影响，格鲁吉亚的读者不能很好地理解原意。如果翻译由懂得中格文化的翻译者相互合作，会达到很好的效果。①

安娜教授的看法指出了中国文学走向海外将面临的困难和障碍，格鲁吉亚单边对中国文学的研究团队固定，力量有限，所以两国文学交流发展需要双方共同付出努力。近年来，中国图书出版行业在中国文学走出国门方面也进行过各种尝试。目前，中国文学走向海外的途径主要有三条：一是国内外出版社之间的版权交易；二是新闻出版总署等部门通过"中国图书对外推广计划"等项目资助国外译者和出版商翻译出版；三是国外出版商直接取得中国作家的授权翻译出版。前两种方式约占90%，是中国文学"走出去"的主渠道。

据相关报道，为促进中国文学"走出去"，中国出版传媒股份有限公司推出了"外国人写作中国计划"。邀请了顾彬、狄伯杰、吉莱等一批了解中国、热爱中国的外国学者、汉学家，讲述自己的"中国

---

① 整理自格鲁吉亚伊利亚州立大学安娜副教授在兰州大学文学院暑期学校的学术讲座，兰州大学网站：http://news.lzu.edu.cn/c/201907/58477.html。

故事",撰写中国题材的图书,目前已与印度、土耳其、格鲁吉亚、波兰等国 19 位汉学家、中国问题研究专家签约。2018 年,在第 20 届第比利斯国际书展上,中国图书进出口(集团)总公司携《习近平谈治国理政》《习近平讲故事》等一批当代中国优秀图书首次亮相该书展,得到了当地媒体和民众的广泛关注,此次参与当地书展也是中国文学"走出去"的一次有益尝试。

此外,中国文学走进格鲁吉亚,离不开格鲁吉亚本土出版文化市场的推介,对格鲁吉亚出版市场的深入了解也有利于中国文学在当地的推广。据报道,截至 2015 年,格鲁吉亚大约有 100 多家已注册的出版社,其中 55 家比较活跃。这些出版社大部分都是小型出版社,大中型出版社在格鲁吉亚的图书出版市场上所占份额较小。并且,目前格鲁吉亚大部分的出版活动主要集中在格鲁吉亚的首都和政治、经济、文化及教育中心第比利斯。55 家活跃的出版社中大部分是在第比利斯开展业务的,另外还有两家在格鲁吉亚西南部靠近黑海岸的巴统市。2015 年,格鲁吉亚曾作为法兰克福书展的主宾国,这让全球的目光投向了格鲁吉亚的出版和文化市场。

从 2013 年开始,格鲁吉亚图书市场整体呈增长趋势。出版图书的品种数每年都有所增长,平均每年增加约 100 种。根据格鲁吉亚国家议会图书馆统计,2015 年全年格鲁吉亚共出版了 4100 种图书,其中主要出版社共出版了 1491 种图书,包括各类型的文学以及引进版图书,总收入约为 4370 万美元。2013 年到 2015 年之间,格鲁吉亚出版商的销售收入主要来自文学类图书,教材也贡献了相当一部分收入来源。文学类图书中,有 55% 是格鲁吉亚本土文学作品,其余 45% 是引进版文学作品。

在引进版图书方面,格鲁吉亚的引进图书以英语图书为主,其次是德语、法语、俄语,此外还有尼泊尔语等其他语言的图书。值得注意的是,在最近 3 年里,格鲁吉亚引进版文学类图书的数量比起输出的飙升了五倍。

在线上销售方面,目前格鲁吉亚有两个规模最大且经营时间长的网上书店，分别是 saba.com.ge 和 lit.ge。这两个网站的在售图书超过 2500 种，品种丰富，这些图书有格鲁吉亚原创的，也有引进版图书。这些在网上销售的图书定价最高的在 20 拉里（约 50 人民币）左右，最低的则低至 0.25 拉里（约 0.7 人民币）一本。读者也可以在网站上下载免费的电子书。在 lit.ge 上，读者可以下载超过 2500 种不同类型的电子书，这些电子书价格最高的是 13.9 拉里（约 35 人民币），最低的是 0.2 拉里（约 0.5 人民币）。[①]

在网上书店中，读者可以轻松搜索到格鲁吉亚语的中国相关作品，如毛泽东传记、成吉思汗史传、中国佛教、老子《道德经》、孔子《论语》等等。格鲁吉亚网上书城藏书量大，功能完备，在年轻读者中颇受欢迎，因而对中国文学来说，网上推广亦是一个走进格鲁吉亚的良好途径。

四　结语

正如前中国驻格鲁吉亚大使岳斌所说，中格两国在"五通"方面有着诸多契合点和良好发展前景。中格两国同为文明古国，都有着数千年历史和深厚的文化底蕴。在漫长的发展进程中，两国涌现出许多杰出人物，留下了一座座文化古迹，为人类文明进步做出了很大贡献，也给本民族留下了宝贵财富。两国都拥有独特的语言文字，语法和书写体系独树一帜，是世界上公认难度很大的语言。两国的文学瑰宝同样星光璀璨，熠熠生辉，在世界文学史上留下浓墨重彩的记录。

建交以来，中国与格鲁吉亚在教育、文化、旅游等人文领域合作快速发展，取得了丰硕的交流合作成果。"一带一路"倡议提出后，两国交流更是走上新征程，合作往来更加密切。两国文学的交流互鉴

[①] 数据来源：乔治·格格利泽：《中文图书在格鲁吉亚越来越受欢迎》，《国际出版周报》2018 年 6 月 11 日。

随着特定历史时期的更迭而不断变化，在苏联解体前后以及"一带一路"倡议提出后都呈现不同的特点，总结这些交流成果有利于加深两国人民友谊，促进两国关系健康发展，推动两国全方位合作，实现两国共赢发展。

同时，我们也应该看到，中格两种语言难度都比较高，差别也非常巨大，因而在翻译传播过程中，原文的风格不易保留，作品翻译后难免造成原著的较大损耗。如何使得作品在另一种语言呈现时仍具有经典性，从而真正讲好"中国故事"，助力"民心相通"，也是对译者本身母语水平甚至是重写和再创造能力的挑战。值得一提的是，近些年，在"一带一路"倡议提出后，格鲁吉亚"汉语热"随之兴起，从小学生到社会成年人，越来越多的格鲁吉亚人将学好汉语当作目标，当地两所孔子学院也为当地汉语推广提供助力。随着当地学生汉语水平的不断提高，高水平翻译者也将陆续增多，这对两国文学的交流发展将起到推进作用，相信未来两国文学的翻译传播、交流发展都将日益繁荣兴盛。

参考文献

［1］翁义钦：《格鲁吉亚文学掠影》，《苏联文学》1988年第3期。

［2］玛琳娜·吉布拉泽：《格鲁吉亚汉学发展与汉语教学》，《世界汉语教学》2004年第4期。

［3］乔治·格格利泽：《中文图书在格鲁吉亚越来越受欢迎》，《国际出版周报》2018年6月11日。

［4］格鲁吉亚伊利亚州立大学安娜副教授为兰州大学文学院暑期学校作学术讲座，兰州大学网站：http：//news.lzu.edu.cn/c/201907/58477.html。

［5］《走出去，中国文学正以蓬勃之势》，《中华读书报》http：//epaper.gmw.cn/zhdsb/html/2017－09/20/nw.D110000zhdsb_20170920_

1-06.htm。

［6］中国驻格鲁吉亚大使岳斌：《丝绸之路经济带将见证中格合作的美好明天》，新华网：http://www.xinhuanet.com/world/2015-04/21/c_1115043641.htm。

第七章

中国与格鲁吉亚在"一带一路"建设中的文化交流与合作

王 辉

格鲁吉亚第比利斯开放教育大学孔子学院

中国与格鲁吉亚的交往有着悠久的历史,早在两千年前,古代的"丝绸之路"就已经将两国人民紧密地联系在一起。1992年,中国与格鲁吉亚正式建立外交关系以后,双方的关系一直发展得很顺利。2013年,中国提出"一带一路"倡议后,中格关系更是取得了极大的发展与提升,并进一步加强了两国人民在人文、教育等方面的交流与合作。

格鲁吉亚一开始就积极参与"一带一路"倡议,也是首批在"一带一路"倡议下签署合作备忘录的国家之一。鉴于格鲁吉亚对中国有着特殊的意义,研究中国与格鲁吉亚在"一带一路"建设中的文化交流与合作就显得十分必要。

一 引言

"一带一路"是"丝绸之路经济带"和"21世纪海上丝绸之路"的简称,是中国国家主席习近平于2013年9月、10月分别提出的合作倡议。这一伟大构想旨在推动中国与"一带一路"沿线国家的合作与交流，打造政治互信、经济融合、文化包容的"利益共同体、命运共同体、责任共同体"，进一步构建人类命运共同体。可以说，在"一带一路"倡议中，经济融合只是重点，而文化的交流与发展才是核心。中国文化源远流长，博大精深，一直以来，不仅在增进中外人民的友谊中扮演着重要的角色，也为我国的长期战略发展提供更好的舆论环境。

格鲁吉亚位于欧亚大陆的十字路口，是"一带一路"沿线重要的国家之一。1992年6月，中国与格鲁吉亚建交，两国建交以来，双方关系发展很顺利，这也为后来两国的友好发展奠定了坚实的基础。2006年4月，时任格鲁吉亚总统萨卡什维利访华，拉开了新世纪格鲁吉亚与中国交往的新篇章。2015年9月，李克强总理在大连会见格鲁吉亚总统加利巴什维利，进一步促进了两国的发展。2016年6月4日，张高丽副总理访问格鲁吉亚，与格总统和总理会见，双方就自贸协定谈判达成一致，推动了中格自贸协定谈判进程；[①] 2018年1月1日中格自贸协定生效，这是中国与欧亚地区国家签署的第一个自贸协定，也是"一带一路"倡议提出后，我国签署并实施的第一个自贸协定；2019年5月，国务委员兼外交部长王毅访问格鲁吉亚，这是23年来中国外交部长首次访问格鲁吉亚，具有里程碑式的重要意义。

格鲁吉亚作为"一带一路"沿线重要国家之一，随着两国交往的日益频繁，将在中国"一带一路"倡议实施中扮演着重要的角色。自改革开放以来，我国经济迅速发展，人民生活日新月异，综合国力日渐强盛。因此，以格鲁吉亚为例，研究双方在"一带一路"建设中的交流与合作，促进"一带一路"民心相通具有重要意义。

在"一带一路"背景下，特别是自中格自贸协定生效以来，中

[①]《张高丽访问格鲁吉亚》，新华网，2016年6月4日，http：//www.xinhuanet.com//politics/2016-06/04/c_1118989995.htm。

格两国经贸交流取得了长足的实质性发展,实现了互利共赢。但在当前"一带一路"相关研究中,涉及中外双方政治、经贸领域的交流与建设的研究较多,但对中国与格鲁吉亚之间政治、经贸文化领域的研究却很少,而关于两国文化交流与建设领域的研究更是寥寥无几。

一直以来,国家间的政治与经贸关系是国际社会中广泛关注的问题,但是随着全球化的发展,文化间的关系显得愈加突出。一方面,随着"一带一路"倡议的深入,中国越来越重视对外文化交流,文化软实力也在树立国家威望、提升国家形象、增强国家对外影响力方面扮演着越来越重要的角色。另一方面,"一带一路"倡议的顺利实施,既有利于创造良好的外部环境,让"一带一路"沿线国家人民更容易接纳和支持,更有利于实现"民心相通"。因此,研究"一带一路"背景下中国与格鲁吉亚文化交流与合作,对于中国文化交流战略的持续发展有着重要意义。

国外关于文化及文化软实力的研究比较多,如塞缪尔·亨廷顿在《文明的冲突与世界秩序的重建》一书中从"文明冲突"的角度阐述文化软实力的作用,提出在社会发展的过程中,文化的作用是必不可少的,世界各国的博弈表面上是基于经济层面,而实际上是基于文化层面的;[1] 早在20世纪90年代,约瑟夫·奈对"软实力"这一概念做了定义:"软实力是一种能力,它通过吸引力而非威逼或利用达到目的,这种吸引力来自一个国家的文化、政治价值观和外交政策。"

国外对"一带一路"倡议的研究大多是基于"古丝绸之路"探究新时期"一带一路"的特点及影响。比较有代表性的如牛津大学历史学家彼得·弗拉科潘在《丝绸之路:一部全新的世界史》一书中通过对世界史的重新解读,阐述了"一带一路"在新时期的奥妙所在,强调"一带一路"正在悄无声息地将亚洲屋脊上的交流网络编织在一

---

[1] 萨缪尔·亨廷顿:《文明的冲突与世界秩序的重建》,新华出版社2010年版。

起,"丝绸之路"的光辉历史或被重写。①

国外学者的研究无论是基于文化领域还是针对"一带一路"的背景,大多集中在国际政治层面,涉及国家之间的文化交流与建设层面较少,这也为本文的研究提供了更大的空间。

自"一带一路"倡议提出后,国内很多专家学者对"一带一路"沿线国家开始大范围的研究和讨论,并涌现了很多与之相关的研究成果。但是纵观这些研究著作,大部分研究集中于交往历史比较悠久、关系比较密切的国家。如梁福兴、罗丹的《"一带一路"背景下中越两国骆越文化旅游产业合作发展研究》②,阐述了中越两国较好的旅游合作基础和现实条件,并提出通过文化旅游创新发展论坛与项目投资与合作等途径促进两国文化旅游产业发展。

目前国内关于中国与格鲁吉亚在"一带一路"的研究主要集中在政治、经贸和教育方面,涉及中格之间的文化领域的交流与建设研究成果寥寥无几。

二 文化交流与合作的理论分析

文化交流与合作是推动国家之间关系发展的重要方式,而"一带一路"倡议在新时期对于文化交流与合作有着特殊历史贡献。中格之间文化交流与合作既能促进两国相互了解、加深彼此感情,又能促进两国现代文化的发展。

1. 文化的定义

"文化"是一个非常广泛的概念,很难给它下一个精准科学的定义。关于"文化"一词的记载,最早见于《易经》贲卦,"刚柔交错,天文也;文明以止,人文也。关乎天文以察时变,关乎人文已化成天

---

① [英]彼得·弗拉科潘:《丝绸之路:一部全新的世界史》,浙江大学出版社2016年版。
② 梁福兴、罗丹:《"一带一路"背景下中越两国骆越文化旅游产业合作发展研究》2016年第6期,第47—49页。

下"。后来，西汉的刘向在《说苑·指武》中第一次将"文"与"化"相结合，提出"圣人之治天下也，先文德而后武力，凡武之兴，无不服也。文化不该，然后加诛"，这里的"文化"本意为"以文教化"，指的是对人性情的陶冶，品德的教养。后来，文化发展为广义与狭义的两种概念。广义的文化指的是"人类宇社会实践过程中所创造出来的物质和精神财富总和"；而狭义的文化指的是"在历史上一定的物质生产方式发生和发展的社会精神生活形式的总和"。英国文学家泰勒在《原始文化》中提出经典文化学说，即"文化是包括知识、信仰、艺术、道德、法律、习俗"和任何人作为社会成员而获得的能力和习惯在内的复杂整体。

由此可见，不同时期，由于人们对文化的认知不同，所以对文化的定义也不尽相同，在这里，我们将文化作为一种思想、价值、传统或类似方面的广义的意识形态。

2. 文化交流与合作的形式

根据文化行为主体的不同，我们将其归为官方和民间两种形式。

官方文化交流与合作是以政府为主导，通过政府间正式的文化交流项目实施的，如官方协议、国际文化会议、文化部门人员之间的访问、文化业务的开展及文化成果的展览等。

而民间的文化交流与合作则是一种民间行为，文学艺术展览、语言文化教学、新闻传媒报道、民间艺术人员往来、体育文化交往、文化遗产保护及文化产业贸易等都属于民间文化交流与合作的范畴。通过开展民间文化交流，促进中华文化"走出去"，让中华文化"走进去""融进去"，并真正做到落实"民心相通""文化互鉴"。

三 中国与格鲁吉亚文化交流与合作的基本形式

早在两千多年前，"丝绸之路"就将中国与格鲁吉亚两国人民紧紧地联系在一起,中格友好交往史上也涌出了许多佳话。公元12世纪,格鲁吉亚著名诗人就在他的著作《虎皮骑士》中写道:公元19世纪末,一位姓刘的中国人在格鲁吉亚黑海沿岸培育出了适合当地气候和土壤条件的"刘茶",这种茶受到了当地及周边地区人民的极度欢迎。

1. 官方正式往来

1992年,两国正式建立外交关系后,双方的文化交流与合作日渐广泛。

(1) 早期阶段 (1992—1999)

20世纪90年代是双方文化交流与合作的早期发展阶段,两国开展了一系列官方代表团访问活动。

1993年6月2—4日,格国家元首、议会主席谢瓦尔德纳泽正式访华,双方签署联合声明、两国外交部合作议定书、两国政府经贸合作协定、鼓励和保护协定以及科学、文化、卫生、农业、旅游、海关、体育、邮电领域的合作协定等17个文件,为两国关系的发展奠定了基础。1998年7月,格文化部部长阿萨季阿尼访华,[①] 1998年9月8—15日,格议会移民和格侨事务委员会主席沙拉泽访华,格鲁吉亚早期来华的官方访问进一步加强了中格之间的友好关系。

(2) 发展阶段 (2000—2012)

进入21世纪以来,中格文化交往又迈入了一个新时期。2001年4月12—14日,国务院副总理李岚清对格进行正式友好访问,分别会见格总统谢瓦尔德纳泽、议长日瓦尼亚、国务部长阿尔谢尼什维利。双方签署了经济、文化和教育等协议;[②] 5月26—27日,应格鲁吉亚对外友好和文化关系协会邀请,浙江衢州市代表团访格,双方就衢州市与库塔伊西建立友好城市关系进行了探讨,并签署了一

[①] 中国新闻网:《中国同格鲁吉亚的关系》,2013年3月21日,https://www.chinanews.com/gj/zlk/2014/01-15/163_2.shtml。

[②] 东方新闻:《李岚清到抵格鲁吉亚访问》,2001年4月13日,http://news.eastday.com/epublish/gb/paper148/20010413/class014800004/hwz360388.htm。

系列有关两市经济和文化的合作意向书,这为中格之间的城市交流开辟了先河。

2003年10月,格鲁吉亚旅游局局长瓦扎·舒伯拉泽出席在北京举行的世界旅游年会。

2006年4月10—14日,格总统萨卡什维利对中国进行国事访问,国家主席胡锦涛在人民大会堂举行了欢迎仪式,两国针对双边关系和国际问题进行探讨并达成了广泛共识。此次访问促进了双方在政治、经贸、文化及旅游等领域的全方位合作,继而造福两国人民;[1] 2008年6月24日,格鲁吉亚"丝绸之路"格中友好协会和中国驻格鲁吉亚大使馆在第比利斯联合举办格文版《时空中的中国文化》一书首发式。[2]《时空中的中国文化》是由刘光文女士和格汉学家共同编纂成书,由中国驻格鲁吉亚大使馆赞助出版,是格国内第一部综合介绍中国历史、宗教、哲学、艺术、文学的格文著作,受到了格学术界的高度关注;7月9日,中国青铜器展览开幕式在格鲁吉亚第比利斯国家博物馆举行,中国驻格鲁吉亚大使王开文、格文化部部长切瓦尔伊什维利、格国家博物馆馆长洛尔特基帕尼泽及政府官员、社会各界人士出席了本次活动。本次展览在第比利斯持续了两个月,对增进中格两国人民相互了解和友谊有重要作用。

2009年12月22日,庆祝新中国成立60周年的"中国万花筒—现代生活面面观"图片展开幕式在格鲁吉亚西部城市库塔伊西的大卫·卡卡巴泽画廊举行,[3] 中国驻格鲁吉亚大使宫建伟、库塔伊西代市市长戈尔德纳鲁泽分别致辞,格民众对中国图片高度赞赏,本次图片展取得了圆满的成功。

2010年9月28日,中国艺术品展开幕式在格鲁吉亚国家博物馆

---

[1] 中国网:《格鲁吉亚总统萨卡什维利14日结束对话访问》,2006年4月14日,http://www.china.com.cn/txt/2006-04/14/content_6184344.htm。

[2] 中华人民共和国驻格鲁吉亚大使馆:《格文版〈时空中的中国文化〉首发式在第比利斯举行》,2008年6月25日,https://www.fmprc.gov.cn/ce/cege/chn/whjl/t468870.htm。

[3] 中华人民共和国驻格鲁吉亚大使馆:《中国图片展在格鲁吉亚西部城市库塔伊西举行》,2009年12月24日,https://www.fmprc.gov.cn/ce/cege/chn/whjl/t647488.htm。

所属的绍瓦·阿米拉纳什维利举办,该艺术展是新中国成立61周年前夕由中国大使馆和格国家博物馆联合举办的,展出的120多件展品均是中国国家博物馆在不同时期收藏的艺术珍品,包括象牙工艺品、传统服饰、瓷器、丝绸织品、绘画、雕刻、佛像等,本次艺术展促进了中格文化的进一步交流与发展;11月23日,中国驻格鲁吉亚大使陈建福会见格鲁吉亚文化部部长尼克洛兹·鲁鲁阿,双方就加强两国间文化合作与交流交换了意见,此次会面使两国之间的文化建设迈上了一个新的台阶。

2012年9月,格鲁吉亚文化部部长鲁鲁阿访华并出席了"格鲁吉亚文化日"活动,中国文化部部长蔡武在北京会见了鲁鲁阿。会后双方共同签署了《中华人民共和国文化部和格鲁吉亚文化和古迹保护部2012—2015年文化合作议定书》,开辟了两国文化关系建设的新思路,进一步推动了两国官方和民间文化交流共同发展,为两国夯实坚实的友谊奠定了基础。

(3) 新发展阶段 (2013—2020)

随着"一带一路"倡议的提出,中格两国文化交流不断深化,合作领域不断拓宽。

2013年11月4日,中国驻格鲁吉亚大使岳斌会见格文化与古迹保护部部长奥吉沙利亚,双方认为古丝绸之路作为一条文化纽带,将两国的文化关系密切联系在一起,相信在双方共同努力下,中格文化合作必将取得新的进展。

2015年10月14—16日,中国与格鲁吉亚政府共同举办的首届"丝绸之路"国际论坛在第比利斯召开,来自38个国家的政府代表和12个国际组织代表,以及150多家中方企业参加了论坛,本次论坛让古老的"丝绸之路"散发出生机与活力,对丝绸之路沿线国家经贸与文化建设有重要意义。[1]

---

[1] 新疆维吾尔族自治区发展和改革委员会官网:《丝绸之路国际论坛在格鲁吉亚首都第比利斯召开》,2015年10月26日,https://www.sogou.com/link?url=DSOYnZeCC_qycPIsAHV-vv2QJ6AJM-tu129faqO6m7jHEJjl1k3hZBbwfeHNvomoV。

2016年2月6日,时任中国驻格鲁吉亚大使季雁池在华凌帕佛伦斯酒店举行首届汉学家新春招待会,格教育与科技部部长萨尼基泽、副部长沙尔瓦什泽及外交部、文化部官员,汉学家协会、"丝绸之路"文化研究中心、第比利斯自由大学孔子学院、格有关大中院校领导、主流媒体及汉语学习者150余人参加了活动;4月9日,时任中国驻格鲁吉亚大使季雁池会见格中"丝绸之路"文化研究中心主席刘光文教授等代表,季大使鼓励丝路中心将"丝绸之路"沿线国家也作为中心研究内容,不断丰富"丝绸之路经济带"精神内涵,此次会议对中格友好的民意基础发挥着重要的作用。

2017年1月26日,时任中国驻格鲁吉亚大使季雁池在华菱帕佛伦斯酒店举行第二届汉学家招待会,格外长贾涅利泽、议会文化教育委员会主席亚希、伙伴基金主席萨加涅利泽,格外交部、教育部、文化部官员,汉学家协会、"丝绸之路"文化研究中心、第比利斯自由大学孔子学院、汉语教学点负责人,主流媒体等130余人参加了会议,本次招待会推动了中格教育文化事业的发展,使汉语教学开展及中华文化传播迈上了新台阶。① 11月28日,第二届"一带一路"国际论坛在第比利斯举行,来自60多个国家和国际组织的2000多名政要嘉宾、智库学者和商业代表参加了论坛,该论坛是除中国以外,第一个以中央政府的名义举办的有关"一带一路"的峰会论坛,体现了格鲁吉亚对"一带一路"倡议的大力支持,也表明了格鲁吉亚与中国开展交流与建设的决心。

2019年5月24日,中国国务委员兼外交部长王毅访问格鲁吉亚,分别拜会了时任格鲁吉亚总理马穆卡·巴赫塔泽、格鲁吉亚总统萨洛梅·祖拉比什维利、格鲁吉亚外交部长扎尔卡利亚尼,双方就加强中格之间贸易关系,深化两国务实合作,推进人文交流等方

---

① 中华人民共和国驻格鲁吉亚大使馆:《驻格鲁吉亚大使季雁池夫妇举行第二届格鲁吉亚汉学家春节招待会》,2017年1月27日,https://www.fmprc.gov.cn/ce/cege/chn/xwdt/t1434653.htm。

面达成了共识；① 6月29日，"埃塔隆中国年"中学生知识竞赛颁奖仪式在格鲁吉亚科学教育文化体育部举行，驻格使馆临时代办左洪波、格教育部副部长阿布拉泽、格议会教科文委员会主席贾什等出席。该竞赛作为格鲁吉亚最大的全国性知识竞赛，吸引了两万余所中学的四万多名学生参与，对汉语在格发展及中国文化的传播起到了重大的推动作用；7月1日，国务院总理李克强在大连会见时任格鲁吉亚总理巴赫塔泽，双方表示支持共建"一带一路"，扩大双边贸易规模，深化人文领域交流与合作，不断促进两国人民之间的友谊，实现互利共赢。10月23日，第三届"丝绸之路"国际论坛在第比利斯成功落下帷幕，在本次论坛中，加强与中方的合作，积极与"一带一路"倡议对接成为与会各国代表的共同呼声。12月27日，格鲁吉亚国家博物馆中国藏品展正式开幕，中国驻格鲁吉亚大使李岩、格国家图书馆馆长罗德基帕尼泽、格各界艺术爱好者、中资企业、孔子学院代表共100余人参加了开幕式，中国藏品作为中国文化的载体，对格民众对中国文化的了解，增进两国友谊有着重要意义。

2020年1月13日，中国驻格鲁吉亚大使李岩会见格新任科学、教育、文化、体育部部长齐亨克利，就中格双边关系及科学、教育、文化、体育等合作领域交换了意见，此次会谈为汉语教学在格发展、壮大，推动两国人文领域合作交流起到了积极作用。②

2. 民间文化交流

（1）早期阶段（1992—1999）

"国之交在于民之亲，民相亲在于心相通"，通过民间文化交流，促进人们相互了解与信任，增进心灵之间的对话，从而搭建起一个友谊与合作之桥。

---

① 中国政府网：《格鲁吉亚总统祖拉比什维利会见王毅》《格鲁吉亚总理巴赫塔泽会见王毅》《王毅同格鲁吉亚外长扎尔卡利亚尼举行会谈》，2019年5月24—25日，http：//www.gov.cn/index.htm。

② 中华人民共和国驻格鲁吉亚大使馆：《驻格鲁吉亚大使李岩会见格教育、科学、文化、体育部部长》，2020年1月14日，https：//www.sogou.com/link？url＝MRoBrhLn5VMmGBHpBqe4bLdL677hul5NITPG27ztBHi0LA5v1CimP4qKPenT1Icoz98T－pCQ7Y8。

1998年是中格文化往来非常活跃的一年。8月,格圣山歌舞团来华参加中国第四届国际民间艺术节;10月,中国煤矿艺术团赴格参加第二届国际艺术节。这两次互访的艺术活动奠定了中格民间文化的交流与合作基础。

(2) 发展阶段(2000—2012)

中格民间文化交流步入发展阶段后,文化交流的渠道逐渐拓宽,形成了文化合作的基本格局。

2002年10月,中国图片展在格鲁吉亚首都第比利斯举行;2005年7月1—6日,中国著名轮椅女画家秦百兰个人画展在第比利斯画廊成功举行。中国驻格鲁吉亚大使王开文和格文化部副部长克瓦里阿尼共同主持了画展开幕式,画展吸引了格中友协、格文化界、新闻界及格华侨华人上百人参加,受到了广大人民的推崇与喜爱。[①]

2006年9月29日—10月26日,"中国景德镇瓷器展"和"'舞动的北京'图片展"在第比利斯历史博物馆举行,此次艺术展在格鲁吉亚民众之间反应极其热烈,民众对中国瓷器的精湛技艺赞不绝口,对北京建设取得的成就更是惊叹不已。此次展览加深了格民众对中国传统及现代的了解,格电台、广播、报刊等媒体均对此次展览给予了很高的评价,把展品称为"中国奇迹"。

2008年7月23日,格鲁吉亚首都第比利斯举办"中国主题日"民俗表演活动,本次表演在民俗村举行,来自天津华夏未来少儿艺术团的小演员和四川川剧团的演员们为格观众献上了精美绝伦的歌舞、乐曲、武术、舞龙舞狮等表演,"变脸"等中华特色的精彩民俗艺术节目更是在格民俗界产生了强烈凡响。

2010年2月13日,中国大使馆在第比利斯举办首届2010年驻格使馆、中资机构暨华人华侨春节联欢会,整个春节联欢会充满了浓浓的节日气氛;9月27日,中国古典文学名著《聊斋志异》格鲁吉亚文

[①] 中华人民共和国驻格鲁吉亚大使馆:《著名轮椅女画家秦百兰画展在第比利斯举行》,2005年7月6日,https://www.fmprc.gov.cn/ce/cege/chn/whjl/t202596.htm。

版选集首发式在第比利斯举行。该书系由著名旅格华人、"丝绸之路"格中文化交流中心主任刘光文教授提议并主持翻译，中国大使馆资助出版。刘光文女士为推动中格文化交流作出了重要贡献，在她的努力下，格文版《孙子兵法》和《中国文化》也相继出版；11月25日，第比利斯智障人教育培训学校举办"中国日"活动，该校智障学生精心准备了以中国民间故事为题改编的情景话剧，并带来了用中文演唱的国歌和儿歌《两只老虎》的精彩演唱，此次"中国日"活动办得非常成功。

2011年1月30日，第二届春节联欢晚会在第比利斯"缪斯"国际文化中心举行，晚会所有的节目均为自编自演，包括歌舞、戏曲、乐器、诗朗诵和小品等，第比利斯自由大学孔子学院的学生也带来了精彩的和声和歌舞节目。第比利斯音乐学院女高音歌唱家还用中文演唱了歌曲《茉莉花》《美丽的夜莺》等。本次联欢会不仅营造了春节的气氛，更唤起了海外华人华侨对祖国的自豪感。

2012年12月，为庆祝中格建交20周年，两国政府文化部商定互办文化日，甘肃省歌剧院带来的《敦煌韵》大型舞剧描绘了中国大唐盛世，表达了中国人民在历史上与各民族和睦相处的愿望，并将新年祝福送给格鲁吉亚人民，此次文化日活动将两国关系推到了一个新的历史台阶。[①]

(3) 新发展阶段（2013—2020）

随着中国与格鲁吉亚文化往来日益密切及取得的巨大成就，两国关系进入新发展阶段后，中格民间文化交流拉开了新序幕。

2013年3月27—28日，兰州大学武术队受邀与格鲁吉亚武术协会进行武术文化交流，双方联合举办了"中国—格鲁吉亚武术交流会"，中国武术是中国文化和民族精神的体现，本次交流会激发了格民众学习武术的热情，也推动了中格武术文化交流与建设；9月9日，"对话

---

① 网易新闻：《中国与格鲁吉亚建交20周年专访》，2012年6月7日，http：//news.163.com/12/0607/08/83CQRLD200014JB5.html。

兵马俑—欧盟与中国雕塑家作品巡演"开幕式在格鲁吉亚采南达利市恰夫恰瓦泽故居博物馆举行，该作品展由中国陕西省博物馆、比利时的"现代雕塑中心"、格鲁吉亚丝绸之路集团等单位联合举办，共展出30件中欧艺术家作品，此次展览对促进东西方文化交流意义重大，通过无声的艺术语言增进彼此之间的友谊；12月7日，由格妇女俱乐部举办的圣诞慈善义卖活动在第比利斯喜来登酒店开幕，中国大使馆设的中国展区布满了具有中国特色的商品和美味小吃，宣传中格关系的小册子受到了大家的热烈欢迎，本次义卖活动使格鲁吉亚民众对中国文化产生了浓厚的兴趣。

2014年7月5日，"南京青奥同心结文化交流—中国与格鲁吉亚"活动在南京市第五高级学校举行，此次活动拉开了中国与格鲁吉亚校级教学合作的序幕。

2015年10月11日，中国驻格鲁吉亚大使岳斌参加首届格鲁吉亚"中国日"活动，格教育与科技部部长萨尼吉泽、第比利斯市市长纳尔马尼亚、格国家旅游局局长乔戈瓦泽及格鲁吉亚近万名民众参加。"中国日"活动的成功举行，是中格民间文化交往的一个里程碑，更有助于格民众与中华文化零距离接触，对培育更多的中格文化友好事业的传播者有重要意义。

2016年3月13日，在国家大剧院管弦乐团2015—2016音乐剧的毕业音乐会上，格鲁吉亚籍女钢琴家蒂雅·布尼亚季什维利与乐团首席指挥吕嘉合作，在音乐会上演奏舒曼钢琴协奏曲，并在音乐会结束后开启了中国的巡演，让更多的中国人了解格鲁吉亚的艺术文化；6月22日，格鲁吉亚美酒节在上海罗斯福公馆举行，使中国人民深度了解了格鲁吉亚的葡萄酒历史及文化。10月10日，格鲁吉亚驻中国大使馆一秘缇娜婷·茜茜娜什维利拜会中国美术家协会，双方就组织格鲁吉亚美术家参加2017年北京国际美术双年展及双方文化艺术合作前景进行了探讨。此次会面奠定了中格美术界交流的基调，为双方开展长久深入的合作打下了坚实的基础。

2020年1月11日，格鲁吉亚中国涉外教育学院举行了开业庆典和剪彩仪式，旨在为格鲁吉亚民众提供更多学习汉语及了解中国文化的机会。

3. 教育部中外语言交流合作中心文化教育建设

教育部中外语言交流合作中心孔子学院是我国为了满足国外民众学习汉语的热情，创办的汉语学习和中华文化推广的中外合作非营利性机构，它是采用中外合作的形式开展、通过双方共同建立而形成的教育平台。为了满足格民众学习汉语和了解中华文化的需求，教育部中外语言交流合作中心相继创办第比利斯自由大学孔子学院和第比利斯开放大学孔子学院。

（1）早期阶段（1992—1999）

汉语早在沙皇时期就被官方引进到了格鲁吉亚，经过发展，汉语学习人数有了一定的规模。1991年，格鲁吉亚亚非学院创立，它成了整个外高加索首个设立汉语专业的高等学府；1992年，中国与格鲁吉亚建交后，格鲁吉亚学习汉语的人数逐渐增加；同年，亚非学院正式开设了中文系，在创建初期，由于缺乏汉语老师和学习教材，汉语课在开展的过程中面临了很多困难；1992年，刘光文女士受邀担任亚非学院中文系老师，格鲁吉亚汉语发展开始步入了正轨，并为以后的孔子学院的建立奠定了基础。

（2）发展阶段（2000—2012）

进入21世纪后，随着"汉语热"在全球的广泛兴起，2002年，格鲁吉亚教育部向中国提出申请，希望中方能派中文教师在格鲁吉亚教授汉语，此后每年都会有1—2名教师来第比利斯自由大学中文系教授汉语；2010年开始，格鲁吉亚中小学也向格教育部申请汉语老师，希望他们可以在中学任教，并教授汉语课程；2010年11月26日，第比利斯自由大学孔子学院举办了揭牌仪式，孔子学院的建立为格民众学习汉语和了解中国文化提供了宽广的平台；[①] 2012年2

[①] 中华人民共和驻格鲁吉亚大使馆：《驻格鲁吉亚大使陈建福出席第比利斯自由大学孔子学院揭牌仪式》，2010年11月28日，https://www.fmprc.gov.cn/ce/cege/chn/kxjy/t772652.htm。

月6日，兰州大学2012年孔子学院春晚巡演团在格首都第比利斯举行首场演出，中国驻格鲁吉亚大使陈建福，格鲁吉亚外交部、科技和教育部、文化部和古迹部、格中友好协会、华人华侨、中资企业代表500余人参加了此次活动，孔子学院春晚巡演活动为中格民间表演艺术提供了一个交流的契机，更为中格两国搭建了一座超越国界、民族与时代的桥梁。

（3）新发展阶段（2013—2020）

"一带一路"倡议提出后，中格两国的文化交往迈上了一个历史新台阶。

2013年11月23日，第六届"孔子学院杯"武术散打赛开幕，武术散打比赛是由第比利斯自由大学孔子学院和格武术协会联合举办的，参赛的武术散打选手来自格鲁吉亚和伊朗两国，本次比赛对中国武术文化的传播产生了深远的影响。

2014年1月27日，第比利斯自由大学孔子学院举办春节联欢晚会，作为孔子学院一年一度的重大活动，它不仅为汉语专业的学生提供了一个展示自我的平台，更能有效地传播中国的语言与文化；9月26日，在新中国成立65周年前夕，圣安德里亚大学举办"中国日"活动，"中国俱乐部"的学生制作了有关中国历史文化及当代发展的宣传片和图片，并表演了中国传统舞蹈，受到了广大活动参与者的一致好评；9月30日，中国驻格鲁吉亚大使岳斌参加了第比利斯自由大学孔子学院成立四周年活动。孔子学院成立四年来，在汉语教学和中华文化推广上取得了优异的成绩，也为中格文化合作与交流做出了重大贡献。

2015年1月29日，第比利斯自由大学孔子学院举办第二届"格鲁吉亚中小学汉语知识竞赛"，吸引了来自12所中小学500多名学生参赛，有效地扩大了汉语在格的传播范围；[1] 2月5日，第比利斯自由

---

[1] 教育部中外语言交流合作中心官网：《第比利斯自由大学孔子学院举办格鲁吉亚中学生中国知识竞赛》，2010年5月8日，http://www.hanban.org/article/2018-05/08/content_730412.htm。

大学孔子学院举办"羊年春节联欢晚会";4月17日,格鲁吉亚首届"中国之声"中国歌曲大赛总决赛在第比利斯自由大学孔子学院举行,中国驻格鲁吉亚大使岳斌为冠军选手颁奖,此次歌曲大赛让更多的格鲁吉亚民众了解中国的歌曲文化;5月15日,第比利斯自由大学孔子学院举办"格鲁吉亚第四届中国诗歌朗诵大赛",中国驻格鲁吉亚大使岳斌、自由大学校长奇科瓦尼、格鲁吉亚外交部官员共200余人参加了活动,诗歌大赛展示了中国的诗词文化,受到了格民众的一致好评;5月22日,第八届"汉语桥"世界中学生中文比赛格鲁吉亚决赛在格鲁吉亚举办,这是"汉语桥"比赛首次走进格鲁吉亚,学生们通过参加比赛展示自己的汉语学习成果,也推动了中格之间文化的交流;10月11日,"孔子学院日"系列活动之"中华文化走进社区"活动在Dedaena公园举办,此次活动是由中国驻格鲁吉亚大使馆、第比利斯市政府、第比利斯自由大学孔子学院联合举行的,吸引了格鲁吉亚万余人参加。

2016年3月31日,时任故宫博物院院长单霁翔在第比利斯自由大学孔子学院举办题为"故宫的世界,世界的故宫"文化讲座,该讲座不仅宣传了故宫文化,更是让人们了解到故宫藏品背后的文化底蕴及相关文化产业的发展;8月16—29日,兰州大学承办格鲁吉亚部分校长及汉语项目主管赴华文化参访项目,该项目为巩固和拓宽汉语教学点,促进教育高层领导对中国文化的了解有着积极作用;8月27日,"2016年格鲁吉亚学生文化之旅夏令营"在中国开启了为期两周的文化之旅,加深了格鲁吉亚学生对中国人民和中国文化的了解,使中外师生友谊逐步升华。

2017年1月24日,教育部中外语言交流合作中心举办格鲁吉亚与"一带一路"研讨会,时任中国驻格鲁吉亚大使季雁池出席并致辞,他介绍了中格在"一带一路"建设中取得的成就,并强调了人文交流对促进两国民心相通的重要意义。孔子学院为中格在"一带一路"中的文化建设贡献了力量。11月16日,第比利斯开放大学孔子课堂举行揭牌仪式,这是格鲁吉亚首个孔子课堂。① 中国驻格鲁吉亚参赞左洪波、格教育部官员、兰州大学副校长潘保田、开放大学师生及华人华侨出席了开幕式,孔子课堂将为格鲁吉亚人学习中文及中国文化搭建桥梁,并进一步推动中格两国教育文化之间的交流;随着"一带一路"倡议的推进,中国在格鲁吉亚的影响力与日俱增,格鲁吉亚政府官员也越来越重视汉语学习。孔子课堂自成立以来,陆续为格鲁吉亚官员开设汉语课,培养了越来越多的中格友好使者;12月23日,第比利斯开放大学孔子课堂的一节国画课让格鲁吉亚民众热情高涨。

2018年2月10日,第比利斯开放大学孔子课堂首届"春节联欢晚会"拉开帷幕,本届春晚不仅为汉语学生提供了一个展示自我的舞台,更为格鲁吉亚民众展示了中国的艺术文化。② 孔子课堂成立后,还开展了"中华文化进校园"文化系列活动,陆续走进第比利斯开设汉语教学点的学校,这些文化展示活动为推广中国文化,促进中格文化交流,提升孔子课堂的影响力起着积极作用;3月3日,孔子课堂推出了制作元宵节灯笼活动,使学生们感受到中国传统佳节的氛围。为了满足格鲁吉亚民众学习中国文化的需求,孔子课堂老师结合学生实际情况,策划推出了"相约星期六"系列文化活动,每周六都会举办书法、绘画、中国结、剪纸、武术、茶艺、围棋、汉语角等相关主题的文化活动,逐渐形成了孔子课堂自己的特色品牌,并一直延续了下来;4月3日,孔子课堂举办首届中文歌曲大赛决赛,该比赛既检验了孔子课堂的教学水平,又传播了中国的艺术文化;4月26日,孔子课堂举办首届"孔子课堂杯"围棋大赛,本次大赛不仅为围棋爱好者提供一个切磋棋艺的平台,还对进一步推广中国围棋文化,促进两国教育发展作出了贡献;5月7—8日,第比利斯开放大学、兰州大学

---

① 兰州大学新闻网:《兰州大学与第比利斯开放大学共建孔子课堂》,2017年11月22日,http://news.lzu.edu.cn/c/201711/46386.html。

② 教育部中外语言交流合作中心官网:《第比利斯开放大学孔子课堂首届春节联欢会精彩绽放》,2018年2月19日,http://www.hanban.org/article/2018-02/19/content_719034.htm。

联合主办的"全球视野中的'一带一路'国际论坛"在第比利斯开放大学举行，本次论坛为各国专家学者构建了交流合作的平台，有助于推动"一带一路"倡议中教育文化的交流与发展；5月9—10日，兰州大学共建孔子学院/课堂联席会暨2018年理事会在第比利斯开放大学举行，会议的成功召开对中格两国文化教育发展作出了突出的贡献；10月22日，由中国社会科学院、第比利斯开放大学及孔子课堂联合举办的"一带一路"五周年中格合作新前景圆桌会议在孔子课堂举办，本次会议为专家们提供了一次深入交流的机会，并谱写了中格合作的新篇章。11月24日，孔子课堂举办中小学汉语教学点校长论坛，此次论坛既对中小学汉语教学点的开辟和建设有指导作用，也为孔子课堂的科学发展奠定基础；11月24日，孔子课堂还举行了一周年庆典活动，孔子课堂成立以来的一周年里，累计汉语学员达到2000余人，覆盖了格鲁吉亚大、中、小学22个教学点，举办了30余场文化活动，对汉语教学和文化推广取得了优异的成绩；12月15日，首届"中国风"趣味运动会在孔子课堂举行，此次活动以喜闻乐见的形式推广中国文化，受到了当地民众的一致好评。

2019年2月2日，孔子课堂举办2019年春节联欢晚会，使格民众了解到了中国的春节习俗，提高了民众学习中国文化的热情和兴趣；3月16日，孔子课堂举办首届中小学生中国元素绘画比赛，此次比赛拉近了学生与中国文化的距离；[1] 5月18日，第二届"孔子课堂杯"围棋大赛在孔子课堂拉开帷幕，与首届"孔子课堂杯"相比，本次围棋大赛的选手水平更高，并进一步地宣传了中国的围棋文化；[2] 6月15日，第十二届"汉语桥"世界中学生中文比赛在孔子课堂举行，这是孔子课堂成立来首次承办"汉语桥"大赛，受到了社

---

[1] 教育部中外语言交流合作中心官网：《妙手绘丹青演绎中国风》，2019年3月24日，http://www.hanban.org/article/2019-03/24/content_767418.htm。

[2] 教育部中外语言交流合作中心官网：《第比利斯开放教育大学孔子课堂举办第二届"孔子课堂杯"围棋大赛》，2019年5月20日，http://www.hanban.org/article/2019-05/20/content_773612.htm。

会各界的一致好评，并扩大了孔子课堂的影响力；① 7月15—28日，2019年孔子课堂赴华夏令营在中国展开语言文化之旅，本次夏令营活动为格学生提供一个了解中国文化的机会；11月16日，孔子课堂举办第二届中文歌曲大赛，本次大赛比首届的汉语水平更高，表演也更加成熟，对中华文化推广有重要意义；12月14日，孔子课堂举办第二届"中国风"趣味运动会；12月21日，孔子课堂迎来了成立两周年庆典暨孔子学院揭牌仪式，② 中国驻格鲁吉亚大使李岩、格鲁吉亚驻华大使阿尔赤卡岚第亚、格鲁吉亚鲁斯塔维里国家科学院主席兹瓦德·加布森尼亚、第比利斯大中小学教学点校长、驻格中资企业等参加了庆典仪式，孔子学院已经成为格鲁吉亚了解中国的一个窗口，并为两国教育文化交流与发展作出了突出的贡献。

四 结语

自"一带一路"倡议提出以来，中国与"一带一路"沿线国家的政治联系、经贸往来、教育文化交流等都备受国际社会关注。"国之交在于民之亲，民相亲在于心相通"，"丝绸之路"为我们留下了丰富的历史遗产。在21世纪的新时代，"一带一路"不仅继承了"丝绸之路、商贸之路"的使命，它还被赋予了新的时代内涵，即构建"民心相通之路"。

格鲁吉亚作为"一带一路"沿线重要国家之一，非常重视与中国在各领域之间的合作与交流。双方通过官方平台、民间组织、孔子学院等开展一系列文化交流活动，不仅为中国塑造了良好的国际形象，也为格鲁吉亚人民了解中国提供了重要窗口。今天，中国与格鲁吉亚

---

① 教育部中外语言交流合作中心官网：《第十二届"汉语桥"世界中学生中文比赛格鲁吉亚赛区决赛举行》，2019年6月24日，http://www.hanban.org/article/2019-06/24/content_778570.htm。

② 教育部中外语言交流合作中心官网：《第比利斯开放教育大学孔子课堂成立两周年庆典暨孔子学院揭牌仪式举行》，2019年12月24日，http://www.hanban.org/article/2019-12/24/content_797058.htm。

通过文化交流与合作建设，传承弘扬了"和平合作、开放包容、互学互鉴、互利共赢"的丝绸之路精神，同时，也打造了政治互信、经济融合、文化包容的"利益共同体、责任共同体、命运共同体"。

虽然，在中格文化交往的过程中，遇到了一些困难和挑战，但双方通过多种形式的文化交流，加强教育旅游文化的合作、完善文化产业合作机制、创新文化合作新形势，实现了文化交流与合作的可持续发展。

综上所述，中国与格鲁吉亚在文化交流的过程中取得了很大的成就，特别是"一带一路"倡议提出后，双方的文化交流领域得到进一步拓展，同时，我们也应该正视客观存在的挑战，构建中格文化交往的新格局，保证"一带一路"的安全畅通，从而实现中华民族伟大复兴的"中国梦"。

参考文献

[1] 龚天颖：《"16+1"合作下中国对中东欧文化外交研究》，北京外国语大学，2019 年。

[2] 朱小雪：《"一带一路"文化外交问题研究》，湖南大学，2017 年。

[3] 杨荣国、张新平：《"一带一路"人文研究：战略内涵、现实挑战与实践途径》，《甘肃社会科学》2018 年第 6 期。

[4] 李凤亮、罗小艺：《跨文化交流视域中"一带一路"文化产业合作》，《西北大学工业学报》（社会科学版）2018 年第 4 期。

[5] 刘翠霞、高宏存：《"一带一路"文化产业国际合作优势选择与重点领域研究》，《东岳论丛》2019 年 10 月第 10 期。

[6] 李国青、刘晓宇：《中华文化在"一带一路"沿线国家传播的出路》，《北方经贸》2018 年第 11 期。

[7] 梁福兴、罗丹：《"一带一路"背景下中越两国骆越文化旅游产业合作发展研究》，《广西社会科学》2016 年第 6 期。

［8］［美］萨缪尔·亨廷顿：《文明的冲突与世界秩序的重建》，新华出版社2010年版。

［9］［英］彼得·弗拉科潘：《丝绸之路：一部全新的世界史》，浙江大学出版社2016年版。

［10］孔子学院总部官网：http：//www.hanban.org/

［11］中华人民共和国驻格鲁吉亚大使馆：http：//ge.china-embassy.org/chn/

［12］新华网：http：//www.xinhuanet.com/

［13］中华人民共和国外交部：https：//www.fmprc.gov.cn/web/

［14］中国一带一路网：https：//www.yidaiyilu.gov.cn/index.htm

［15］中国政府网：http：//www.gov.cn

［16］网易新闻：https：//news.163.com/

［17］兰州大学新闻网：http：//news.lzu.edu.cn/

Part 1

China's Economic and Social Development

Chapter 1

China's Social Development History and Prospect

Zhang Yi

Director, Professor

National Institute of Social Development, CASS

    The development of China's society, first of all, is reflected in the growth of population size and the change of place of employment, followed by a magnificent upsurge of urbanization and the development echelons in the proportion of employment in the three industrial structures, and finally, by the optimization of class structure, the upgrading of consumption level and the expansion of per capita housing area of families, as well as the improvement of human capital and the expansion of social mobility channels. China has changed from a poor society to a well–off society. At the same time, China has also enhanced the per capita education level and extended the per capita life expectancy. China has, on the whole, changed from the stage of popularizing nine–year compulsory education to the stage of mass higher education, and has also changed from low life expectancy at the founding of People's Republic of China to high life expectancy—the average life expectancy in 2018 reaching 77 years old, which makes China top all the developing countries in the world.

As the most commonplace explanation in the social sciences, social development implies a transformation of social structure, social organization mode, social production mode and social lifestyle from a relatively low level to a relatively high level. Since the industrial society appeared in human history, development has always been regarded as a transformation of the human society from agricultural one to industrial one and finally to a post-industrial one, or referred to as the process of modernization. [1] Regardless of the macro society level, or micro community and organization level, the social development of China is always full of words and expressions related to industrialization and modernization with top–bottom or bottom–top significance of daily life.

China's development in the sense of modernization is objectively reflected in the process of changes in various social fields driven by economic growth. Economic growth and population growth are tied together. The structural changes of children's population, labor force population and elderly population affect the overall economic growth rate and its growth model from the distribution ratio of accumulation and consumption. Therefore, the social construction and social development of China in the past 70 years is firstly the process of demographic transition in the dialectical change of population growth rate and economic growth rate.

I The Expansion of Population Size and the Extension of Life Expectancy Per Capita

Since the founding of the People's Republic of China, the population as

---

[1] Wang Yuan, Kong Weiyan, "China's Social Development Trends in the Next 30 Years and Suggestions for Promoting Shared Development", *Macroeconomics*, Vol. 5, 2019.

a preset variable has affected economic and social development. From the land reform, equivalent land ownership to the cooperative, and then to the establishment of the three-level ownership system based on the people's commune team, and the nationalization and collectivization movement of urban enterprises, to a certain extent, solved the problem of people's urgent needs of food, and also improved the people's stable living standards and medical standards to a certain extent, which led to the rapid growth of the population. ① In return, the rapid growth of population has brought pressure on economic and social development. In order to overcome the pressure brought by the population growth faster than the economic growth rate, the country embarked on a journey of family planning, which advocated that a couple should have only one child, and tried to control the population size within 1.2 billion in 2000. In 2000, the family planning law was promulgated to control the impact of population growth on the national economy and social development.

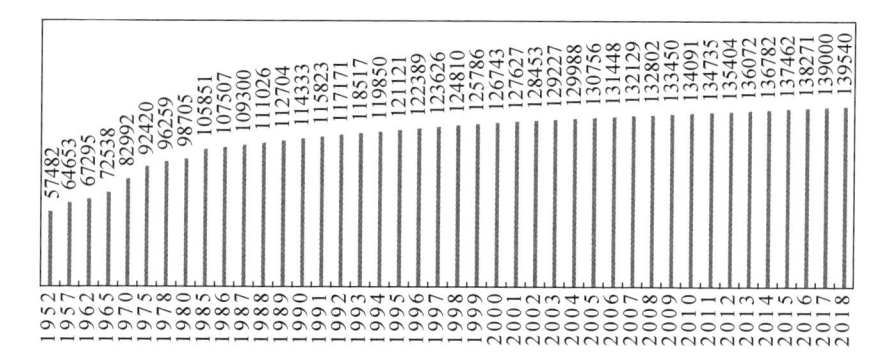

Figure 1-1 China's population growth trend in the 70 years since the founding of the People's Republic of China

---

① Except for the population loss in the "three-year difficult period" from 1959 to 1961, the population in other historical periods showed a trend of growth.

China's birth rate pattern has been gradually shifted from high growth to low growth in the 21st century. However, due to the influence of the huge population base, the new growth of population is still very considerable every year, so the population has been breaking new highs repeatedly. At the beginning of the founding of the People's Republic of China, the actual population in 1949 exceeded 450 million and reached 540 million, 660 million in 1960, 830 million in 1970, 980 million in 1980, 1.14 billion in 1990, 1.26 billion in 2000, 1.34 billion in 2010, and 1.395 billion by the end of 2018. [1]

During the planned economy, due to the low production efficiency, the increment of land output is difficult to supply the food demand brought by population growth. After the reform and opening-up, both rural and urban areas have fully liberated the productive forces, improved the relations of production and superstructure, and made them adapt to the growing productive forces, thus arousing the people's enthusiasm for production. China's grain production has been growing rapidly and historically. Chinese farmers have also changed their labor occupations in the form of migrant workers. They have left their hometown to work and do business in cities, which not only meets the needs of urban labor force but also provides the agricultural industry with labor and capital, thus fundamentally changes the traditional appearance of villages and towns.

Under the condition of low productivity level, it is difficult to "feed" or "nourish" the stock population with more and more people. However, in the reform to gradually coordinate the productive forces and production relations with gradual implementation of the household contract responsibility system and removal of the constraint on labor mobility, the timely reform of

---

[1] The population figures for 2017 and before are from table 2-1 of *China Statistical Yearbook in 2018* and *2018 Statistics Bulletin of the National Economic and Social Development of the People's Republic of China*.

the household registration system, and the gradual growth of township enterprises and private enterprises, the increase of the total population and the growth of the number of labor force have not kept pace with the improvement of living conditions. China has encountered the problem of starvation at the stages of more than 500 million people, 600 million people, 700 million people, 800 million people and 900 million people. In a growth practice of more than 1 billion people, China has hardly encountered the problem of starvation. More and more facts show that the increase in population is accompanied by the improvement of quality of life. In the period of a planned economy, the ration system of grain, cloth, meat, and oil was abolished by the economic development after the reform and opening up, as well as the price double-track system.

In the composition of productive forces, science and technology are the most positive progressive factors. Before the reform and opening-up, the agricultural production teams, production brigades or people's communes were maintained in a reproduction structure combining human and animal power. Under the condition of given land fertility, the food increment provided by agricultural labor force "involution" is extremely limited. In 1952, the number of employed people in the primary industry accounted for 83.5% of the total employment in the country. At the beginning of the reform in 1978, 70.5% of the employed people were still working in the primary industry. In other words, with the slow development of agricultural science and technology and the difficulty in liberating the productive forces in the relations of production, even if more than 70% of the country's labor and employment personnel are put into the primary industry, the food produced by them can hardly meet the needs of the population.

However, after the reform and opening-up, with the opening up of rural areas and the implementation of household contract responsibility system, on the one hand, agricultural output has been greatly increased, on the other hand, a large number of surplus rural labor force has been separated out to work in cities. In China, family planning reduced the number of children in the family, the time for the family to take care of their children, and the amount of family chores. First, the husband was liberated to work in the city, and then the wife took the children to work in the city.

It should be said that during the 43 years after the reform and opening-up, China has maintained an average annual growth rate of about 9.5%, which has promoted social and community development, and people's living standards. At the same time, the proportion of employees in China's primary industry has rapidly decreased to 60.1% in 1990, 50% in 2000 and 27% in 2017. That is to say, China now feeds nearly 1.4 billion people with the grain produced by about 27% of the labor force and employment, and has greatly increased the amount of food consumption of the Chinese people. In 2017, China's per capita grain consumption has decreased to about 130.1 kg per year, but the consumption of meat has increased to 26.7 kg per year, milk consumption has increased to 12.1 kg, and the consumption of dried and fresh fruits has increased to 45.6 kg. [①]

The improvement of nutritional status and medical security has rapidly extended the average life expectancy of Chinese population. In 1949, when the People's Republic of China was founded, the average life expectancy of the Chinese population was only 35 years. In 1957, the figure was extended to 57 years. Finally, the average life expectancy reached 64 years in 1964. Practice has proved that as long as the war is eliminated and a relatively fair production and living environment is formed, the life expectancy of the population will rapidly grow. After the reform and opening-up, the average life expectancy of Chinese people has been greatly

---

① Data source: see table 6-4 of *China Statistical Yearbook* in 2018.

increased, reaching 68 years in 1981, 69 years in 1990, 71 years in 1996, 73 years in 2005, 75 years in 2010, 76 years in 2015 and 77 years in 2018. ①

In the growth of life expectancy per capita, women have shown more surviving advantages than men. At the time of the fourth census in 1990, the average life expectancy of the female population was 70.5 years and that of the male population was 66.8 years. At the fifth census in 2000, the average life expectancy of women was 73.3 years old and that of men was 69.6 years old. At the sixth census in 2010, the average life expectancy of the female population was 77.4 years and that of the male population was 72.4 years. In 2015, the average life expectancy of the female population was 79.4 years and that of the male population was 73.6 years. ② The most enviable aspect of China's social development is the extension of the average life expectancy of the population. The increase of the average life expectancy of the population in turn verifies the sharing speed of social progress and social development.

II The Great Development of Education and the Promotion of Human Capital

Since the founding of the People's Republic of China, the greatest manifestation of China's social development is the improvement of the average national education level.

Around 1949, the illiteracy rate in China was as high as 80%. From 1949 to 2000, China has devoted more than 50 years to improving the literacy rate of the whole people and eliminating illiteracy, and finally

---

① Data source: see table 2-4 of *China Statistical Yearbook* in 2018.
② At present, the longest life expectancy in Asia is Japan, with an average life expectancy of 87.32 years for women and 81.25 years for men.

completed the task of getting rid of illiteracy in a country with the largest population. As early as in the period of cooperation, collectivization and nationalization, the government began the nationwide literacy campaign and the adult literacy promotion campaign. Governments at all levels and mass organizations have widely held night schools and literacy classes in factories, rural areas, streets and troops, compiled literacy textbooks, and combined the improvement of literacy rate with daily life, mutual education of the common people, development of young people, and women's liberation movement, which formed a fever of centralized learning in fields, workshops, factories and military garrisons.

After years of effort, the adult literacy rate has increased year after year. In the second census in 1964, the number of illiterate and semi‐illiterate people (those aged 13 years and above who were illiterate or with little literacy) dropped to 33.58%, 22.81% in 1982[1] and 15.88% in 1990. After nearly 50 years of effort, the illiteracy rate was finally reduced to 6.72% in the fifth census in 2000.

At the same time of eliminating illiteracy, China has also vigorously set up education and expanded the enrollment scale of education at all levels. At the beginning of the 1950s, the government set up a primary school in several cooperatives or in a township to adapt to the increase of school‐age population. After the establishment of the people's communes and production brigades, the degree of organization at the grass‐roots level was further strengthened. Under the leadership of the people's commune, almost all the production brigades with the conditions have set up primary schools. Therefore, it can be seen from figure 2 that the 1950s and 1960s have witnessed the fastest growth in the number of primary school students in

---

[1] Data source: table 4‐4 of *China Statistical Yearbook*, 2004. In 1964, the illiterate population was 13 years old and over, and in 1982, 1990 and 2000, the illiterate population was 15 years old or above.

China.

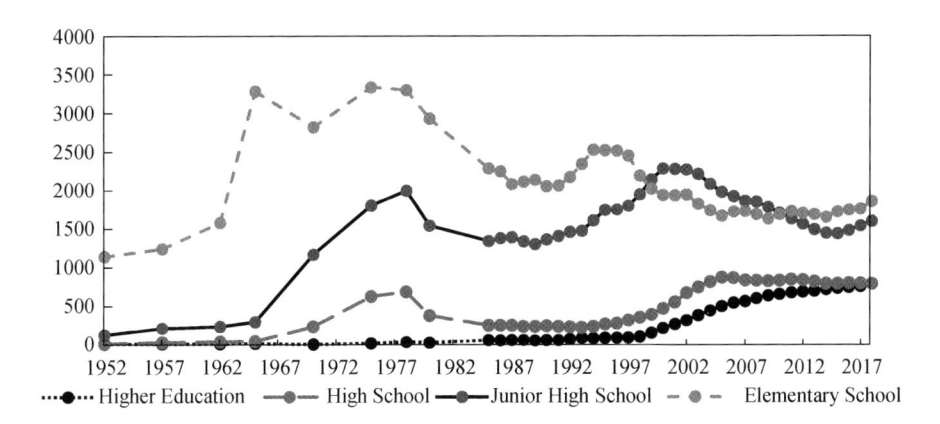

Figure 1 – 2 Trend of Enrollment in Schools at all Levels since the Founding of the People's Republic of China (Unit: 10, 000)

In 1952, the enrollment of primary schools in China reached 11.493 million. However, the enrollment of junior high schools is only 1.422 million, that of high schools is only 141,000, and that of ordinary colleges and universities is 79,000. Because of the income gap and the basic pattern of college enrollment at the beginning of the founding of the People's Republic of China, the source of students receiving education in colleges and universities is basically the children of relatively wealthy families in cities or counties. After the completion of the socialist transformation in 1957, the number of students enrolled in ordinary primary schools increased to 12.49 million, that of ordinary junior high schools rose to 2.17 million, that of ordinary high schools rose to 323,000, and that of colleges and universities rose to 106,000. It can be seen that at that time, the number of students enrolled in junior high school or above was still very limited. In the 1960s, with the population explosion in the middle and early 1950s, the enrollment of ordinary primary schools in China increased rapidly. By 1965, the number of students enrolled in ordinary primary schools reached 32.96

million, and in 1975 it reached 33.52 million. Since then, it has declined slowly. Due to the influence of birth control and family planning, the number of school-age children began to decline, and the number of primary school students also began to decline. However, the enrollment of ordinary junior high schools has greatly increased, reaching 18.1 million in 1975. The enrollment of ordinary high schools has also reached a historic 6.331 million. Under the influence of concept that "the schooling system should be shortened and education should be revolutionized", the time of primary school education should be shortened to five years, two years for junior high school and two years for senior high school. And high school combined with the local characteristics, created a lot of matching professional employment, such as agricultural machinery class, carpentry class, casting class and so on. However, due to the history reason, the enrollment of higher education stopped. After 1966, the number of students in higher education began to decline. In 1970, only 42,000 workers, peasants and soldiers were recruited.

After the reform and opening-up, on the one hand, the implementation of the household contract responsibility system, on the other hand, the commune or township government's control of the production brigade has been relaxed. In addition, the demand for labor force from rural families and township enterprises has led to a shrinking trend in the number of students enrolled in ordinary junior high schools and that in ordinary high schools. After the enrollment reached 20.06 million in 1978, it dropped to 15.509 million in 1980, 13.494 million in 1985 and 13.094 million in 1989. After reaching 6.929 million in 1978, it dropped to 3.834 million in 1980, only 2.575 million in 1985 and 2.283 million in 1993.

After the end of the Cultural Revolution, the college entrance examination system① was resumed in 1977, and the enrollment of higher education began to rise slowly. Because of the small number of high school students, there is a situation that junior high school entrance examination is difficult to high school entrance examination. Generally speaking, from the beginning of resuming the college entrance examination to 1997, the enrollment of colleges and universities has been on the rise, but the enrollment of ordinary high schools has declined rapidly. For example, in 1993, the number of students enrolled in Colleges and universities reached 924,000, but that of ordinary high schools was only 2.283 million. ②In 1989, the enrollment rate of high school to higher education was 24.6%, increased to 45.1% in 1997 and 83.4% in 2003. But in 2003, the enrollment rate of junior high school to senior high school was

---

① In October 1977, the State Council approved the *Opinions of the Ministry of Education on the Admission Work of Colleges and Universities* in 1977, which stipulates that all workers, peasants, educated youths going to the countryside and returning to the city, demobilized soldiers and fresh graduates who meet the requirements can participate in the college entrance examination. The conditions here are relaxed to senior high school graduates in 1966 and 1967. Therefore, there is a big year gap among the students. In the winter of that year, more than 270, 000 students were enrolled. Since some people missed the opportunity of the college entrance examination, another examination was held in July 1978, and 402, 000 people were admitted. Grade 77 was enrolled in the spring of 1978 and Grade 78 in the autumn of 1978. But this is not to say that there was no enrollment during the cultural revolution. In fact, enrollment began to resume in 1971 by adopting the method of "voluntary enrollment, recommendation by the masses, approval by leaders, and review by schools", and the "revisionist enrollment and examination system" was abolished. The main recruitment was workers, peasants and soldiers with better family background. Because students need to have more than 3 years of "practical experience", are not limited by their educational level, and are recommended to be free of examination and given 19.5 yuan of food and subsidies, the phenomenon of "get in by the back-door" is prominent, and the academic performance is not ideal. However, many colleges and technical schools have been restored and built in this period.

② During this period, the combination of junior high school and senior high school reduced the accessibility of educational resources. The increase in school accommodation, tuition and books also makes it difficult for some low-income families to provide their children with the necessary learning expenses. On the other hand, it reduces the enrollment rate of ordinary junior high school and ordinary high school. Of course, some families still choose to arrange their children to drop out of school for employment because of the employment opportunities provided by migrant workers.

only 60.2%.

After the reform and opening-up, the widening gap between urban and rural areas gradually makes rural basic education tend to be vulnerable. The 1982 Constitution clearly stipulates that the state should popularize compulsory education. In 1985, *the Decisions of the Central Committee of the Communist Party of China on the Reform of the Education System* emphasized the implementation of nine-year compulsory education. In 1986, the *Law of the People's Republic of China on Compulsory Education* was implemented on July 1, 1986 after deliberation and approval by the Sixth National People's Congress. Since then, China has embarked on the road of administering education according to law. In 1992, the State Education Commission issued the detailed rules for the implementation of the *Law of the People's Republic of China on Compulsory Education*, which strengthened the education work in primary and junior high schools. After that, the enrollment rate of junior high school and senior high school has gradually rebounded. The enrollment of junior high school students reached 17.523 million in 1995 and 22.956 million in 2000. The enrollment of senior high schools reached 2.736 million in 1995 and 4.727 million in 2000.

The increase in the number of students enrolled in junior high school and senior high school education during this period is also closely related to the increase of government investment in education, the increase of per capita disposable income in rural areas, and the reduction of the number of children caused by family planning. The latter support may be greater than other factors, because Chinese families place a high value on the education of their children. Since the reform and opening-up, the rapid growth of the national economy provided opportunities for upward mobility of Chinese people, which also encouraged families to actively invest in their children to receive modern education.

The changes in the number of students enrolled in primary schools and junior middle schools after the mid-1990s are basically in line with the changes in the family planning policy. The population born in the process of the rising birth rate in the middle and late 1980s, after increasing the number of primary school students in the early 1990s, has also increased the number of junior high school students in the middle and late 1990s. As shown in Figure 1 - 2, the curve of the number of junior high school students exceeds that of primary school students. Until 2011, the number of primary school students again exceeded that of junior high school students. This is the result of the impact of the same period group born in the process of fertility rising in the middle and late 1980s into the vigorous period of marriage and childbirth after 2005.

However, the expansion of university enrollment has led to the growth of enrollment in ordinary high schools. From 1990 to 1997, the enrollment of higher education in China increased from 609,000 to 1 million, only less than 400,000. But in 1999, it increased to 1.597 million students on the basis of 108.4 enrollment in 1998—a net increase of 513,000 in a year. In 2000, there were 609,000 more students than in 1999, reaching 2.206 million. In order to alleviate the employment pressure of the labor market and improve the quality of the whole people, more than 3.2 million students were enrolled in 2002, 4.47 million students were enrolled in 2004, 5.46 million in 2006, 6.07 million in 2008, 7.21 million people in 2014, and 7.91 million people in 2018. Because the growth rate of high school enrollment cannot keep up with that of higher education enrollment, the number of high school enrollment in 2018 is very similar to that of university enrollment, only 7.93 million. In the process of family planning, which reduces the number of primary school students, the number of junior high school students has also declined and necessarily a decline in the number of high school students.

Table 1 – 1　　Population with Different Educational Levels Per 100,000 Population from the Second to the Sixth Census　Unit: person

	1964	1982	1990	2000	2010
College degree and above	416	615	1,422	3,611	8,930
High School	1,319	6,779	8,039	11,146	14,032
Junior High School	4,680	17,892	23,344	33,961	38,788
Primary School	28,330	35,237	37,057	35,701	26,779

Note: the data of the first census is missing. Other data are from figure 3 – 6 of 2012 *China Statistical Yearbook*.

The development of education at all levels has rapidly promoted China's human capital. As can be seen from Table 1 – 1, in 1964, there were only 416 people with "college degree or above" per 100,000 population, which rose to 615 in the third census in 1982, 3,611 in the fifth census in 2000, and 8,930 in the sixth census in 2010. But the most rapid expansion is the "high school" education level of the population. At the second census in 1964, there were only 1,319 people with this educational level per 100,000, which rose to 6,779 in the third census in 1982, 8,039 in the fourth census in 1990, and 14,032 in the fifth census in 2000. As far as the labor force population is concerned, its quality has also been greatly improved. From 2006 to 2016, the average education level of the national labor force increased from 6.1 years to 10.0 years. The average education level of urban labor force has increased from 7.8 years to 11.2 years. The rural area has increased from 5.6 years to 8.5 years. In 2017, according to the data obtained from the GSS national sampling survey of the Chinese Academy of Social Sciences, 47.1% of the population born in 1990—2000 received "college degree or above". This means that nearly 50% of the population born after 1990 received a college degree.

Table 1 – 2   **Educational Level of Population of Different Birth Periods**   Unit: %

Birth Period	Junior High School and below	High School and Polytechnic School	College and above	Total
1949—1959	82.10	14.20	3.70	100.00
1960—1969	74.60	19.30	6.10	100.00
1970—1979	69.70	16.50	13.80	100.00
1980—1989	52.20	19.50	28.30	100.00
1990—2000	26.20	26.70	47.10	100.00

Data source: GSS national sampling survey of Institute of Sociology, Chinese Academy of Social Sciences, 2017.

In 2018, China's gross enrollment rate of higher education has reached 48.1%, higher than the average level of middle and high - income countries[1]. After 72 years of the founding of the People's Republic of China, China has changed from elite education stage to mass education stage. The future reform trend is to expand the nine - year compulsory education downward to kindergarten stage and upward to senior high school stage. [2]If free education can be extended downward and upward for three years, and tuition and miscell-aneous fees can be exempted, the average education level of China's population will be improved faster in the future.

---

[1] The gross enrollment rate after the enrollment of vocational education is included.

[2] The revised *Law on Compulsory Education of the People's Republic of China* in 2006 clearly stipulates that the implementation of compulsory education does not charge tuition and miscellaneous fees. In 2007, the tuition fees and miscellaneous fees of students in rural compulsory education stage were exempted, and textbook fees were exempted in 2007. In 2008, tuition fees and miscellaneous fees of urban compulsory education stage were exempted, and textbook fees of students in compulsory education stage of families enjoying minimum living security for urban residents were exempted.

Ⅲ　Rapid Urbanization and Improvement of Employment Structure

At the beginning of the founding of the People's Republic of China, the urban economic recovery needs the support of certain labor force, so there is a relatively rapid wave of urbanization. In 1949, the proportion of urban population in the total population was only 10.64%, but it reached 19.75% in 1960, almost reaching the urbanization rate of 1% per year.

After the reform and opening-up amid the start of commodity economy, the progress of agricultural production technology and the large-scale flow of rural surplus labor force to cities and towns have accelerated the pace of China's urbanization. The level of urbanization based on resident population has increased year by year. It reached 19.39% in 1980, 26.41% in 1990, 36.2% in 2000 and 49.95% in 2010. Since the 18th National Congress of the Communist Party of China, China's urbanization level has been steadily advancing, with an annual average increase of more than 1.2%. This has enabled more than 80 million agricultural transfer population to become urban residents, raising the urbanization rate of China, the world's most populous country, to a new history record, reaching about 59.6% in 2018.

The household registration system has been greatly reformed in different cities. In the policy allocation based on urban policies and classification except for megacities, other cities have liberalized the settlement restrictions. However, the devotion of farmers to the rural land and the improvement of market economy and rural social construction have gradually weakened the attraction of urban household registration. Practice has proved that as long as the urbanization process can adhere to the principle of equalization of basic public services, as long as the rural revitalization can adhere to the concept of farmers as the center, the farmers will no longer bind to the non-agricultural household registration. Now, on the contrary, it is difficult for people with non-agricultural household registration to change their household registration into agricultural one. It can be seen from here that the reform and opening up has brought earth shaking changes to Chinese society.

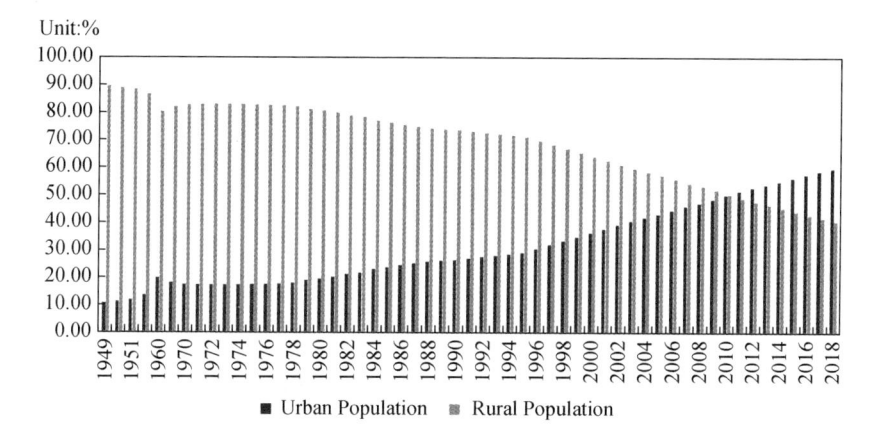

Figure 1-3 Urbanization Trend of the People's Republic of China in the Past 70 years

With the rapid development of urbanization, China has rapidly transformed from a village society to an urban society, from a settled life to a migrant life, from a self-sufficient and semi self-sufficient society to a market society, and from a traditional society to a modern society. This is the most significant event in human progress after the Renaissance. Urbanization is not only a transformation process of rural population to the city, but also a positive influence on urban production and lifestyle on rural areas. China's urbanization has not only successfully solved the employment problem of rural migrant workers, but also children's school enrollment. Although the solution to this problem is not satisfactory in megacities, the vast majority of the children of migrant workers are able to go to school under the system of "two mains" (the education funds are mainly invested by finance, and the schooling degree is mainly by public schools).

The portable and transferable social insurance policy also enables migrant workers to obtain the same rights as the urban labor force, and can participate in the social insurance of urban enterprise employees in the inflow place. According to the current growth rate, the urbanization rate of China's permanent population will exceed 75% in 2035 and 80% in 2050. While building China into a modern power in an all-round way and realizing the great rejuvenation of the Chinese nation, it has transformed the vast majority of China's population into urban population, greatly improving the quality of daily life of the Chinese people, enhancing the sense of happiness and security of Chinese people's life, and also making a significant contribution to the urbanization of the world's population.

At the same time, the tide of urbanization with migrant workers as the main force has also changed the employment structure of Chinese people rapidly, which makes the labor force flow from the primary industry to the secondary industry, and then to the tertiary industry. At the beginning of the founding of the People's Republic of China, the proportion of employees in the primary industry was as high as 83.5%, that in the secondary industry was only 7.4%, and that in the tertiary industry was only 9.1%. The implementation of the strategy of giving priority to the development of secondary industry and China's transformation from an agricultural country to an industrial one rapidly increased the proportion of employees in the secondary industry. By the time of reform and opening-up in 1978, the number of employees in the primary industry decreased to 70.5%, that in the secondary industry increased to 17.3%, and that in the tertiary industry increased to 12.2%.

Nevertheless, the proportion of agricultural workers is still very large. However, when the well-off society of food and clothing was realized

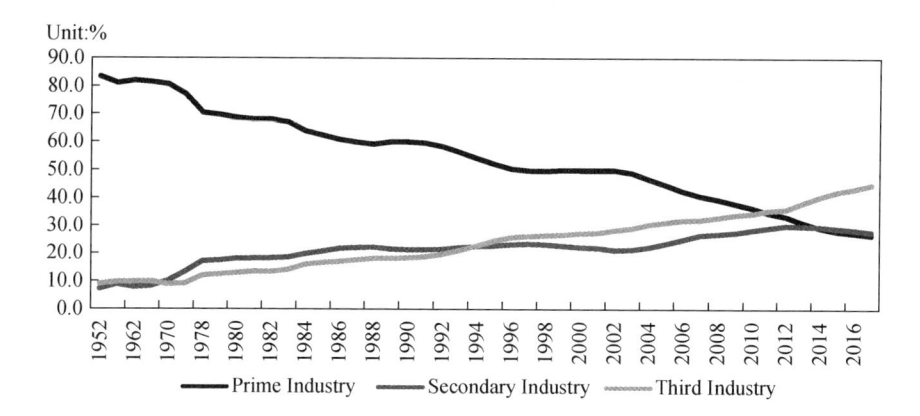

Figure 1–4 The Number of Employed People in Three Industries Since the Founding of the People's Republic of China

in 1990, the proportion of employees in the primary industry decreased to 60.1%, that in the secondary industry rose to 21.4%, and that in the tertiary industry rose to 18.5%. Therefore, before the mid–1960s, the proportion of employees in the tertiary industry was higher than that in the secondary industry. However, from the mid–1960s to 1994, the proportion of employees in the secondary industry once again exceeded that in the secondary industry. In other words, in 1994, the proportion of employees in the tertiary industry reached 23%, which once again exceeded the proportion of employees in the secondary industry. Since then, driven by the rapid economic development, the proportion of employees in the tertiary industry grew faster than that in the secondary industry for a long time, strengthening the characteristics of post–industrialization. This is the most significant change in employment structure since the founding of the People's Republic of China 72 years ago. With the requirements of market economy and social development, the demand for service industry is growing. After China has become a big manufacturing country, it has begun to transform into a big service industry country.

In addition, the further strengthening of agricultural modernization, land circulation and the use of chemical fertilizers have gradually reduced the number of employees in the primary industry. If the first generation of migrant workers are mainly male, then the demand of women in the second generation of migrant workers increased. This has strengthened the pulling force of the city to the rural middle-aged and young labor force. Therefore, since China's grain production is rising, the number of employees in the primary industry has plummeted. In 2000, the number of employees in the primary industry dropped to about 50%, that in the secondary industry reached 22.5%, and that in the tertiary industry rose to 27.5%. In 2010, the proportion of employees in the primary industry decreased to 36.7%, that in the secondary industry rose to 28.7%, and that in the tertiary industry reached 34.6%.

In 2011, the proportion of employees in China's three industrial structures experienced a second fundamental change: the proportion of employees in the primary industry dropped to the second place, to 24.8%, to 29.5% in the secondary industry, and 35.7% in the tertiary industry, becoming the sector with the most labor force. This is a perfect transcendence of the proportion of employees in the tertiary industry to that in the primary industry.

In 2015, the third epoch-making change took place in the structure of China's labor force employees. For the first time, the proportion of employees in the primary industry was lower than that in the second industry, falling to 28.3%, the proportion of employees in the secondary industry rose to 29.3%, and the proportion of employees in the tertiary industry rose to 42.4%. In 2018, the proportion of employees in the primary industry continued to decrease to 26.1%, the proportion of employees in the secondary industry decreased to 27.6%, while the proportion of employees in the tertiary industry increased to 46.3%. In the third transformation, after the decline of employees in the primary industry, the number of employees in the secondary industry also began to decline significantly.

In the future, with the progress of agricultural science and technology, as well as the improvement of agricultural robots and agricultural mechanization, the proportion of employees in the primary industry will gradually decrease. When the last generation of traditional agriculture descends in history, the characteristics of modern agriculture will be further strengthened. In this stable evolution, while maintaining a certain proportion of employees in the secondary industry, the biggest change in the future will be the continuous increase in the proportion and number of employees in the tertiary industry. The wave of post-industrialization will eventually bring this society into the man – machine society of the combination of machines and people. The biggest characteristic of man–machine society is the reduction of working time and labor intensity, but it is also the extension of people's leisure time and consumption time. Therefore, the demand of man–machine society for service industry will be greatly expanded.

Ⅳ Optimization of Class Structure and Upgrading of Consumption Structure

Since history recorded, China has been characterized by typical agricultural society for a long time. Whether in the north or the south, or in the east or the mid-west, the vast majority of the agricultural population rely on land for production and reproduction to obtain means of living. They even rely on the combination of animal power and human resources to survive and reproduce in the climate constraint. In the whole society, the peasant is the main social stratum.

Since the founding of the People's Republic of China, China has completed the initial industrialization and medium – term industrialization. Whether in the early or middle stage of industrialization, people engaged in industrial labor can always obtain more income than those engaged in agriculture. The consumption structure determined by the income structure encourages farmers to "jump out of the agricultural industry" to change their life style.

After the reform and opening – up, the mode of economy and organization based on the three levels of the people's commune, production brigade and team has been replaced by towns, administrative villages and natural villages, and the household contract responsibility system has also been widely promoted. In order to solve the problem of income, farmers first go out to work in the slack season, and then stay in the cities where they enter for a long time to become migrant workers. The channel of social mobility is gradually opened up. In this way, when farmers transform themselves into working class by going to cities to work and do business, they also transform their children into "national cadres", "non-manual workers" or "white-collars" by educating their children to participate in the college entrance examination.

After the reform and opening – up, the social mobility of Chinese farmers paralleled on the two roads of the transformation of workers and middle – class, and more farmers became industrial workers in 2000. Therefore, China's social mobility and class structure transformation are significantly different from those in the West. The West first ushered in industrialization and formed a large working class, and then after the World War II, it ushered in post industrialization and transformed the working class into the middle class. As the most populous country, China has continued industriali-zation in many provincial capital cities (i. e. second-tier cities) while post – industrialization in big cities, which is manifested as industrialization and post–industrialization in the same time and space, as well as large – scale and parallel industrialization and middle – class transformation in the same time and space.

It is precisely because of the dual characteristics of social transformation that China has solved the unbalanced development in the process of social transformation, resolved the social risks brought about by the transformation process to a certain extent, and maintained the long-term stability and harmonious development of society. The institutional change with the characteristics of progressive reform has created the economy and society outside the system by means of incremental reform, and created huge individual enterprises and township enterprises, forming a trend of absorbing rural surplus labor. The price double track system is used to construct different reforms within and outside the system. Finally, the integrated transformation of market economy is completed.

Although the reform of state-owned enterprises has not been completed, private enterprises have successfully occupied an important share with the market-oriented grass-roots growth, and become the main battlefield to solve the problem of labor employment. Now, the private economy has contributed 50% of the tax revenue, more than 60% of GDP, accounting for 70% of technological innovation and new products, solved more than 80% of urban employment, and contributed more than 90% to the new created employment opportunities.

The diversified development pattern of China's economy has successfully completed the modernization tasks proposed in various historical periods. In 1990, China achieved the goal of a well-off society with adequate food and clothing. In 2000, the overall goal of well-off society was achieved. In the course of continuous development, the grand goal of "building a well-off society" is put forward. Later, China adjusted "building a well-off society" to "building a well-off society in an all-round way", and now China continue to design it as "building a well-off society in an all-round way", and strive to make sustained efforts in economic, political, cultural, social and ecological civilization, so as to make the construction of people's livelihood step by step.

The process of industrialization and post-industrialization in China has rapidly increased the per capita disposable income of urban and rural residents. In 1978, the per capita annual disposable income of national residents was 171.2 yuan, including 343.4 yuan for urban residents and 133.6 yuan for rural residents. In 2000, the annual per capita disposable income of national residents was 3,721.3 yuan, including 6,255.7 yuan for urban residents and 2,282.1 yuan for rural residents. In 2010, the per capita annual disposable income of national residents was 12,519.5 yuan, including 18,779.1 yuan for urban residents and 6,272.4 yuan for rural residents. In 2018, the per capita disposable income of national residents increased to 28,228 yuan, including 39,251 yuan for urban residents and 14,617 yuan for rural residents.

The increase of the per capita disposable income of the national residents has created conditions for the poverty-stricken population to get rid of poverty, and the number of the poor population has dropped rapidly. At the beginning of reform and opening-up, according to the poverty line determined as 2,300 constant yuan in 2010, the proportion of rural poverty-stricken population in the total rural population reached 97.5% in 1978, but it dropped to 49.8% in 2000, 17.2% in 2010 and 1.7% in 2018. The number of poor people in rural areas has dropped to almost 16.6 million. According to the United Nations poverty standard of 2%, it can be said that absolute poverty has been eliminated on the basis of the constant price of 2,300 yuan in 2010.

The great success of targeted poverty alleviation has reduced the scale of poverty-stricken population in social strata and supported the optimization process of social strata.[1] This has brought about great changes in the class structure of China. In 2017, according to the GSS sample survey of the Chinese Academy of Social Sciences, the proportion of the employer class was 4.93%, that of the old middle class was 12.83%, that of the new middle class was 23.22%, that of the working class was 31.28%, and that of the peasant class was 27.74%. It can be seen from here that China is no longer a country dominated by the peasant class. The percentages of Chinese traditional industrial workers also began to shrink in the process of post-industrialization. Since the reform and opening-up, the scale of China's middle class has been expanding continuously. Under the influence of domestic and international situation, China has accelerated the pace of de-industrialization, which makes some of the employees who should have been in the working class into the middle class.

Table 1-3   The Changing Trend of Class Structure in China   Unit: %

Year	Employer Class	Old Middle Class	New Middle Class	Working Class	Farmer Class
2001	2.78	10.61	6.79	28.21	51.61
2006	3.15	11.51	7.77	30.61	46.96
2010	3.66	11.03	12.68	36.21	36.52
2013	4.62	13.85	15.74	35.46	30.32
2015	5.06	14.92	18.91	32.79	28.32
2017	4.93	12.83	23.22	31.28	27.74

Data source: GSS survey of Chinese Academy of Social Sciences in 2017.

The change of class structure in China has changed China from a country dominated by peasants to a country dominated by middle class. In

---

[1] Li Qiang, Yang Yanwen, "Social Development, Society Building and the Innovation in Sociological Studies during the 12th Five-Year Plan", *Sociological Study*, Vol. 2, 2016.

this process of transformation, the consumption structure will be upgraded rapidly. ①

In the traditional agricultural society, farmers mainly live on food crops and are often threatened by hunger. Even after the founding of People's Republic of China for a long time, due to the low efficiency of the agricultural sector, as well as a lack of science and technology and mechanization in the process of agricultural production, the grain yield per unit has been depressed for a long time.

Only when the reform takes the lead in making major breakthroughs in rural areas, increasing grain production, increasing market supply, and meeting the needs of people's life, can the grain coupon system go out of the historical stage with the abundance of market commodities. After the implementation of the household contract responsibility system, farmers' enthusiasm for production has been mobilized, and grain output has been increased year by year, thus solving the long-term "food shortage" problem in China. Shenzhen, China's special economic zone, took the lead in breaking through the barriers, abolished the restrictions on grain coupons, and used the price mechanism to regulate the distribution of grain and oil, thus forming a market demand system. In 1991, Guangdong Province and Hainan Province carried out the reform of purchasing and selling grain at the same price. In 1992, it was carried out throughout the country. In October of the same year, the socialist market economic system was established at the 14th National Congress of the Communist Party of China. The prices of grain, oil and non-staple food were liberalized throughout the country, and the supply was allocated by market mechanism. Since then, China's consumer goods market has gradually transited from the shortage stage to the sufficient

---

① Zhang Yi, "The Advent of Postindustrial Society and Middle-Class Society", *Jinagsu Social Science*, Vol. 1, 2016.

supply stage.

After 72 years of development, after the rapid increase in the proportion of the middle class, the consumption structure of Chinese people has undergone significant changes. In terms of Engel's Coefficient, in 1949, China's cities were as high as 60.2%, and the rural areas was even higher. In 1956, the socialist transformations of agricultural, second and service industries were completed. In 1957, the Engel Coefficient of the city was 58.4%, and that of the rural areas was still as high as 65.7%. In 1979, it was 57.5% in urban areas and 64.0% in rural areas. In 2000, it dropped to 39.2% in urban areas and 49.1% in rural areas. By 2010, it was 37.5% in urban areas and 41.1% in rural areas. In the new era, the living standard of Chinese people has been improved rapidly. In all household consumption, the proportion of expenditure on food isgetting lower and lower. The national Engel Coefficient has been reduced to 28.4%, which shows that Chinese people have shifted their main consumption to education, health care, tourism, housing improvement and so on. The consumption pattern of Chinese people has also changed from imitation to individualization, diversification and customization.

In terms of food consumption structure, for rural residents, the grain consumption at the beginning of reform and opening-up in 1978 was relatively high, which was 247.8kg per household. The figure then increased to 257.2kg in 1980 and 262kg in 1990. After that, it began to decline and dropped to 249.3 kg in 1998. However, the consumption of pork and mutton has gradually increased. In 1978, the average annual consumption per capita of rural households was 5.7 kg, which increased to 11.3 kg in 1990 and 13.2 kg in 1998 respectively. After entering the new era, the annual per capita food consumption of rural households decreased to 178.5 kg in 2013 and 154.6 kg in 2017. Meanwhile, the per capita annual meat consumption of rural households increased to 22.4 kg (including pork, mutton and beef) in 2013 and 23. 6 kg in 2017.

Similarly, in food consumption, for urban households, the average annual food consumption decreased rapidly. For example, the per capita food consumption was 134. 7 kg in 1985, 130. 7 kg in 1990 and 86. 7 kg in 1998. However, the consumption of pork increased first and then decreased. In 1985, the average household consumption was 16. 7 kg, increased to 18. 5 kg in 1990, and decreased to 15. 9 kg in 1998. The average annual consumption of beef and mutton per capita was only about 2kg in 1985 and increased to 3. 34kg in 1998. After entering the new era, the per capita annual food consumption of urban households decreased to 121. 3 kg in 2013 and 109. 7 kg in 2017. However, the annual per capita consumption of meat continued to grow, reaching 28. 5 kg in 2013 and 29. 2 kg in 2017.

In terms of durable consumer goods, whether in rural areas or cities and towns, by 2000, the National Bureau of Statistics still counted "overcoat", "blanket", "wardrobe", "sofa", "bicycle" and "sewing machine" as household durable consumer goods. For example, in rural households, the number of bicycles per 100 households increased from 30. 1 in 1978 to 137. 2 in 1998; the number of sewing machines per 100 households increased from 19. 8 in 1978 to 65. 8 in 1998; the number of watches per 100 households increased from 27. 4 in 1978 to 154. 6 in 1998. In 1998, there were 191. 1 woolen coats, 142. 1 blankets, 84. 0 wardrobes, 207. 6 sofas, 182. 1 bicycles and 56 sewing machines for every 100 families in cities and towns. After entering the new era, the so-called "Laosanjian" (three kinds of household durable consumer goods in old times), such as bicycles, sewing machines and watches, have fully met the needs of both rural and urban areas. It is difficult to regard these consumer goods as durable consumer goods. For the "Xinsanjian" (three new kinds of household durable consumer goods), namely, household cars, mobile phones and computers, in every 100 rural households, the number of household cars in 2013 was 9.9, which increased to 19.3 in 2017; in 2013, the number of mobile phones was 199.5, which increased to 246.1 in 2017; in 2013, the number of computers was 20, increasing to 29.2 in 2017. In every 100 urban households, the number of household cars in 2013 increased from 22.3 to 37.5 in 2017; the number of mobile phones in 2013 was 206.1, which increased to 235.4 in 2017; the number of computers in 2013 was 71.5, which increased to 80.8 in 2017.

In terms of family housing area, the average per capita housing area in rural China was only 8.1 square meters in 1978, increased to 17.8 square meters in 1990 and 23.7 square meters in 1998. The per capita housing area in cities and towns was only 3.6 square meters in 1978, increased to 6.7 square meters in 1990, and increased to 9.3 square meters in 1998. In 2016, the per capita housing area of rural residents has reached 45.8 square meters, and that of urban residents has reached 36.6 square meters. By 2018, the per capita housing construction area of urban residents will reach 39 square meters, and that of rural residents will reach 47.3 square meters. [1]

The expansion of the middle class and the consumer market have improved the living standard of the whole society, improved the nutritional conditions, reduced the labor intensity and increased the life expectancy per capita. China's development model has also transited from investment driven to consumption driven. China has entered the middle-class society for the first time in history, China has entered the network society for the first time, and China has also entered the automobile society for the first time. These changes will have an extremely strong impact on China's future social

---

[1] After 2000, China's real estate is calculated by building area. The data in 2018 are from the "sustained and rapid development of the construction industry, significant improvement of urban and rural appearance—the 10th series report on economic and social development achievements of the 70th anniversary of the founding of the People's Republic of China" issued by the National Bureau of Statistics. National Bureau of Early Statistics.

development.

China's development will inevitably enter the stage of population debt in the future. The aging level began to increase rapidly. By the end of 2018, the proportion of the population aged 60 and above in the total population has reached 17.9%, and the proportion of the population aged 65 or above in the total population has increased to 11.9%. After experiencing a slow aging speed in the 13th Five-Year Plan period, China will enter a rapid aging stage in the 14th Five-Year Plan period. The marriage rate of young people has begun to decline with rising divorce rate. The result of years of delay in the age of first marriage has reduced the birth rate. Currently, only by transforming a country with a large population into a country of rich human resources can the impact of labor aging be alleviated. The development model based on labor-intensive industries, which relies on cheap labor, land, and sufficient supply of capital at the expense of the environment has gradually declined. After entering the middle and high income stage, only by rapidly developing science and technology, automation equipment and artificial intelligence, and strengthening the production and reproduction of robots, can we finally solve the problem of labor shortage in the future. China is still a big country in education and enrollment, but it is not a powerful country in education. Only by continuously increasing the reform of education system and scientific research system and mobilizing the enthusiasm of teachers and researchers can we promote the development of productive forces and form innovative forces as soon as possible. In addition, after entering the post-industrialization stage, the original industrial bases of China began to decline, and it was difficult for the old industrial bases in the north to form new production capacity, and the regional development gap seemed to continue to widen, which delayed the replacement of the old industries to a certain extent. The urbanization rate is increasing day by day, but the quality of urbanization needs to be further improved. [1]

References

Zhang Yi, "The Advent of Postindustrial Society and Middle – Class Society", *Jinagsu Social Science*, Vol. 1, 2016.

Li Qiang, Yang Yanwen, "Social Development, Society Building and the Innovation in Sociological Studies during the 12th Five – Year Plan", *Sociological Study*, Vol. 2, 2016.

Xu Yanhui, Gong Ziyu, "Social Quality and the Citizenization of Migrant Worker", *Economist*, Vol. 7, 2019.

Wang Yuan, Kong Weiyan, "China's Social Development Trends in the Next 30 Years and Suggestions for Promoting Shared Development", *Macroeconomics*, Vol. 5, 2019.

---

[1] Xu Yanhui, Gong Ziyu, "Social Quality and the Citizenization of Migrant Worker", *Economist*, Vol. 7, 2019.

Chapter 2

Analysis and Forecast of China's Economic Structure

Lou Feng

Professor, Institute of Quantitative and Technical Economics, CASS

In this paper, we consider the main factors affecting the potential growth of China's economy and its transmission mechanism, to construct a model of the Chinese economic system, and forecast the scale and structure of China's economy over the next 17 years. In the benchmark scenario for 2016—2020, 2021—2025, 2025—2030, and 2031—2035, China's gross domestic product (GDP) forecast growth rates are 6.5%, 5.6%, 4.9%, and 4.5%, respectively. In 2035, China's GDP scale will be 10.1 times greater than in 2000, 4.0 times greater than in 2010, and 2.0 times greater than in 2020. Over the next 17 years, investment-driven economic growth will gradually become increasingly led by consumption demand. In the face of slowing growth in developed economies and a gradual reduction of its domestic labor force, China needs to strengthen research and education investment; improve investment efficiency, total factor productivity, and technological progress; promote the transformation and upgrading of the manufacturing industry; and accelerate tax reforms in the financial system and modify the income distribution system.

Ⅰ Introduction

Since the reform and opening-up, Chinese economy has experienced about 10% average annual growth rate. However, at later stage of global financial crisis, with the low growth rate of overseas developed economies and the gradually shrinking of new domestic workforce, as well as the constraints of domestic resources and environment, what lies ahead for China's potential economic growth?

A wealth of literature has focused on the medium – and – long term forecast of Chinese economy, including the forecasts conducted before 2009 and the ones after the start of the global financial crisis.

Adopting DRC – CGE model to forecast Chinese economy to 2045, Jianwn He and Louis Kuijs (2007) predict that the average annual growth rates of Chinese economy are 8.3%, 6.7%, 5.6% and 4.6% respectively during 2005—2015, 2015—2025, 2025—2035 and 2035—2045. According to Kuijs (2009), the potential GDP growth rate is likely to moderate in the coming 10 years (7.7% and 6.7% respectively in 2015 and 2020 based on Cobb – Douglas production function) due to the deceleration of working population and TFP despite still sizeable capital deepening. Li & Liu et al. (2011) forecast Chinese economy to 2030 under baseline, accelerated transformation of development pattern, and risk scenarios, and predict it will grow annually by 7.9%, 7.0% and 6.2% respectively during 2011—2015, 2016—2020, and 2021—2030 under baseline scenario.

According to Goldman Sachs (2009), the GDP growth rates of China will be about 7.9%, 5.7%, 4.4% and 3.6% respectively during 2011—

2020, 2021—2030, 2031—2040 and 2041—2050.

Based on adjusted Barro's Growth Model, HSBC (2012) forecasts the average annual growth rate of China could stay at over 5% in the next 4 decades, specifically, 6.7%, 5.5%, 4.4% and 4.1% respectively during 2010—2020, 2020—2030, 2030—2040 and 2040—2050; and China will be the most rapidly expanding economy during 2010—2020. However, some Asian countries will surpass China successively since 2020.

Adopting the growth model consisting of capital stock, workforce, human capital and technological progress, PwC (2008) reports that the average annual growth rate of Chinese economy will be about 6.8% at US dollar exchange rates and 4.7% in PPP terms. PwC also states that although Chinese economy grows fastest among BRICS countries in the next several years, its growth rate will probably be surpassed by India in 2015 and by Brazil in 2025 due to the fast aging of population in China etc.

According to Dwight H. Perkins and Thomas G. Rawski (2008), Chinese economy can sustain rapid growth during 2005—2025, and the average annual growth rate of the real GDP is about 6%—8%, which is feasible during 2005—2015, but the upper end of this range appears to be unrealistically high for 2015—2020.

Hu Angang (2008) states that the average annual growth rate of China's GDP is 7.5%—8.5% during 2006—2020, and could exceed 8.5% if the TFP growth rate remains the same as in the past 30 years as the economy growth rate in the future is mainly driven by the growth rate of TFP. Hu Angang, Yan Yilong & Wei Xing (2011) further point out that the potential growth rate of Chinese economy is between 5.9%—9.2% during 2010—2030, and the appropriate growth rate could be 7.5% during 2011—2030 (8.0% and 7.0% respectively during 2011—2020 and 2020—2030) under ecological constraints and if the government would pursue economic growth quality instead of rapid growth.

Applying an extended Lucas – type growth model and after decomposing the growth rate based on the contributing factors, Wang Xiaolu, Fan Gang and Liu Peng (2018) predict that the average annual growth rate of China will be about 6.7% during 2008—2020 under the scenario of "every contributing factor changes at the current trend". According to them, the average annual growth rate can be around 9.3% under three optimistic yet probable assumptions, including the growing government's management cost restricted by future political reform, the growth rate of human capital improved by better education, and the falling consumption suppressed by a series of policies.

After analyzing natural constraints of energy and environment, urbanization and technological progress, Zhang Ping and Wang Hongmiao (2011) predict that the potential average annual growth rate of China will be around 9.5%, 7.3% and 5.8% respectively during 2010—2015, 2016—2020 and 2020—2030 by using China's aggregate production function.

The above literature shows that many researchers and institutions are precautious after the international financial crisis, and they think the average annual growth rate will be less than 8% in the next 15 years, for example, HSBC (2012) reports 6.7% and 5.5% respectively during 2010—2020 and 2020—2030. But some optimistic researchers believe China can sustain the growth rate of 8% in the coming several decades. Robert W. Fogel (2007), a Nobel Prize laureate in Economics, estimates that the average annual growth rate of China's GDP could be around 8.4% in 2000—2040, higher than that of the US, the EU, Japan and India etc. due to inter – industry population transfer and the improvement of workforce quality in the coming three decades. Mundell (from *Securities Times*), another Nobel Prize laureate in Economics, pointed out at the 4th Northeast Asia Economic Cooperation Forum that the average annual growth rate of China's

GDP should be no lower than 8% in the next 15 to 20 years, could sustain a fast growth rate even in 2030, and would become the biggest economy in the world by 2050. Lin Yifu indicated in a speech presented in San Francisco in November 2011 that China could retain 8% expansion rate over the ensuing 20 years. According to him, the economy of Chinese mainland in 2008 was equivalent to that of Japan in 1951, South Korea in 1977, and afterwards these countries sustained the growth rate of 9.2%, 7.6% and 8.3% respectively in the following 20 years. He also emphasized that the challenges such as social and economic imbalances should be settled in order to realize fast growth. When writing for the *Financial Times*, Yao Yang (2012) said that based on cross – country comparison, Chinese economy could probably maintain the growth rate of 8% before 2020 with the improvement of the youth's education level and R&D investment etc.

So the forecasts made by different researchers and institutions differ greatly, and no consensus is reached on medium – and – long term potential growth rate of China's economy. With major factors affecting future economic growth of China taken into account, this paper analyzes their transmission mechanism to economic growth and adopts China's Macro Econometric Model to further study the potential growth rate of China's economy for the next decade based on relatively new data, and the rate is compared with some developed economies and other BRICS nations, aiming to provide reference for the future path of China's economic growth.

Ⅱ Decomposition of China's Economic Growth from 1979 to 2018

According to solow's economic growth model, the motive force of China's economic growth during 1979—2018 is decomposed (see Table 2 – 1). From Table 2 – 1, we can see that if capital, labor force and total factor productivity are the main input factors of economic growth, the economic growth of China in the past 39 years mainly depends on investment - driven (the average contribution rate is 61.8%), the contribution rate of labor force to economic growth has decreased from 12.3% in 1979—1985 to 1.29% in 2011—2015, and the contribution rate of total factor productivity to economic growth has increased from 39.7% in 1979—1985, to 60.40% in 2001—2005, and then gradually declined to 45.50% in 2011—2018.

As can be seen from Table 2 - 1, one of the basic development trends of China's three major factors of production is that the actual capital stock used remains basically above a high level of growth. The growth rate of labor force in China is gradually decreasing, which is related to the decrease of the share of the working - age population and the increase of the dependency ratio. Technological progress is considered to be one of the important sources of long - term economic growth. It can be seen that the growth rate of TFP in China was relatively high during 1979—1985. During 2001—2005, the growth rate of TFP in China reached the highest level and contributed 5.92 percentage points to economic growth. After 2006, the growth rate of TFP in China showed a downward trend. The main reason is that China's excess capacity is increasing, the gap with international technology frontier is narrowing, the momentum of utilizing foreign capital is slowing down, and the marginal benefits brought by absorbing and introducing advanced international technology are decreasing.

In order to clarify the internal driving factors of total factor productivity (TFP), we build a model to further subdivide TFP into six sub - elements according to relevant theories.

Table 2-1　　　Decomposition of China's Economic Growth from 1979 to 2018

Year	GDP Growth rate	Capital stock Growth rate	Capital stock Contribution rate	Capital stock Contribution degree	Labor Growth rate	Labor Contribution rate	Labor Contribution degree	TFP Growth rate	TFP Contribution rate	TFP Contribution degree
1979—1985	10.20	8.92	48.00	4.90	3.29	12.30	1.25	4.22	39.70	4.05
1986—1995	10.00	9.48	47.60	4.76	3.21	12.20	1.22	3.74	40.20	4.02
1996—2000	8.60	10.23	58.80	5.06	2.18	9.60	0.83	2.32	31.60	2.72
2001—2005	9.80	8.61	37.30	3.66	0.73	2.30	0.23	5.16	60.40	5.92
2006—2010	11.20	12.07	47.40	5.31	0.42	0.80	0.09	4.53	51.80	5.80
2011—2018	7.80	9.18	53.20	4.15	0.37	1.29	0.10	2.94	45.50	3.55
1979—2018	9.70	10.02	48.70	4.72	1.78	6.40	0.62	3.78	44.90	4.36

Table 2-2　Contribution of Various Factors to TFP Growth Rate (%)

year	TFP	Urbanization and Labor Transfer	Overseas Technology Spillover Effect	Scientific and technological development	Improvement of Human Capital	Market-oriented process	Other factors
1995—2000	2.75	0.63	0.42	0.42	0.32	0.36	0.60
2001—2005	5.92	1.83	1.71	1.09	0.95	0.50	-0.16
2006—2010	5.80	1.74	1.39	1.28	1.20	0.53	-0.34
2011—2018	3.55	1.57	0.95	1.54	1.36	0.32	-2.19
1995—2018	4.36	1.44	1.12	1.08	0.96	0.43	-0.67

Note: Since some of the indicators in the table had not been counted before 1994, the table starts from 1995.

1. Urbanization and labor transfer

As the labor productivity of the primary industry in China is far lower than that of the secondary and tertiary industries, with the increasing urbanization rate, more and more rural population will continue to move to cities and towns, from the primary industry to the tertiary or secondary industry, thus, the overall labor productivity will tend to continue to improve. From Table 2 – 2, it can be seen that the contribution of urbanization and labor transfer to the growth rate of total factor productivity averaged 1.44 percentage points between 1995 and 2016, and the contribution of urbanization and labor transfer to the growth rate of total factor productivity was the largest among the six sub – factors.

2. Foreign technology spillover effect

Generally speaking, while providing funds to the host country, FDI also produces positive technology spillover effects on the host country from two ways of management and technology, thus improving the total factor productivity of the host country. The larger the proportion of FDI, the stronger the positive spillover effects. This report uses this variable to reflect the impact of foreign capital technology on China's total factor productivity. From Table 2 – 2, it can be seen that the average contribution of foreign technology spillover effect to total factor productivity is 1.12 percentage points during 1995—2018, ranking second among the six sub-factors. From different stages, the average contribution of technology spillover effect to total factor productivity in foreign countries shows a trend of rising first and then falling. The contribution of technology spillover effect to total factor productivity reached the peak of 1.71 percentage points during 2001—2005, when the effect of WTO accession was significant. However, due to the narrowing gap between China and the international technology frontier, the marginal benefits brought by learning, imitating and absorbing international advanced technology and management are gradually decreasing. From 2011 to 2018, the contribution of foreign technology spillover effect to total factor productivity has dropped to 0.95 percentage points, which is 0.76 percentage points lower than that of 2001—2005.

3. Scientific and technological progress

This variable is measured by the real growth rate of R&D funds. According to economic theory, R&D investment is an effective way to improve total factor productivity and a significant factor affecting total factor productivity. Table 2 – 2 shows that the contribution rate of scientific and technological progress to total factor productivity is generally on the rise, especially in recent years, which may increase. It is related to the strengthening of R&D investment and fiscal and tax incentives for independent innovation in China in recent years. From 1995 to 2016, the contribution of scientific and technological progress to total factor productivity averaged 1.08 percentage points.

4. Improvement of human capital

According to the theory of human capital, education is an effective way to improve the quality of workers and increase human capital. The proportion of education expenditure in GDP of a country can often measure the strength of human capital. Human capital is a significant factor affecting productivity. However, due to the lack of reliable data on family education expenditure in China, this paper uses financial education expenditure in GDP. The proportion is used to measure the impact of education on total factor productivity. Table 2 – 2 shows that the contribution of human capital to total factor productivity is increasing, especially since 2011. This is related to the substantial increase in education investment in recent years.

5. Market-oriented process

According to economic theory, generally speaking, the higher the degree of marketization, the more market competition will be promoted, thus speeding up the improvement of technological progress and enterprise management level, which is conducive to the improvement and development of total factor productivity. This report uses the data of China's provincial market index in Fan Gang, Wang Xiaolu and Zhu Hengpeng's "China's Marketization Index: Relative Process of Marketization in Various Regions 2018 Report", and estimates the total national market index. Its indicators mainly include five sub–indices: the relationship between government and market, the development of non–state–owned economy, the development of product market, the development of factor market, the development of intermediary organizations and the law. They are used to measure the depth and breadth of market – oriented reform in provinces, autonomous regions and municipalities directly under the Central Government. They basically summarize the main aspects of market-oriented process. From Table 2 – 2, it can be seen that during 1995—2018, with the gradual reduction of the dividend of market – oriented reform, the contribution of market – oriented process to total factor productivity gradually declined, with an average contribution of 0.43 percentage points approximately.

6. Other influencing factors

Other influencing factors are other factors besides the above five seed elements, such as scale economy effect, management and management ability, foreign patent use and technology purchase, resource constraints and so on. Table 2 - 2 shows that the contribution of other factors to China's total factor productivity is positive and negative. It is worth noting that in recent years, other factors have a negative impact on the contribution of China's total factor productivity, which may be related to such factors as the serious reduction of economies of scale caused by excess capacity, the weakening of enterprise's profitability caused by the high cost of factors of production, and the remarkable decrease of investment return.

III Transmission Mechanism of Main Factors on Potential Economic Growth

This paper researches by employing the Macroeconomic Forecasting Model of China (2018 Version) which developed by Institute of Quantitative & Technical Economics, Chinese Academy of Social Sciences, and the new version has the following characteristics: (i) it uses co - integration theory to perform co - integration test on every equation, and introduces Error Correction Model (ECM) to analyze the long - term equilibrium relationship implied in economic theory as well as short - term fluctuation among variables; (ii) with "LS - LM model + Phillips curve" as core theory, the LS - LM model of China is developed after estimation of China's consumption, investment, net exports and currency demand functions, and then the model of Lucas aggregate supply function of China is built by fitting Expectations - augmented Phillips Curve. In addition, the aggregate supply and aggregate demand are effectively connected by introducing China's tax and money supply policies; (iii) the model helps with the analysis of monetary policy by enhancing the financial module through incorporation of more financial variables and addition of behavioral functions of central and commercial banks; (iv) the model moderately reduces dummy variables to avoid the degree of freedom loss during fitting process as possible.

The model of 2018 version consists of nine modules, i. e. output, price, income & consumption, government tax, finance, trade, population & employment, investment and savings, including 253 variables, 216 equations and 37 exogenous variables.

In order to forecast China's economy in 2035, the transmission mechanism of the influence of TFP, urbanization and international economic environment on potential economic growth is set as follows.

(1) TFP and Potential Economic Growth

Firstly this paper estimates China's GDP equation with Cobb – Douglas production function, which is the long – term equilibrium equation of production function:

$$ECMGDPC = LOG(GDPC/LTOT) - TFP - 0.71518 * LOG$$

Where GDPC is China's GDP (at 1980 constant prices), LTOT is the total employment, TKC is capital stock (at 1980 constant prices), and ECMGDPC is the error correction term.

According to economics, GDP minus non – constant part of long – term equilibrium equation is the time series of TFP, which is taken as explained variable to construct TFP equation as follows:

$$TFP = -2.4691 + 0.0042 * RUB + 0.0654 * RRD + 0.0081 * RFDI + 0.1028 * RFEDUGDP$$
$$(-15.9705) \quad (2.6312) \quad (1.5816) \quad (2.5680) \quad (4.0532)$$

($R^2 = 0.9036$, AIC = -3.5121, DW = 1.7392)

Where TFP is total factor productivity; RUB is urbanization rate, i. e., the ratio of urban population to total population, which means overall labor productivity will be enhanced with the continual growth of urbanization rate as more rural population will transfer to cities and towns to participate in the tertiary or secondary industries, which are more productive than the primary industry in China. RRD is the real growth rate of R&D expenditure, and the

R&D inputs are effective in improving TFP according to economics; RFDI is the ratio of foreign direct investment (FDI) to total investment, and generally speaking, in addition to fund, the host country's TFP will be raised thanks to FDI positive spillover effect in management and technology, and more FDI means more positive effect, so RFDI is used to denote the effect of foreign capital and technology on China's TFP; RFEDUGDP is the ratio of fiscal expenditure on education to GDP, and according to human capital theory, education is effective in increasing labor quality and human capital, so a country's human capital, a significant influencing factor on productivity, can be measured by the proportion of educational funds in GDP. We use the ratio of fiscal expenditure on education to GDP to denote the influence of education on TFP due to the lack of reliable data on family educational expenditure.

The short-term fluctuation equation of production function is built by applying co-integration theory, also called co-integration equation, as follows:

D (LOG (GDPC/LTOT)) = 0.4849 * D (LOG (GDPC (-1) /LTOT (-1))) - 0.1594 * D (LOG (GDPC (-2) /LTOT (-2)))

(5.1153)   (-2.9506)

+1.0112 * D (LOG (TKC/LTOT)) - 0.5649 * D (LOG (TKC (-1) /LTOT (-1))) - 0.1203 * ECMGDPC (-1)

(18.6228)   (-5.9477)   (-2.2069)

(R^2 = 0.9279, AIC = -5.8249, DW = 1.9787)

(2) Urbanization, Global Economy and China's Potential Economic Growth

The process of urbanization affects the investment in infrastructure, the changes of global economy first influences exports and then influences investment in manufacturing. Put it all together, both the process of domestic urbanization and the changes of global economy affect the investment as well as capital information and capital stock, and then affect the potential economic growth in the medium and long term. So the investment equation is set as follows.

LOG (INVC) = 1.1752 * LOG (INVC (−1)) − 0.6273 * LOG (INVC (−2)) + 0.2332 * LOG (LOANTT)

(7.5230) (−3.9399) (1.9983)

+ 0.0277 * RUB + 0.0816 * LOG (WGDPC)

(2.7722) (1.9445)

(R^2 = 0.9958, AIC = −2.1841, DW = 2.1049)

Where INVC is investment in fixed assets (at 1980 constant prices), and INVC (−1) and INVC (−2) are INVCs with one and two lag terms respectively, representing inertia of investment in fixed assets; RUB refers to the urbanization rate, which directly affects the investment in fixed assets as higher urbanization rate means more investment in roads, transportation facilities and real estate etc; In addition, with accelerated global economic integration, the effect of the global economy on China's investment in manufacturing becomes more prominent by affecting China's exports, so the variable "WGDPC" (world GDP, at 1980 constant prices) is included in the investment equation to denote the transmission mechanism of this global factor on China's investment; LOANTT is the total loan, another variable influencing investment except the urbanization rate and the world economy.

Ⅳ China's Macroeconomic Growth Forecast

(1) Prediction and analysis of China's GDP 2019—2035

Table 2 − 3   Forecast of China's Potential Economic Growth Rate for 2019—2035

	Baseline scenario	Rapid growth scenario	Slow growth scenario
2019	6.4	6.5	5.7
2020	6.2	6.3	5.5

(Contd.)

	Baseline scenario	Rapid growth scenario	Slow growth scenario
Average in 13th Five – Year Plan period (2016—2020)	6.5	6.6	6.0
2025	5.4	5.8	4.9
Average in 14th Five – Year Plan period (2021—2025)	5.7	6.0	5.2
2030	4.8	5.3	4.0
Average in 15th Five – YearPlan period (2026—2030)	5.0	5.5	4.3
2035	4.3	5.0	3.4
Average in 16th Five – Year Plan period (2030—2035)	4.4	5.1	3.6

In the baseline scenario, the average GDP growth in 2016—2020, 2021—2025, 2026—2030, and 2031—2035 were 6.5%, 5.6%, 4.9%, and 4.5%, respectively. In the rapid growth scenario, if China successfully implements reforms such as steadily rising urbanization, promoting the transformation and upgrading of the manufacturing industry, enhancing the international competitiveness of products, and further increasing the proportion of financial education funds in the GDP, improving the quality of workers, strengthening R&D investment, improving the added value of the products, and deepening the market reforms, then for the Plan periods in 2019—2020, 2021—2025, 2026—2030, and 2031—2035, the four period, we predicts China' GDP growth may remain an average GDP growth of 6.6%, 6.0%, 5.5%, and 5.1% respectively. However, in the

Chapter 2 Analysis and Forecast of China's Economic Structure 171

slower growth scenario, the average GDP growth rate of GDP is just 6.0%, 5.2%, 4.3%, and 3.6%, respectively in the four periods.

For the baseline of the above three scenarios, the contribution of the capital stock, the labor force, and the total factor productivity (TFP), to GDP growth for in the last 2019—2035 years is shown in Table 2 – 4.

Table 2 – 4 Decomposition of China's Potential Economic Growth Rate for 2019—2035 Under the Benchmark Scenario

Year	GDP growth	Capital Stock Contribution rate	Capital Stock Contribution degree	Labor Contribution rate	Labor contribution degree	Total Factor Productivity Contribution rate	Total Factor Productivity contribution degree
2019	6.4	53.4	3.4	1.3	0.1	45.3	2.9
2020	6.2	52.6	3.3	1.3	0.1	46.1	2.9
2016—2020	6.5	53.4	3.4	1.3	0.1	45.3	2.9
2025	5.4	48.4	2.6	0.7	0.0	50.9	2.7
2021—2025	5.6	49.9	2.8	1.0	0.1	49.2	2.8
2030	4.8	45.0	2.1	-0.6	0.0	55.6	2.6
2026—2030	4.9	46.4	2.3	0.0	0.0	53.6	2.6
2035	4.3	41.7	1.8	-2.0	-0.1	60.4	2.7
2031—3035	4.5	43.0	1.9	-1.5	-0.1	58.5	2.6

(2) Prediction and Analysis of the Three Industrial Structural Changes

According to the forecasting, under the benchmark scenario, in 2035 China's fixed price GDP scale will be 10.06 times higher than in 2000, 3.99 times that for 2010, and 2.02 times 2020's value. For the period 2016—2035, the growth of the national economy is not only reflected in this rapid increase, but also in a revised economic structure which involves three industries at different rates of growth, the result of a long – term focus on qualitative aspects. Over the next 20 years, the three industry trend is roughly as follows: (1) in respect of industry structure, the proportion of the three industries in the economy changes steadily, namely, the proportion of the primary industry and the secondary industry decreases each year, and the tertiary industry proportion increases each year; (2) during the period 2019—2035, the proportion of the primary industry is stable, only decreasing by 1.7 percentage points; the secondary industry added value accounted for in the proportion of GDP has dropped by 10 percentage points. The tertiary industry has maintained its largest share in the national economy, and moreover, the proportion of the tertiary industry in 2016 is more than 50%, and its position in the national economy is further consolidated. In 2035, the value – added proportion of each industry's added value in the national economy was 7.4%, 29.9%, and 62.7%.

Table 2 – 5   China's GDP and Three Industrial Structures for 2019—2035 under the Benchmark Scenario

Year	GDP (trillion yuan, Current price)	GDP (trillion yuan, 2000 year price)	GDP growth rate (%)	Value added ratio of Primary industry (%)	Value added ratio of Secondary industry (%)	Value added ratio of Tertiary industry (%)
2019	975025	706672	6.4	8.9	38.8	52.3
2020	1054977	749216	6.2	8.8	37.7	53.5
2025	1528683	982356	5.4	8.4	34.4	57.3
2030	2146049	1243063	4.8	7.9	32	60.1
2035	2940260	1603369	4.3	7.4	29.9	62.7

Note: the values in 2019—2035 years are forecasting data

(3) Forecast and analysis of China's economic structure (investment, consumption, net exports)

According to the forecasting result of the Macroeconomic Forecasting Model of China (as shown in Table 2 – 6), during the period 2019—2035,

China's economic growth and its structure will change significantly. From the perspective of its consumption structure, the proportions of rural residents' and urban residents' consumption in final consumption, will increase year by year, especially for urban residents. The proportion of government consumption in total consumption decreases each year because of China's strategic decision to boost urbanization. In addition, with the rapid development of urbanization, the urban population will continue to expand; hence, the income and social welfare of urban residents will be further increased. On the other hand, the series of policies to curb government's expenditures on food and drinking has been successful, and thus, its relative proportion has gradually declined.

From the perspective of economic growth, from 2016, the proportion of final consumption will exceed the rate of capital formation, thus consumption will become the main driving force for China's economic growth. Over the next 15 years, economic growth driven by investment will gradually change, becoming increasingly consumer demand – led, which will undoubtedly help to improve the investment structure and investment efficiency.

Table 2 – 6   Forecast of China's Economic Growth Structure
(constant price) in 2019—2035

year	Consumption ratio of rural residents	Consumption ratio of urban residents	Government consumption ratio	Final consumption ratio	Capital formation ratio	Net export ratio
2019	8.46	30.28	10.82	49.56	49.07	1.37
2020	8.51	30.54	10.66	49.70	49.01	1.29
2025	8.76	31.75	9.98	50.48	48.55	0.97
2030	9.01	32.88	9.47	51.37	47.89	0.74
2035	9.19	35.25	8.31	52.75	46.75	0.50

(Contd.)

year	Consumption ratio of rural residents	Consumption ratio of urban residents	Government consumption ratio	Final consumption ratio	Capital formation ratio	Net export ratio
Average in 13th Five – Year Plan period 2016—2020	8.42	30.01	11.01	49.44	49.10	1.46
Average in 14th Five – Year Plan period 2021—2025	8.66	31.27	10.23	50.16	48.75	1.09
Average in 15th Five – Year Plan period 2026—2030	8.91	32.43	9.67	51.01	48.17	0.82
Average in 16th Five – Year 2031—2035	9.12	34.21	8.81	52.15	47.26	0.59

V Conclusions and Suggestions

Historical world economic development proves that when an economy develops rapidly and reaches a certain level, the speed of economic growth then slows before moving to a gradual declining stage. China is still a developing country, its technological progress and innovation still have scope for improvement, and there still is a huge market demand for escalating consumption and investment.

First, deepening the reform of the administrative system and actively changing the functions of the government is essential. The key to advancing the structural reform of the supply – side and encouraging enterprises is to improve the relationship between the government and market. Because the traditional supply – side factors of production (such as capital and labor) have shown a decreasing return to scale, future sustainable development must rely on new factors such as TFP (as the representative of information technology, innovation, management, etc.), and these new factors of production, cultivation, development, and growth need a free market environment. Therefore, the government should deepen the reform of the administrative system, through the establishment of a legal "power list" and "negative list" to determine the reasonable boundaries of government and market, minimize government interference for micro market transactions, and improve the government's decision – making. This should also help to increase efforts to further open the market, stimulate the vitality of the market, let the market play a decisive role in the allocation of resources, establish a price formation mechanism, and a transmission mechanism of cost and return on investment. Market development should help promote private capital market through "widespread entrepreneurship and innovation", and prevent putting the market in the cage of power.

Second, we recommend breaking the monopoly, reforming the state – owned enterprise system, and creating a full and fair market environment for competition. Historic evidence validates that monopoly not only hinders the intensification of market contradictions, industrial transformation and upgrading, but also constrains the innovation of technology and management level, and leads to social conflicts; moreover, it hinders the efficiency of resource allocation and fair distribution of social wealth effect. At present, the factors that seriously hinder China's enterprise R&D initiative come from two aspects: the short – term behavior of enterprises, and the monopoly of enterprises. As R&D requires a lot of money and manpower for long – term investment (while the returns are not immediately apparent), a pursuit of short – term interests of enterprises holds no advantage for R&D. In addition, when several enterprises benefit from the special monopoly status given by the government, they do not have enough incentive to carry out research and development. This pursuit of short-term benefits and excessive reliance on government monopolies and subsidies is a common problem for most state-owned enterprises in China. However, because China still has some monopoly and industrial policies, and the opening degree of telecommunications and other service areas is not high for private capital, it is difficult for private capital to enter fields with competition. Thus, it is not only useless to the effective allocation of resources, but also disadvantageous to the development of private capital. An unfair system seriously hinders the technological innovation and incentive mechanism of the producer. Therefore, China should reform state-owned enterprises and change their cadre appointment system, eliminate monopoly, introduce competition, and evaluate the mechanism of state-owned enterprises, eliminate short-term behavior, further liberalize high-end manufacturing industries and market access of modern service industries, which are important for fostering independent research and innovation driven economy. Whether or not China can avoid the middle-income trap with independent research and become an innovative economy, a key factor is the reform and promotion of state-owned enterprises, to become the backbone of independent R&D and technological innovation waits to be seen. Therefore, as regards social management, the Chinese government should create a market environment for fair competition by introducing relevant laws and regulations, improving and accelerating the establishment of a unified, open, competitive, and orderly market system, to break geographical segmentation and industry monopoly, and thus, better stimulate economic vitality and market creativity.

Third, we suggest enhancing the capability of independent innovation and facilitating scientific and technological innovation. Core technology is the basis of competition among modern enterprises. They must focus on scientific research and technological innovation in order to build their own core technology, and to enhance their long – term survival and development. At present, China's economic development is in a critical period of industrial restructuring and upgrading; hence, there is an immediate need to strengthen and rely on scientific and technological innovation. On the one hand, with the development opportunity of the "supply – side structural reform", China should formulate and improve relevant planning and industrial policies to promote independent innovation, ability, and willingness among enterprises. Furthermore, the Chinese government should establish and perfect the risk investment mechanism innovation, promote the development of risk investment institutions, ensure tax reforms and optimization of enterprise science and technology R&D management regulations, encourage and guide enterprises to strengthen R&D investment, and improve the willingness of independent innovation in terms of science and technology policy, and restructure investment and financing systems. Besides, China should strengthen the protection of intellectual property rights; improve the scientific and technological achievements and industry support system, technical service system, and technology property rights trading system; and establish the external environment protection of intellectual property rights of enterprises to ensure the independent innovation of enterprises' economic and social benefits.

Finally, China should substitute quality and efficiency for quantity and increase capital utilization and labor productivity. While increasing scientific and technological innovation and striving to improve TFP, the "supply – side structural reform" also need to improve supply efficiency and supply quality of traditional production resources. China's population growth trend in the short term cannot be changed effectively—based on the fact that in order to adapt to the modern economic development needs, it needs to increase investment in human capital, promote the demographic dividend bonus to personnel changes, improve the quality of the labor force to counteract the negative effects of human resources based on the meaning of "demographic dividend". However, through the construction of a unified labor market, China needs to optimize the allocation of labor, reduce labor costs and free flow, promote the orderly flow of labor between urban and rural areas, enterprises, universities, scientific research institutions, technical personnel, and extend the retirement age to the aging population. Finally, China should accelerate the implementation of financial sector reform, improve the efficiency of capital use, change monopoly profiteering of financial enterprises, accelerate the construction of multi – level financial system coordinated with the real economy, diversification of the organization system and three – dimensional service system, effectively integrate a variety of financial resources, accelerate the reform of the financial markets, and effectively reduce the cost.

References

Chow, Gregory C. (2005), *China's Economic Transformation*, Beijing: China Renmin University Press (in Chinese).

Coopers, Price Waterhouse (2008), The World in 2050——Beyond the BRICs: A Broader Look at Emerging Market Growth Prospects, *PricewaterhouseCoopers LLP economics group*.

Fogel, Robert W. (2007), Capitalism and Democracy in 2040: Forecasts and Speculations, *NBER Working Paper*, 13184.

HSBC (2012), the World in 2050, *HSBC Global Research*.

Hu, Angang (2008), "The Quantitative Evaluation and Prospects of China's Economic Power (1980—2020)", *Journal of Literature, History and Philosophy*, No. 1 (in Chinese).

Hu, Angang, Yan, Yilong & Wei, Xing (2011), *China 2030: to Common Wealth*, Beijing: China Renmin University Press (in Chinese).

Kuijs, Louis (2009), China through 2020 —— A Macroeconomic Scenario, *World Bank China Office Research Working Paper*, No. 9.

Li, Shantong & Liu, Yunzhong (2011), *Chinese Economy 2030*, Beijing: Economic Science Press (in Chinese).

Lin, Justin Yifu (Dec. 30, 2011), China to maintain 8% growth rate for over 20 years, *China Business Network*, Retrieved July 26, 2012, from the World Wide Web: http://www.yicai.com/news/2011/11/1236989.html (in Chinese).

Perkins, Dwight H. and Rawski, "Thomas G. (2008), Forecasting China's Economic Growth to 2025", *China Business Review*, 35, No. 6, 34 - 9, 45 N/D.

Research Group of Input - Output Table of China 2007 (2011), China's Economic Prospect for the 12th Five - Year Plan Period and 2030, *Statistical Research*, Vol. 28, No. 1 (in Chinese).

Robert A. Mundell (Sept. 4, 2008), Chinese Economy can Grow Fast to 2030, *Securities Times* (in Chinese).

Sachs, Goldman (2009), the Long - Term Outlook for the BRICs and N - 11 Post Crisis, *Global Economics Paper*, No 192.

The World Bank, DRC of the State Council the PRC (2012), China 2030, Building a Modern, Harmonious, and Creative High - Income Society, the World Bank.

Wang, Xiaolu, Fan, Gang & Liu, Peng (2018), "Transformation of Growth Pattern and Growth Sustainability in China", *Economic Research Journal*, No. 1 (in Chinese).

Yao, Yang (July 4, 2012), Why I'm still Bullish on China's Growth. *FT Chinese*. Retrieved July 24, 2012, from the World Wide Web: http://www.ftchinese.com/story/001045324 (in Chinese).

Zhang, Ping & Wang, Hongmiao (2011), "China's Economic Outlook into 2030: Transformation, Simulation and Policy Suggestions", *China Economist*, Vol. 6, No. 4.

Zhangjun, Zhang Jipeng (2016), "The Estimation of China's Provincial Capital Stock: 1952—2000", *Economic Research Journal*, No. 10 (in Chinese).

Part 2

Georgia's Economic and Social Development

Chapter 3

Georgia's Economic Development and Prospect

Ouyang Xiangying

Professor, Institute of World Economics and Politics, CASS

Located in the Eurasian junction, Georgia is known as the "Eurasian Crossroads" and is the intersection of Eurasian history, cultural integration, and economic and trade exchanges. It is also the gateway to the ancient Silk Road and the modern Eurasian traffic corridor. Its geographic location and strategic position are crucial. The development of China – Georgia relations will promote the development strategy of the two countries under the Belt and Road Initiative, strengthen people – to – people bonds, achieve common prosperity, which is in line with the long – term interests and fundamental interests of the two countries.

I The Basic Situation of Georgia and the Relationship between China and Georgia

Georgia is a country with good economic developing conditions. The comprehensive score of the business environment is at the forefront of the former Soviet Union region. In 2000, Georgia joined the World Trade Organization (WTO). Currently, Georgia is one of the countries with the most freedom regarding world trade policy. Including the foreign trade system and the customs clearance procedures, lower import tariffs and less non-tariff control measures. Georgia is also one of the world's least tax – paying single tax countries, with a total tax level of 16.5%, selected by *Forbes* magazine in the United States and ranked fourth in the global tax index. According to the World Bank's *Business Environment Report 2017*, Georgia ranks 16th out of 190 countries.

China was one of the first countries to recognize Georgia's independence and establish diplomatic relations with Georgia. Since the establishment of diplomatic relations in 1992, China and Georgia have achieved fruitful cooperation in various fields. The two have signed a series of cooperation agreements such as the *China – Georgia Economic and Trade Agreement* and the *Agreement on Encouraging and Mutual Protection of Investment*. In 2017, China and Georgia signed a free trade agreement and entered into force on January 1, 2018. According to the Agreement, the two sides canceled the tariffs on most of the goods trade products, and made a high – quality market opening commitment to many service departments, and improved the rules on intellectual property rights, environmental protection, e – commerce, and competition. The purpose of signing the Agreement is to create a more open, convenient and stable business environment for the enterprises of the two countries, comprehensively enhance the level of pragmatic cooperation between the two countries, and lay the foundation for achieving common prosperity. The author of this article will analyze how effective the agreement is and what direction it should work in the future.

II The Preliminary Effect Evaluation of the China – Georgia Free Trade Agreement

The signing of the China – Georgia Free Trade Agreement is a major event in the development of economic and trade relations between the two countries. The content of the agreement is very detailed, and the tariff list covers a very large number of goods. Georgia has implemented zero tariffs on 96.5% of China's products, which covers 99.6% of Georgia's total imports from China; China's 93.9% of Georgia's products have zero tariffs which accounts for 93.8% of China's total imports from Georgia. China's concession table for Georgia contains more than 7,000 items, the vast majority of goods are category A, a category allows the tariffs to be abolished and bound to 0 from the date of entry into force of the agreement. Georgia's classification of China's concessions is more detailed, and the same is true for most commodities.

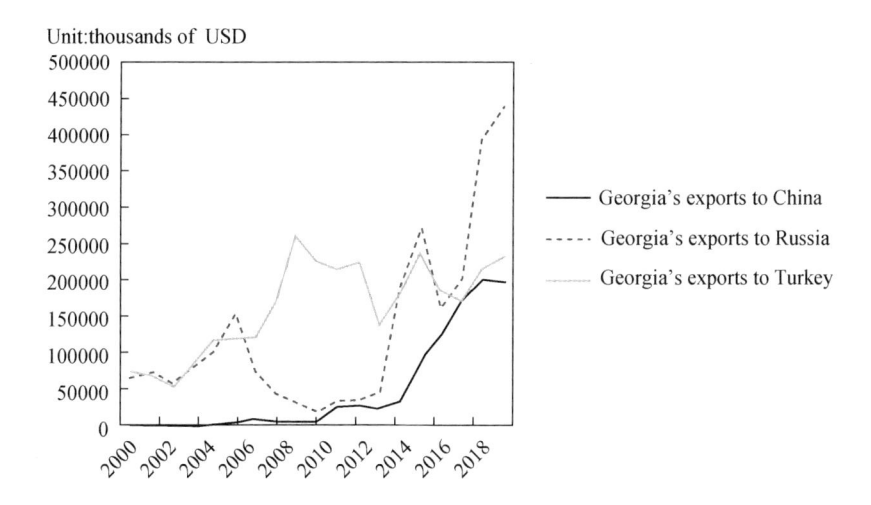

Figure 3–1　Georgia's Exports to Major Trading Partners (2000—2018)

Source: Georgia Statistics Bureau. Author homemade.

Unit: thousands of USD

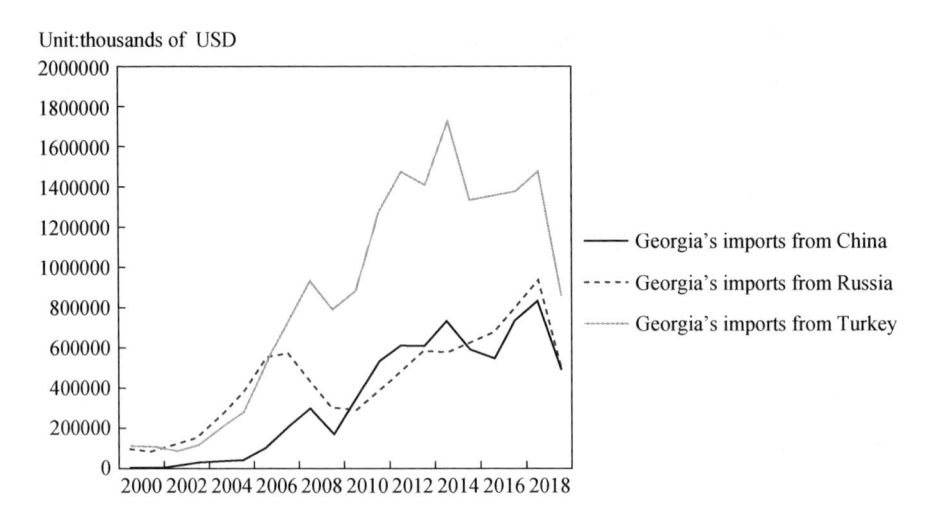

Figure 3–2 Imports of Georgia from Major Trading Partners (2000—2019)

Source: Georgia Statistics Bureau. The data for 2019 is January – July. Author homemade.

After the signing of the China – Georgia Free Trade Agreement, China – Georgia economic ties were further strengthened. At present, China is the fifth – largest trading partner of Georgia, the third – largest export market, the second – largest wine export market and a major source of investment. The main export commodities of Georgia are automobiles, ferroalloys, copper ore, etc. The main imported commodities are petroleum products, automobiles, and medicines. In 2018, Georgia's exports to China worth about 200 million USD, and imports from China amounted to about 830 million USD. For the first time, the bilateral trade volume exceeded 1 billion USD, and the pace of building a trading relationship between China and Georgia is accelerating than that of Georgia – Turkey and Georgia – Russia.

Table 3-1   2017—2019 grid exports to major countries

Unit: thousands of USD

	Export	Export to Russia	Export soil
2017	201701.71	396672.04	216673.60
2018	198034.35	437303.54	232714.29
2019 (until July)	66493.72	303813.42	135103.65

Source: Georgia Statistics Bureau. Author homemade.

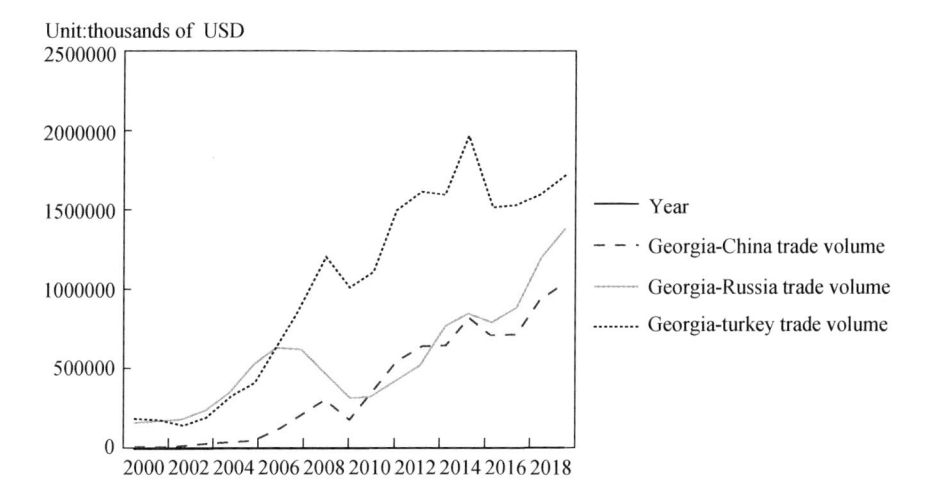

Figure 3-3   Bilateral Trade Volume between Georgia and Its Major Trading Partners (2000—2018)

Source: Georgia Statistics Bureau. Author homemade.

However, we should also see that 2018 is the first year that the China - Georgia FTA came into force. Compared with the bilateral trade volume of 9.3 million US dollars in 2017, it has increased in 2018, but the amount of growth is not much. From January to July in 2019, Georgia's total exports to China fell by 37% compared with the same period in 2018, and the number of imports from China also declined slightly about 2%. Although we do not make emergency efforts and are too eager to hope for rapid growth in bilateral trade, growth is undoubtedly beneficial to the economic development of the two countries. Compare the trade volume between China and neighboring countries, for example, the trade volume between China and Vietnam exceeds 100 billion USD in 2018. The trade volume between China and Kazakhstan in 2018 is more than 10 billion USD (shrinking due to the decline in international raw material prices, and over 20 billion USD in 2013). In the first half of 2019, the bilateral trade volume between China and Azerbaijan reached a total of about 1.3 billion USD in the whole year of last year. In 2018, the bilateral trade volume between China and Kyrgyzstan was also 1.5 billion USD. Starting from the long – term interests of the two countries, we should find the main factors that restrict the development of bilateral trade and address them one by one, and truly promote the Belt and Road Initiative docking between China and Georgia.

Table 3 – 2   Georgia's Bilateral Trade Volume of Recent Years with Major Trading Partners (2017—2018)

Unit: millions of USD

Years	Georgia—China volume	Georgia—Russia trade volume	Georgia—Turkey trade volume
2016	721	882	1527
2017	934	1184	1590
2018	1032	1373	1706

Source: Georgia Statistics Bureau. Author homemade.

Ⅲ The Main Factors

We believe that the factors restricting the further development of China – Georgia economic and trade relations vary. Among them, there are many objective reasons, and the market in both countries needs to be further cultivated and improved.

First of all, a peaceful and stable environment is essential. In recent years, Georgia has pursued pragmatic diplomacy and balanced diplomacy fully exerted the role of economic diplomacy, and focused on restoring the development and relations with the Eurasian countries, including adhering to the pragmatic policy toward Russia, actively developing relations with the EU. The relationship with China is also one of the key development directions of Georgia. The economic growth of China and Georgia also benefits from this. However, influenced by the Russian – Georgian war in the past few years and local conflicts in the surrounding areas, some business people are cautious about investing in Georgia and doing business there. Although in 2016, the Ministry of Commerce of the People's Republic of China has announced that Georgia has become one of the safest countries in the world after Singapore and South Korea, this mainly refers to the domestic security situation. Frankly speaking, whether Georgia will be involved in the geopolitical conflicts of big countries is still a problem that some big companies are worried about.

Secondly, subject to the economic volume and the total population. In 2016, the grid GDP was 14.3 billion USD, up 2.7% year – on – year, and the per capita GDP was 3,853 USD. In 2017, the grid GDP was 15.16 billion USD, up 5% year – on – year. As of 2019 In January, the total population of Georgia was 3.724 million. What does it mean? Compare the population of Chinese cities: Beijing has a permanent population of more than 20 million, Tianjin has a resident population of more than 15 million, and Jinan has a resident population of more than 8 million. The population is more than 3 million. Therefore, the population of 3.72 million is about the size of a prefecture – level city in China. The per capita GDP is 5,000 USD, reflecting that the economic structure of Georgia is still dominated by low value – added products, while the population is related to consumer consumption. Demand and consumption power are closely related. Georgia is a very beautiful country, known as "the back garden of God". Accelerating industrialization and implementing fertility encouragement policies may change this aspect. The only solution is to change the economic structure of Georgia and to include Georgia in the track of relying on high technology for rapid development, but this is not an easy task.

Third, the lack of the driving effect of brand – name products. A large number of goods between China and Georgia are exempt from each other. It is reasonable to say that the bilateral trade volume should increase rapidly, but it does not. The Georgian products that Chinese people are familiar with are still red wine, and Georgia knows that Chinese products should be Huawei mobile phones. The lack of the driving effect of brand – name products will directly affect the bilateral trade volume. China has long since become the most complete manufacturing country in the world. Machinery, electronics, complete sets of equipment, communications and automobiles have good products with good quality and low price. Georgia's mineral water and handicrafts are also very good and need to do some promotional activities in China.

Finally, Georgia should pay more attention to the Chinese market. China is the largest market in the world, and it has strong digesting ability for both high – end machinery and equipment and ordinary agricultural products. Georgia should attach great importance to the development of the Chinese market, and at the same time increase the opening up of Chinese enterprises so that the free trade agreement can bear fruit.

Ⅳ Future Development and Cooperation Direction

I suggest that the two sides should focus on cooperation in the following areas.

The first is infrastructure construction. In recent years, China's achievements in infrastructure construction have attracted worldwide attention. Our roads, bridges, tunnels, communications, water supply, power supply, and other projects are blooming everywhere and exported to many countries around the world. Why is China able to export infrastructure? It is because China's infrastructure construction has several characteristics. First, the constructing speed is fast. Second, the quality is good. The third is a low price, and the fourth is experienced. Since the reform and opening-up, China's infrastructure has not only achieved modernization in large and medium-sized cities but has also been upgraded in small cities and small towns. Georgia should have some experience. The No. 9 tunnel in Kwishsh quarter in central Georgia is more than 8.3 kilometers long. It is the longest railway tunnel ever built in Georgia and the "throat" project of the Georgian railway modernization project. Since 2011, the builders of China Railway 23rd Bureau Group Co., Ltd. have worked hard to adopt dozens of international advanced construction techniques, overcoming the engineering and technical problems of surrounding rock settlement, flammable gas release and rock fragmentation, ensuring that the tunnel will pass through the high standards on time. The same thing happened in Tajikistan, Pakistan, Ukraine, Belarus, Maldives, Hungary, and many other countries. These projects were completed, delivered and used, and received praise from the local government and people. The Kwishsh quarter tunnel should also serve as a model window for overseas infrastructure construction and promote further cooperation between China and Georgia in the field of infrastructure.

The second is to develop the digital economy. Georgia is more concerned about the development of the digital economy. In 2016, it ranked 64th in the global innovation index. In recent years, China's digital economy has developed rapidly, and its comprehensive strengths such as economic scale, patent application, and technology utilization ranked second in the world, second only to the United States. Therefore, the digital economy is also the development focus of the EU, Russia and Central Asia and China in recent years. Georgia should also join the process to transform the original industrial enterprises and agricultural product sales systems with the Internet and mobile communication technologies to serve the economic development of the country.

The third is to promote financial cooperation. China – Georgia has achieved certain results in the field of financial cooperation. On September 21, 2017, China Export Credit Insurance Corporation (hereinafter referred to as "China Credit Insurance") and the Georgia Partner Fund signed the *China Export Credit Insurance Corporation and Georgia Partner Fund Framework Cooperation Agreement*. According to the Agreement, the two sides will establish a financing and insurance cooperation platform in the fields of infrastructure, energy, machinery, logistics, electricity, and large – scale complete sets of equipment. Financial assistance and industrial docking will become an effective model for cooperation between China and Georgia.

The fourth is to vigorously develop tourism. Georgia has a wealth of tourism resources, and there is a strong demand for tourism in China. There are many Chinese, and they have achieved rapid accumulation of wealth, eager to travel around the world and broaden their horizons. In 2018, the number of mainland citizens leaving the country was nearly 150 million. China's per capita travel (including domestic travel) five times a year, this rate of development is very fast. For Chinese tourists, although Georgia is not a traditional hot tourist destination, it was strong in the first half of 2018, with a heat increase of 216%. This is not a single phenomenon. In the same period, the number of new tourists in Serbia and Turkey increased by 383% and 265% respectively, followed by Morocco,

Russia, and Iceland. The per capita spending of tourists in Europe and Oceania is significantly higher than that of Asian countries, which is about 10,000 yuan. The tourism industry is green, sustainable and has low barriers. Georgia can develop special tourism projects such as cultural festivals and food festivals to attract more Chinese tourists.

With the smooth progress of the Belt and Road Initiative overall project, China – Georgia needs to achieve strategic docking at a higher level, truly realize a pattern of each having something of the other and promote the common prosperity of the two countries.

Chapter 4

Georgia's Social Development: Status Quo and Prospects

Ma Feng

Associate Professor, National Institute of Social Development, CASS

Georgia is not only an important country along the Belt and Road, but also a significant junction of the Belt and Road. So far, Georgia is the only Eurasian country concluding the free trade agreement with China. Joint efforts made by China and Georgia and people of the both countries to build the Belt and Road have not only created a new opportunity of development for both countries and their people, but also promoted the inheritance of friendship established by people of both countries in the age of the ancient Silk Road. Since its independence, Georgia has realized historical changes in social development from a highly centralized planned economy to a market economy. The Belt and Road Initiative proposed by China has brought a precious opportunity for Georgia to reverse its economic decline. Georgia has also deemed the Silk Road economy as an important support to realize its strategic development goals. Currently, Georgia has a relatively stable social situation, and maintains good relations with its surrounding countries. Though Georgia is still unavoidably affected by the tension between western powers and Russia and party strife, these adverse factors are not strong enough to shake Georgia's resolution to get involved in the Silk Road construction. [1]

In terms of economic profile, Georgia has realized steady economic and social development in recent years. Since "Georgian Dream" won through in the parliamentary elections of Georgia held in October 2012, it has provided significant political premise to the stable development of Georgia. "In June 2018, Kvirikashvili announced his resignation, and Bakhtadze took over as prime minister. Currently, 'Georgia Dream – Democratic Georgia' is running the parliament, central and local governments, and maintains certain control capability." [2] This provides relatively favorable political conditions to the social development of Georgia. The reality and prospect of Georgia's social development is of great significance for us to get a deeper understanding of the social development stage and policies of the countries and regions along the Belt and Road in different stages of development, deepen bilateral cooperation and make people of both countries benefit from the outcome.

I China and Georgia: Belt and Road Initiative, a New Tie to Promote Social Development

Georgia is one of the first countries supporting and participating in the Belt and Road Initiative, and connecting its economic and social sectors

---

[1] Lu Ping, "Proposal regarding Georgia and the Silk Road Economic Belt: Attitude, Significance and Prospect", *Academic Journal of Russian Studies*, Issue 5, 2016, p. 75.

[2] Georgia profile (updated: January 2019), Ministry of Foreign Affairs: https://www.fmprc.gov.cn/web/gjhdq_676201/gj_676203/yz_676205/1206_676476/1206x0_676478/.

associated with its national development with the Initiative. Most countries along the Belt and Road have responded and supported the Belt and Road Initiative proposed by China, and Georgia was especially enthusiastic about it. Despite the tangles, doubts and challenges of some countries, Georgia extended its warmest welcome to BRI. Georgian leaders have stressed at one time and another the importance of the Silk Road Economic Belt and its significance to Georgia's economic development, and expressed strong willingness of involvement. They have taken concrete measures to promote its development, and demonstrated their firmly support to the construction of the Silk Road Economic Belt with their practical actions."[1] "In recent years, Georgia has been dedicated to national stability and economic development, and made active progress in improving relations with surrounding countries. Georgia is willing to continuously participate in the Belt and Road construction together with China, and take this opportunity to promote cooperation with China in various fields, boost regional connectivity, and make Georgia become the passage and corridor connecting the Eurasia"[2], said Georgian President Zourabichvili when meeting with Chinese State Councilor and Foreign Minister Wang Yi at Tbilisi presidential palace on May 24, 2019.

"Georgia is one of the first countries supporting the Belt and Road Initiative", and "Georgia hopes to strengthen cooperation with China in such fields as business, trade, investment, traffic, infrastructure construction and high-tech through the Belt and Road construction, and promote connectivity and people – to – people exchanges with China and other countries along the Belt and Road"[3], said Georgian Prime Minister

---

[1] Lu Ping, "Proposal regarding Georgia and the Silk Road Economic Belt: Attitude, Significance and Prospect", *Academic Journal of Russian Studies*, Issue 5, 2016, p. 76.

[2] Georgian President Zourabichvili met with Wang Yi, Ministry of Foreign Affairs: https://www.fmprc.gov.cn/web/wjbzhd/t1666381.shtml.

[3] Georgian Prime Minister Bakhtadze met with Wang Yi, Ministry of Foreign Affairs: https://www.fmprc.gov.cn/web/wjbzhd/t1666386.shtml.

Bakhtadze when meeting with State Councilor and Foreign Minister Wang Yi in Tbilisi on May 24, 2019.

In addition, on July 1, 2019, Georgian Prime Minister Bakhtadze, when attending the World Economic Forum's Annual Meeting of the New Champions held in China, further said to Li Keqiang, Premier of the State Council of the People's Republic of China, that "Georgia and China have maintained close high-level exchanges and firm political mutual trust. Georgia actively supports the Belt and Road construction, and welcomes Chinese enterprises to expand their investment in Georgia, as well as is willing to expand bilateral trade and strengthen cooperation with China in people-to-people exchanges and other fields for mutual benefit and win-win."① Prime Minister Li Keqiang said that "Georgia is the first Eurasian country concluding the free trade arrangement with China. China is willing to connect both sides' development strategies better, bring the geographical advantage of Georgia into full play, and carry out the Belt and Road cooperation under the principle of extensive consultation, joint contribution and shared benefits".②

The conclusion of China-Georgia free trade agreement has strongly promoted the bilateral economic and trade relation. "According to data of the National Bureau of Statistics, from January to March 2019, the bilateral trade between China and Georgia reached 0.257 billion USD, up 26.8% year-on-year, including Georgia's exports to China of 35.2552 million USD, up 72.6% year-on-year; imports from China of 0.222 billion USD, up 21.6% year-on-year. China is the second largest source of import of Georgia, and the imports from China accounted for 11.2% of

---

① Li Keqiang met with Georgian Prime Minister Bakhtadze, www.gov.cn: http://www.gov.cn/premier/2019—07/01/content_ 5405027.htm
② Li Keqiang met with Georgian Prime Minister Bakhtadze, www.gov.cn: http://www.gov.cn/premier/2019—07/01/content_ 5405027.htm

Georgia's total imports."[1] Moreover, the export of wine to China, which is the major export of Georgia, has also assumed the ascending trend (see Table 3 – 1 and Table 3 – 2), which is objectively helpful to boost development of relevant Georgian industries and income of grape planters.

Table 4 – 1   Statistics of Georgia's Wine Export in 2017—2019[2]

Unit: 10,000 bottles

Year	Importer and quantity						
	China	Poland	US	Belarus	Russia	Ukraine	Kazakhstan
Jan. – Apr. 2019	219	117	22	60	—	—	—
Jan. – Feb. 2019	60	63	—	—	869	98	35
Jan. 2019	28	27	—	—	460	55	15
2018	695	351	—	—	5368	1069	360
2017	760	—	—	—	4780	850	—

Table 4 – 2   Trend of Georgia's Wine Export to China in 2017—2019   Unit: %

Year	Trend—year – on – year growth	
	China	General trend
Jan. – Apr. 2019	22	4
Jan. – Feb. 2019	12	13
Jan. 2019	12	24
2018	—	13
2017	43	54

---

① China – Georgian trade volume up 26.8% year – on – year from Jan. – Mar. 2019, Economic and Commercial Office of the Embassy of PRC in Georgia: http://ge.mofcom.gov.cn/article/jmxw/201905/20190502862441.shtml.

② Table 4 – 1 and Table 4 – 2 are self – made tables with data coming from statistics of relevant Georgian government agencies forwarded by the Economic and Commercial Office of the Embassy of PRC in Georgia. Sources: Georgia's wine export up 4% year – on – year (Jan. – Apr. 2019), http://ge.mofcom.gov.cn/article/jmxw/201905/20190502862442.shtml; Georgia's wine export up 13% year – on – year (Jan. – Feb. 2019), http://ge.mofcom.gov.cn/article/jmxw/201904/20190402853365.shtml; in Jan. 2019, Georgia's wine export up 13% year – on – year, http://ge.mofcom.gov.cn/article/jmxw/201904/20190402853359.shtml; in 2018, Georgia's wine export up 13% year – on – year, http://ge.mofcom.gov.cn/article/jmxw/201904/20190402853345.shtml; in 2017, Georgia's wine export up 54% year – on – year, http://ge.mofcom.gov.cn/article/jmxw/201801/20180102703055.shtml.

The political, economic, social and civil relations between China and Georgia have got even closer in the wake of conclusion of the free trade agreement and implementation of the Belt and Road Initiative, which has strongly promoted the mutual benefit and win – win of both sides. When accepting the credentials submitted by China's new ambassador in Georgia, Georgian president said that "currently Georgia and China had maintained positive momentum for the development of the relationship. Georgia cherishes its relationship established with China, and is willing to continuously strengthen exchanges with China, and looks forward to more fruitful results from cooperation in various fields". ① The cooperation with China within the framework of the Silk Road Economic Belt construction is helpful for the rapid economic growth and livelihood improvement of Georgia, and best serves the interests of Georgia. ②

The Belt and Road cooperation has brought investment from China to Georgia, and provided Georgia's advantageous export items with a vast export market, which has played a positive role in improving Georgia's employment and livelihood and promoting its social development. For example, "the more than 30 Chinese enterprises in Georgia are spreading over industries ranging from investment, engineering contracting, communication, logistics, agriculture, finance, trade, services, etc. The Chinese enterprises and companies have contributed a lot to the social and economic development of Georgia. For example, China Railway 23rd Bureau Group Co., Ltd. employed more than 300 local workers while undertaking the modern railway upgrading project of Georgia, and provided local people

---

① Li Yan presented her credentials to Georgian president in her character as ambassador in Georgia, Embassy of the PRC in Georgia: https://www.fmprc.gov.cn/ce/cege/chn/xwdt/t1682540.htm.

② Lu Ping, "Proposal regarding Georgia and the Silk Road Economic Belt: Attitude, Significance and Prospect", *Academic Journal of Russian Studies*, Issue 5, 2016, p. 76.

with more jobs". [1]

The interaction between the two countries, from high level to civilian, and cooperation in fields ranging from business and trade to culture have paved a solid foundation for enhancing friendship between the two countries and provided a vast development platform. The Belt and Road Initiative has become a new tie for cooperation and social development of both countries.

II Status Quo and Prospects of Georgia

Georgia has gone through an intricate process of development over the past twenty years since its independence, changing politically to capitalism featured by multi – party competition and western democratic election, and economically from a centrally planned economy to a capitalist market economy, which led to fundamental changes in the social development of Georgia. Moreover, factors, such as geopolitics, game of great powers, etc., have also remarkably influenced the political process, economic development and social development of Georgia. Its relationship with Russia and western countries undoubtedly plays a significant role even a decisive role in this regard. Since its independence, Georgia's governance capability which focuses on social development and livelihood improvement has evolved in development.

1. Economic Growth of Georgia

Since its independence, Georgia's economic growth has gone through obvious ups and downs. At the beginning of independence, Georgia experienced sharp economic and national income decline for a while due to collapse of the Soviet Union. The transition from a centrally planned economy

---

[1] Lu Ping, "Proposal regarding Georgia and the Silk Road Economic Belt: Attitude, Significance and Prospect", *Academic Journal of Russian Studies*, Issue 5, 2016, p. 77.

to a market economy led to national economic downturn. Its GDP growth and GDP per capita growth were −44.9% and −45.325% in 1992. Relevant economic data of Georgia began to realize positive growth in 1995. Georgia's GDP per capita was 1,614.64 USD in 1990, then declined continuously, and hit the all-time low of 519.816 USD in 1994 after its independence. Its GDP per capita restored to 1,642.775 USD in 2005, basically the same as that in 1990, which took nearly 15 years. Generally speaking, from 1990 to 2018, the various economic indicators of Georgia have assumed the ascending trend, regardless of the economic growth or GDP per capita, and have realized leap-forward development as compared with the beginning of its independence. As of 2018, Georgia achieved the GDP (current USD) of 16.21 billion USD, GDP growth of 4.717%, GDP per capita growth of 4.633% and GDP per capita (current USD) of 4,344.634 USD. All the above data have hit the all-time high since its independence, which is closely associated with its political stability and efforts to develop economy. Table 4−3 has given a detailed presentation of the comprehensive statistics of Georgia's economic development from 1990 to 2018.

Table 4−3　　Comprehensive Statistics of Georgia's Economic Development 1990—2018

Year	GDP (current USD) Unit: 1 billion	GDP growth (Annual %)	GDP per capita growth (Annual %)	GDP per capita (current USD)
1990	7.754	−14.788	−14.765	1614.64
1991	6.358	−21.1	−21.653	1314.671
1992	3.69	−44.9	−45.325	757.224
1993	2.701	−29.3	−29.841	550.016
1994	2.514	−10.4	−9.01	519.816
1995	2.694	2.6	6.529	578.337
1996	3.095	11.2	15.31	689.017
1997	3.51	10.519	14.121	807.015

(Contd.)

Year	GDP (current USD) Unit: 1 billion	GDP growth (Annual %)	GDP per capita growth (Annual %)	GDP per capita (current USD)
1998	3.613	3.105	5.688	851.516
1999	2.8	2.869	5.008	673.526
2000	3.057	1.838	3.838	749.896
2001	3.219	4.805	6.444	801.99
2002	3.396	5.474	6.424	853.528
2003	3.991	11.059	11.811	1010.008
2004	5.125	5.794	6.452	1305.047
2005	6.411	9.59	10.288	1642.775
2006	7.745	9.42	10.044	1996.057
2007	10.173	12.579	13.168	2635.354
2008	12.795	2.419	2.73	3324.736
2009	10.767	-3.651	-2.791	2822.652
2010	11.639	6.249	7.027	3073.525
2011	14.435	7.222	8.085	3842.618
2012	15.846	6.351	7.137	4249.67
2013	16.14	3.387	3.698	4341.435
2014	16.509	4.624	4.574	4438.687
2015	13.994	2.881	2.719	3756.384
2016	14.378	2.847	2.785	3857.282
2017	15.081	4.833	4.819	4045.417
2018	16.21	4.717	4.633	4344.634

Self-made table, data source: World Bank. [1]

The international financial crisis breaking out in 2008 has brought a

---

[1] The data in the table come from the data published by the WB, and were retrieved from Aug. 20 to Sep. 5, 2019. Sources: GDP (current USD), https://data.worldbank.org.cn/indicator/NY.GDP.MKTP.CD? locations = GE; GDP growth (annual %), https://data.worldbank.org.cn/indicator/NY.GDP.MKTP.KD.ZG? end = 2018&locations = GE&start = 1990; GDP per capita growth (annual %), https://data.worldbank.org.cn/indicator/NY.GDP.PCAP.KD.ZG? end = 2018&locations = GE&start = 1990; GDP per capita (current USD), https://data.worldbank.org.cn/indicator/NY.GDP.PCAP.CD? end = 2018&locations = GE&start = 1990.

negative impact on the economic development of countries across the world. It can be seen that Georgia's economy and national income contracted slightly in 2009 after the 2008 financial crisis, then expanded in 2010, and maintained the growth of over 6% in 2010, 2011 and 2012. Its GDP per capita and GDP also grew continuously. From 2013 to 2016, its economic and national income growth slowed down, which is somewhat associated with the political dispute in that time.

Georgia realized economic growth and national income rise again in 2017 and 2018, and achieved remarkable results. Its political stability is of decisive significance to its economic growth and national income rise. The two negative economic and national income growths happened at the beginning of and after the independence of Georgia were attributable to both the internal and external factors.

2. Social Development of Georgia

(1) Demographic Growth

Table 4 – 4 clearly shows the Georgia's demographic changes since 1990 through such indicators as total population, total labor force, dependency ratio, population ages 65 and above (% of total population), population ages 15—64 (% of total population), etc. It is can be seen that Georgia's demographic changes are closely associated with its national development.

Table 4 – 4　　Comprehensive Statistics of Georgia's Social Development (population) 1990—2018

Year	Total population Unit: 10,000	Total labor force Unit: 10,000	Female population (% of total population)	Dependency ratio (% of working – age population)	Population ages 65 and above (% of total population)	Population ages 15—64 (% of total population)
1990	480.2	239.2170	52.459	51.907	9.31	65.83
1991	483.59	242.4362	52.442	52.73	9.71	65.475

(Contd.)

Year	Total population Unit: 10,000	Total labor force Unit: 10,000	Female population (% of total population)	Dependency ratio (% of working-age population)	Population ages 65 and above (% of total population)	Population ages 15—64 (% of total population)
1992	487.35	246.0919	52.443	53.683	10.181	65.069
1993	491.11	250.0268	52.457	54.647	10.668	64.664
1994	483.6076	248.4436	52.478	55.429	11.084	64.338
1995	465.7722	238.5030	52.498	55.897	11.379	64.145
1996	449.1699	228.3032	52.515	55.889	11.701	64.148
1997	434.9913	219.6503	52.53	55.578	11.896	64.227
1998	424.3607	214.3245	52.545	55.046	12.024	64.497
1999	415.7139	210.1786	52.566	54.452	12.178	64.745
2000	407.7131	200.3899	52.595	53.891	12.409	64.981
2001	401.4373	206.1536	52.634	53.443	12.82	65.171
2002	397.8515	199.2008	52.68	53.089	13.296	65.321
2003	395.1736	203.4586	52.724	52.676	13.773	65.498
2004	392.7340	199.6802	52.753	52.022	14.145	65.78
2005	390.2469	199.1946	52.76	51.07	14.349	66.194
2006	388.0347	199.1317	52.738	50.426	14.506	66.478
2007	386.0158	199.2318	52.693	49.609	14.524	66.841
2008	384.8449	199.7277	52.63	48.779	14.451	67.214
2009	381.4419	198.8971	52.562	48.136	14.364	67.505
2010	378.6695	201.3146	52.498	47.776	14.312	67.67
2011	375.6441	202.9544	52.44	47.923	14.292	67.603
2012	372.8874	205.0357	52.386	48.205	14.315	67.474
2013	371.7668	202.4016	52.339	48.635	14.383	67.279
2014	371.9414	203.4761	52.301	49.225	14.487	67.013
2015	372.5276	206.2766	52.273	49.991	14.615	66.671

(Contd.)

Year	Total population Unit: 10,000	Total labor force Unit: 10,000	Female population (% of total population)	Dependency ratio (% of working–age population)	Population ages 65 and above (% of total population)	Population ages 15—64 (% of total population)
2016	372.7505	203.9265	52.258	50.78	14.73	66.322
2017	372.8004	203.2153	52.255	51.622	14.864	65.953
2018	373.1	203.1381	52.261	52.506	15.012	65.571

Data source: World Bank. ①

The total population and total labor force of Georgia have generally assumed the descending trend since 1990. The descending trend of total population is a continuous process, and there are few rises in middle years. The total labor force has been basically stable since 2000, despite the ups and downs, and generally maintained within a stable range without any obvious ups and downs. Compared with the changes in total population, the total labor force has been stable since 2000. After 2000, the total population is finely agreeable with the total labor force, and has not varied much.

The female population (% of total population) has ascended and then descended since 1990. It climbed up steadily from 1990 to 2008, and then declined continuously. The decline is sharp as compared with the steady rise

---

① Data in the table come from data published by WB, and were retrieved from Aug. 25 to Sep. 10, 2019. Concrete source: population, total, https://data.worldbank.org.cn/indicator/SP.POP.TOTL? end = 2018&locations = GE&start = 1990; total labor force, https://data.worldbank.org.cn/indicator/SL.TLF.TOTL.IN; female population (% of total population), https://data.worldbank.org.cn/indicator/SP.POP.TOTL.FE.ZS? end = 2018&locations = GE&start = 1990; dependency ratio (% of working – age population), https://data.worldbank.org.cn/indicator/SP.POP.DPND? end = 2018&locations = GE&start = 1990; population ages 65 and above (% of total population), https://data.worldbank.org.cn/indicator/SP.POP.65UP.TO.ZS? end = 2018&locations = GE&start = 1990; population ages 15 – 64 (% of total population), https://data.worldbank.org.cn/indicator/SP.POP.1564.TO.ZS? end = 2018&locations = GE&start = 1990.

before 2008. The basic trend has been relatively stable since 2015, and no remarkable ups and downs have been seen. The dependency ratio has gone through a rise, then a long – term decline, and another rise since 1990. Among others, the dependency ratio has declined continuously during the decade from 2005 to 2015.

The population ages 65 and above (% of total population) in Georgia has ascended since 1990. The increase in old people ages 65 above is steady, and the general trend is up despite certain changes. The proportion rose rapidly from 1990 to 2003, and then became moderate after 2003, but has not changed remarkably. Generally speaking, in the 21st century, Georgia's old people ages 65 and above has maintained certain stability and continuity. The proportion of population ages 15—64 has gone through remarkable ups and downs since 1990, namely, a process of down, then up and down, with obvious inflection point and development changes, and prominent features of the times. Generally speaking, the population ages 15—64 (% of total population) in Georgia was 65.571% in 2018, which was close to the 65.83% and 65.498% in 1990 and 2003, respectively. During the 13 years from 2005 to 2018, the population ages 15—64 (% of total population) in Georgia climbed up and then declined, and finally fell back in 2003 which is basically the same as that in the 1990s. The change is significant, and reflects the profound impact of social development on demographic growth.

(2) Education

Education reflects the basic fairness of a society. It is the first step helping members of the society grow and enter the society, also a crucial step in the socialization process. Education boasts significance in social development. It can be said that education, medical care, housing, pension and employment have constituted the lifelong rigid demands of people in social development and indispensable parts of the basic social security. The data in Table 4 – 5 show the changes in Georgia's education since 1990 from four aspects, namely, school enrollment (primary), school enrollment (tertiary), government expenditure on education, total (% of GDP) and government expenditure on education (% of government expenditure).

Table 4 – 5　　Comprehensive Statistics of Georgia's Social Development (education) 1991—2018

Year	School enrollment, primary (% of gross)	School enrollment, tertiary (% of gross)	Government expenditure on education, total (% of GDP)	Government expenditure on education, total (% of government expenditure)
1991	97.291	36.189		
1992	95.475			
1993	86.339			
1994	85.003		6.916	
1995	82.688	44.596		
1996	82.512	42.068		
1997	84.895	45.012		
1998	88.982		2.109	10.851
1999	92.408	36.379	2.155	10.605
2000	95.181	38.325	2.181	12.541
2001	92.782	39.206	2.138	12.362
2002	89.47	41.271	2.235	13.604
2003	88.671	42.51	2.066	12.493
2004	90.71	41.723	2.914	15.037
2005	89.758	45.923	2.484	11.181
2006	93.018	37.434	3.004	12.895
2007	98.36	36.635	2.697	9.487
2008	100.868	34.183	2.92	8.938
2009	101.644	25.723	3.222	8.998
2010	101.77	29.199		
2011	102.845	31.433	2.696	9.269

(Contd.)

Year	School enrollment, primary (% of gross)	School enrollment, tertiary (% of gross)	Government expenditure on education, total (% of GDP)	Government expenditure on education, total (% of government expenditure)
2012	105.5	29.694	1.983	6.708
2013	106.371	35.647		
2014	105.077	40.623		
2015	104.319	45.614		
2016	102.598	51.883	3.785	12.666
2017	102.774	57.528	3.83	12.953
2018	98.631	60.334	3.521	12.951

Data source: World Bank. ①

Primary education, as a fundamental education, forms the foundation and important premise for people to gain a foothold and develop in the society. Georgia's primary school enrollment (% of gross) was volatile from 1990 to 2017, but went upward steadily in the long run, and always had a long-time decline and adjustment at each stage. 1996 saw the all-time low primary school enrollment of 82.512% which was still on the high side. "The educational and technological development of Georgia has been seriously affected by its political and economic situation, and in a hard situation, but the progress of reform is still fast." ②

---

① The data in the Table 4-5 come from the data published by the WB, and were retrieved from Aug. 25 to Sep. 10, 2019. Sources: school enrollment, primary (% of gross), https://data.worldbank.org.cn/indicator/SE.PRM.ENRR? end=2017&locations=GE&start=1990; school enrollment, tertiary (% gross), https://data.worldbank.org.cn/indicator/SE.TER.ENRR; government expenditure on education, total (% of GDP), https://data.worldbank.org.cn/indicator/SE.XPD.TOTL.GD.ZS? locations=GE; government expenditure on education, total (% of government expenditure), https://data.worldbank.org.cn/indicator/SE.XPD.TOTL.GB.ZS? locations=GE.

② Yang Shu, "The Current Educational and Technological Situation of Georgia", *East European & Central Asian Studies*, Issue 5, 1997, p. 94.

The tertiary school enrollment (% gross) cannot clearly reflect the tertiary education development of Georgia since its independence due to missing of some data, but according to the data available, Georgia's tertiary school enrollment (% gross) is on the low side, averagely below 50%, and even below 30% in certain years. For example, the three years, namely, 2009, 2010 and 2012 when Georgia's economy was severely influenced by the 2008 international financial crisis, saw the tertiary school enrollment (% gross) of 25.723%, 29.199% and 29.694%, respectively. After 2012, as the subsequence influence of the crisis eased gradually, Georgia saw a sharp increase in tertiary school enrollment, and this trend remained unchanged until 2017. This is probably associated with the demand for active improvement in self – quality to improve competence in the employment market amid and after the crisis. In 2017, Georgia's tertiary school enrollment (% gross) reached 57.528%. From then on, tertiary education got popularized and brought new opportunity to Georgia's development. Tertiary schools are the primary training place of human resources, and the tertiary school enrollment represents the population quality of a country. Nowadays, the new industrial revolution is rising. Therefore, it is necessary to vigorously develop tertiary education, increase the tertiary school enrollment, adjust specialties and set up new specialties in light of social development and future demand to cultivate talents and expand talent dividend, and further improve the comprehensive competitiveness of the state.

According to the data available, Georgia's government expenditure on education (% of GDP) mostly fell below 3%. Without regard to the discontinuous data, the government expenditure on education (% of GDP) reaches the all – time high or the record high after Georgia's independence of 3.785% and 3.83% in 2016 and 2017, and the all – time low or the record low after Georgia's independence of 1.983% in 2012. The government expenditure on education was stable from 1998 to 2009. The statistical data for this period are continuous and stable. After 2000, the government expenditure on education began to climb up, but was still stable and continuous. On the whole, the changes of this indicator reflect the changes in Georgia's economic development and economic growth trend, and are closely associated with the GDP growth, which shows the resources or newly – added resources invested by Georgia in education. But "Georgia has to reduce its expenditure on education due to continuously increasing budget deficit, which has hindered sound development of the national macroeconomic environment, reduced the administrative efficiency, and weakened the efforts to encourage business activities". [1]

According to the data available, Georgia's government expenditure on education (% of government expenditure) was changeable, and went through significant ups and downs. The overall data analysis showed that the government expenditure on education (% of government expenditure) was around 10%, and hit the record low of 6.708% in 2012, which was also the all – time low since its independence. The changes in Georgia's government expenditure on education (% of government expenditure) reflect the changes in the government's fiscal revenue. The government expenditure on education belongs to expenditure on livelihood. Therefore, it is rigid. The proportion and demand of such expenditure are nearly fixed within certain period of time, but this expenditure is also closely related to the government's financial strength and the state's economic strength. "The government expenditure on education (% of government expenditure) of Georgia is still on the low side as compared with that of developed countries e. g., the average government expenditure on education (% of government

---

[1] Xiao Zhou, "Ups and Downs of Georgia's economy", *Russian, Central Asian & East European Market*, Issue 6, 2003, p. 29.

expenditure) of OECD countries is 11.3%, and that of EU is 9.9%, and the government expenditure on tertiary education (% of government expenditure) is on the decline."[1] On a whole, the government expenditure on education (% of government expenditure) in Georgia is relatively stable. Though it dropped in specific years, or dropped within certain range, it will rebound rapidly thereafter. It is on the decline as a whole. But the discontinuous data showed that this proportion had surged in 2016 and 2017, up from 6.708% in 2012 to 12.666% and 12.953% in 2016 and 2017, respectively. Georgia saw a political stability in 2016 and 2017, which has continued until now.

(3) Employment

While analyzing the employment of Georgia, Table 4 – 6 reveals the employment distribution, total employment and youth employment from 1991 to 2018 from five aspects, namely, employment in the three major industries, namely, agriculture, industry and services, total unemployment, total unemployment of youth ages 15 – 24, etc.

Agriculture is a pillar industry of Georgia. Wine is the major export earner of Georgia and a primary pillar industry in its national economy. Georgia's industrial development is lagging behind, which can be seen obviously from the proportion of employment in industry. The services have played a significant role in Georgia's employment. In recent years, especially since 2016, the employment in services (% of total employment) has been already on a par with that in agriculture. In 2017 and 2018, Georgia's employment in agriculture (% of total employment) was 43.124% and 42.897%, while the employment in services (% of total employment) was 43.704% and 43.881%, respectively.

---

[1] Liu Jin, Wang Yimeng, "Research on Current Tertiary education and Development Trend of B&R Countries (XVII) —Take Georgia as the Example", *Journal of World Education*, Issue 23, 2018, p. 38.

Table 4 – 6   **Comprehensive Statistics of Georgia's Social Development (employment) 1991—2018**

Year	Employment in agriculture (% of total employment)	Employment in industry (% of total employment)	Employment in services (% of total employment)	Unemployment, total (% of total labor force)	Unemployment, youth total (% of total labor force ages 15 – 24)
1991	49.757	10.385	39.858	2.7	5.461
1992	49.65	10.244	40.105	5.4	10.216
1993	49.543	10.103	40.354	5.4	10.223
1994	49.36	10.097	40.544	8.4	15.352
1995	49.165	10.111	40.725	7.6	13.889
1996	48.964	10.134	40.903	11.5	20.317
1997	48.755	10.171	41.074	11.5	20.369
1998	48.553	10.193	41.254	14.53	25.519
1999	52.252	9.449	38.298	13.8	24.24
2000	52.173	9.804	38.023	10.82	20.865
2001	52.792	9.227	37.93	11.16	19.869
2002	53.77	8.22	38.01	12.59	27.489
2003	54.897	8.354	36.748	11.51	24.521
2004	54.002	8.835	37.162	12.62	27.832
2005	54.341	9.292	36.367	13.81	27.979
2006	55.304	9.049	35.646	13.57	29.455
2007	53.431	10.372	36.197	13.28	30.737
2008	52.92	10.461	36.62	17.87	37.174
2009	52.392	10.579	37.029	18.3	40.092
2010	51.843	10.736	37.42	17.41	37.318
2011	51.269	10.94	37.791	17.34	39.252
2012	50.609	11.181	38.21	17.22	35.795
2013	49.695	11.394	38.911	16.94	38.949
2014	48.738	11.675	39.587	14.62	34.564

(Contd.)

Year	Employment in agriculture (% of total employment)	Employment in industry (% of total employment)	Employment in services (% of total employment)	Unemployment, total (% of total labor force)	Unemployment, youth total (% of total labor force ages 15–24)
2015	47.78	11.969	40.251	14.08	33.381
2016	46.824	12.254	40.921	13.97	32.781
2017	43.124	13.171	43.704	13.93	29.103
2018	42.897	13.222	43.881	14.106	30.441

Data source: World Bank. ①

Separately, the employment in agriculture (% of total employment) has assumed a descending trend since 1990, and declined remarkably since 2000; moreover, this trend has not reversed fundamentally until 2018. It has gone through ups and downs over the past nearly thirty years: steady decrease from 1991 to 1998 without remarkable changes, a rapid increase and development from 1999 to 2006, for example, the proportion was 48.553% in 1998, and 52.252% in 1999, up 3.699%, nearly 4%, which is a record high growth from Georgia's independence to 1999. From then on, the employment in agriculture (% of total employment) began to rise until 2007 when it declined continuously to 42.897% in 2018, which is even lower than the 49.757% in 1991 or the beginning of independence. The continuous decline in employment in agriculture (% of total employment)

---

① The data in the Table come from data published by the WB, and were retrieved from Aug. 25 to Sep. 10, 2019. Sources: employment in agriculture (% of total employment), https://data.worldbank.org.cn/indicator/SL.AGR.EMPL.ZS? locations = GE; employment in industry (% of total employment), https://data.worldbank.org.cn/indicator/SL.IND.EMPL.ZS? locations = GE; employment in services (% of total employment), https://data.worldbank.org.cn/indicator/SL.SRV.EMPL.ZS? locations = GE; unemployment, total (% of total labor force), https://data.worldbank.org.cn/indicator/SL.UEM.TOTL.ZS? locations = GE; unemployment, youth total (% of total labor force ages 15–24), https://data.worldbank.org.cn/indicator/SL.UEM.1524.ZS? locations = GE.

which is a pillar industry of Georgia is closely associated with the big environment of the global economy and the small environment of Georgia's economy in the 21st century. The employment in industry and services (% of total employment) also experienced ups and downs, and the overall trend is down and then up. The decline of the employment in agriculture (% of total employment) is to a certain extent associated with the transfer of employment to industry and services, but the employment in agriculture (% of total employment) in Georgia had been maintained at 40% + from 1991 to 2018. Agriculture was still the main source of employment in Georgia. It supports the economic development of Georgia and accumulates materials for the social development.

The employment in industry (% of total employment) declined first and then ascended. From 1991 to 2003, it dropped from 10.385% to 8.354%. The decline lasting more than 10 years has reflected the deficiencies in industrial development, especially in absorption of employment. The employment in industry (% of total employment) has climbed up since 2004, up from 8.835% to 13.222% in 2018, which is a record high since its independence. In particular, the growth has picked up since 2012, which is closely associated with its participation in the Belt and Road construction and investment of Chinese enterprises in Georgia's industry, which has strongly promoted the economy, employment and livelihood improvement of Georgia. The employment in agriculture (% of total employment) has declined while the employment in industry (% of total employment) rose. The rise and decline are complementary, but generally speaking, the employment in industry (% of total employment) is pretty low in Georgia, less than 15%, but it is likely to rise remarkably if the current trend remains unchanged in the future, especially when Georgia maintains its political stability and actively gears to the Belt and Road Initiative.

In Georgia, the employment in services (% of total employment) has gone through a slight rise, a sharp decline and then a steady decline since 1991, but since 2007, it has begun to restore, and then risen continuously. In particular, it has risen acceleratedly since 2015, and reached the record high of 43.881% in 2018 since its independence. Services outstripped agriculture and become the sector with the highest employment, which reflects the economic vitality and gradual recovery, and is closely associated with Georgia's efforts to develop its tourism because it has abundant tourism resources. "Given this, Georgia carried out some transportation projects, such as 'Baku – Supsa', 'Baku – Tbilisi – Ceyhan', etc., developed the 'Silk Road' trade transportation outline, and participated in the production of the outline for tourism infrastructure development under the 'Silk Road' program through the UNWTO and UNESCO. All these undoubtedly will promote the development of Georgia's transportation, trade and tourism." [1]

It can be seen that in Georgia, the employment in industry and services (of total employment) has risen while the employment in agriculture declined over the past thirty years since its independence. According to the overall trend, Georgia's employment in industry and services (% of total employment) started to rise in the 21st century, and has grown rapidly since 2012 when Georgia extricated itself from political unrest, and embarked on political stability and steady economic development. Agriculture and services hold a large stake in Georgia's economic composition, and services outstripped agriculture for the first time in 2017 and became the largest source of employment, 43.704% and 43.124%, respectively. Despite the minor gap, the future development trend is noteworthy. In 2018, the

---

[1] Xiao Zhou, "Ups and Downs of Georgia's economy", *Russian, Central Asian & East European Market*, Issue 6, 2003, p. 29.

proportions were changed to 43.881% and 42.897%. The stake of services was 0.984% above that of agriculture.

From 1991 to 2018, the changes in Georgia's total unemployment were somewhat consistent and tallied with the changes in the total youth unemployment. Both ascended gradually from 1991, and then declined slightly since 2009 but not as low as the beginning of independence. In 1991 or the beginning of Georgia's independence, the total unemployment and total youth unemployment (% of total labor force) were the all-time low of 2.7% and 5.461%, respectively. The total unemployment (% of total labor force) reached the record high of 17.87% in 2008. The youth unemployment (% of total labor force) reached the record high of 40.092% in 2009. Since 2008, Georgia the total unemployment and total youth unemployment (% of total labor force) have been averagely maintained at 15% and 30% around, respectively. The unemployment of youth ages 15—24 was serious. From 1996 when Georgia's youth unemployment (% of total labor force) reached 20.317% to 2018, Its influence on the youth employment was also obvious.

Generally speaking, Georgia's employment structure has gone through remarkable changes since its independence, which can be viewed from the changes in its employment structure. The distribution of employment in agriculture, industry and services has distinctive characteristics and stake in Georgia's national economy. Agriculture has held the dominant position for a long time in its national economy, and always been the biggest source of employment. Since the employment in services exceeds that in agriculture, services and agriculture form the major sectors in Georgia's national economy. Despite the remarkable increase in employment absorbed by industry, its stake is comparatively small. Georgia's total unemployment and total youth unemployment (% of total labor force) have always been on the rise since its independence, and dropped slightly in recent years, but not as low as that at the beginning of its independence. The youth unemployment is noteworthy. In particular, the total youth unemployment (% of total labor force ages 15—24) of around 30% after the 2008 financial crisis was on the high side. An article pointed out that "the livelihood of Georgia's citizens was on the low side according to the statistics. Even according to the official data, more than 20% of the population lived below the poverty line—60% of the average consumption (i. e. , average household consumption) is taken as the relative poverty standard. Experts estimated that about 86% of Georgians were suffering from severe difficulties."[1] It follows that the youth development needs stable environment to provide economic development with sustainable security and promote employment and the youth development.

(4) Health Service

"Georgian government deems its people's health as the foundation of national economic development and national defense. The government developed the national health development planning till 2010 after investigation and appraisal, and proposed to focus on the following aspects to protect and improve its citizens' health, including improving the health of mothers and children, reducing the morbidity and death rate of cardiovascular diseases, strengthening the prevention, research and treatment of tumor, reducing accidental injury, infectious diseases and diseases with social risks, strengthening mental health, and determining a healthy lifestyle to solve the effect of environment on human health."[2]

---

[1] [Georgia] Vladimer. Papava, "Economic Achievements of Post – revolutionary Georgia: Myths and Reality", translated by Wang Fanmei, Qiu Jianmei, Zhang Xuetong and Wang Zixuan, *Journal of University of Science and Technology Beijing (Social Science Edition)*, Issue 6, 2017, p. 64.

[2] Health VIII project delegation, "1989—2001 Georgia's health reform and implication to China—report on the health reform experience of countries in economic transition (Ⅰ)", *Chinese Health Economics*, Issue 6, 2005, p. 73.

Table 4 – 7   Comprehensive Statistics of Georgia's Social Development (health) 1990—2018

Year	Life expectancy at birth, total (years)	Crude deathrate, (per 1000 people, %)
1990	70.386	9.352
1991	70.29	9.51
1992	70.156	9.723
1993	70.003	9.98
1994	69.849	10.27
1995	69.718	10.574
1996	69.635	10.868
1997	69.613	11.132
1998	69.654	11.357
1999	69.756	11.537
2000	69.902	11.68
2001	70.065	11.801
2002	70.22	11.921
2003	70.349	12.054
2004	70.451	12.204
2005	70.538	12.369
2006	70.635	12.542
2007	70.765	12.711
2008	70.946	12.863
2009	71.18	12.922
2010	71.46	13.088
2011	71.773	13.146
2012	72.097	13.168
2013	72.412	13.158

(Contd.)

Year	Life expectancy at birth, total (years)	Crude deathrate, (per 1,000 people, %)
2014	72.707	13.121
2015	72.973	13.062
2016	73.207	12.992
2017	73.414	12.918

Data source: World Bank. ①

Actually, the life expectancy at birth of Georgia has grown continuously since its independence, despite some decline in middle years, the overall trend is upward, and this trend has accelerated obviously since 2008, with the average life expectancy of 70 +. The minimum life expectancy of 69.718 emerged in 1995, and the maximum life expectancy of 73.414 emerged in 2017. The life expectancy was 70.386 at the beginning of its independence, namely, 1990, and then dropped slightly. From 1994 to 2003, the life expectancy was lower than that at the beginning of independence, namely, 1990, until 2004, it reached 70.451, exceeding the life expectancy in 1990.

The crude death rate ascended steadily from 1990 to 2017, but declined after 2013, and reached 9.352% in 1990, which is an all-time low since 1990. The highest crude death rate of 13.168% appeared in 2012. The crude death rate per 1,000 people has been maintained at 10% above since 1994, which is a relatively high proportion, and required Georgia to pay close attention to and improve the health of its people. The downward trend starting in 2013 is of great significance, which has been the

---

① The data in the Table come from the data published by WB, and were retrieved from Aug. 25 to Sept. 10, 2019. Sources: life expectancy at birth, total (years), https://data.worldbank.org.cn/indicator/SP.DYN.LE00.IN? end=2017&locations=GE&start=1990; death rate, crude (per 1,000 people, %), https://data.worldbank.org.cn/indicator/SP.DYN.CDRT.IN? end=2017&locations=GE&start=1990.

first decline over the past two decades since 1990. The crude death rate dropped to 12.918% in 2017, basically close to the 12.204% in 2004. Whether this gradually descending trend is sustainable is subject to further observation.

Ⅲ Conclusion

Regardless of geographically or historically, Georgia has been an important passage and gathering place for exchange of human civilization for thousands of years. Georgia's economic and social development is influenced not only by domestic political environment, but also by its external economic situation and relations with great powers.

Vladimer Papava, a former minister of the Ministry of Economy and Sustainable Development of Georgia, a senior fellow at the Georgian Foundation for Strategic and International Studies, and a professor of Economics at the Tbilisi State University, gave a clear definition of Georgia's position in his article named *A Eurasian or a European Future for Post - Soviet Georgia's Economic Development and the Role of The Belt and Road Initiative*, and a clear statement of Georgia's strategic choice at the geopolitical crossroads. As one of Georgia's elites and a former cabinet minister directly in charge of the economic development of Georgia, he is of the opinion that "comparatively speaking, the European Union (EU) is better than the Eurasian Economic Union (EAEU) regardless in terms of the objective of establishment, economic situation or the incorruptibility of member countries. Moreover, in the long run, Georgia prefers the Europe and Europe – Atlantic mechanism, and joined EU's 'European Neighborhood Policy' and 'Eastern Partnership program' cooperation mechanism, while the EAEU dominated by Russia, although attaining membership of the EAEU is much easier than that of the EU, it rests on a redistribution mechanism for oil and gas revenues, whereby Russia deliberately relinquishes a part of its due gains in favor of other member states in order to not only induce economic interest to remain within the Union, but also to maintain and enhance its political influence via this economic output. This leads to the fragility and instability of the EAEU. A comparison of the EU with the EAEU does not favor the later. The Belt and Road Initiative proposed by China has created new opportunities for the world economy. China has carried out some cooperation with Georgia under the WTO framework. The China – Central Asia – West Asia economic corridor construction under the Silk Road Economic Belt planning will probably become a new opportunity for Georgia's economic development. "[1] China's Belt and Road Initiative has undoubtedly brought new opportunities to the countries along the Belt and Road. This peaceful, prosperous and mutually beneficial initiative was readily embraced by the countries along the Belt and Road because it is a Chinese solution to the post – crisis world development without any geopolitical plot.

In recent years, the political stability and economic and social recovery of Georgia have brought rare opportunity for Georgia's livelihood improvement and national construction. The continuous improvement in business environment and effective containment of corruption in Georgia, as well as active construction of the transit passage connection Europe and Asia constitute the important preconditions for Georgia's redevelopment. The agriculture, industry and service are not only the development strengths of Georgia, but also the weaknesses of its development. The former Georgian Prime Minister Bakhtadze is of the opinion that there are still many problems in Georgia's current economy, including unreasonable economic structure,

---

[1] [Georgia] Vladimer Papava, "A Eurasian or a European Future for Post – Soviet Georgia's Economic Development and the Role of the Belt and Road Initiative", *Global Review*, Issue 2, 2018, p. 1.

weakening industry, heavy rely on service and tourism in national economy, stern employment situation which makes lots of young people go to Russia and EU for jobs, etc. "[1]

The all – round economic and social reform launched by the current Georgian government will further optimize the investment environment, give full play to Georgia's comparative advantage in the global market and the development strength brought by excellent tourism resource, and make it become the new highlight in Georgia's economic development and the new direction for absorbing employment. Employment is vital to people's livelihood, and so does the employment of young people to the social development. According to the analysis on Georgia's education and employment, Georgia still has much room for further development and improvement in education and employment of young people, which can provide the long – term economic and social development with human resource, promote long – term development of Georgia, and expand the economic and social development space of Georgia.

---

[1] Россия — враг? Грузия перетряхнула правительство, https://www.gazeta.ru/politics/2018/06/20_a_11808697.shtml? updated.

Part 3

Communication and Cooperation between China and Georgia

Chapter 5

Prospects of China – Georgia Tourism Cooperation under the Belt and Road Initiative Framework

Zhang Yanlu

Associate Professor

Institute of Russian, Eastern European &
Central Asian Studies, CASS

Nowadays, tourism has been one of the fastest developing industries in the world economy. Tourism cooperation is becoming the trend of bilateral cooperation between countries and regional multilateral cooperation. Known as the "God's garden", Georgia possesses abundant tourism resources, and tourism has become one of the major means adopted by Georgian government to buoy its economy. Though Georgia's tourism is no longer as prosperous as before due to conflicts at home and abroad and world economic crisis since its independence, Georgia still has sound foundation for development. Despite the obstacles to China – Georgia tourism cooperation, desirable cooperation conditions in terms of resource, policy, market, etc. are available now. Therefore, China – Georgia tourism cooperation enjoys broad prospects. If promoted by such means as joint development of the third party market, regional tourism cluster construction, convenient consumption payment methods, etc., China – Georgia tourism cooperation is likely to become a highlight in practical cooperation of the two countries and a model in the Belt and Road cooperation.

Over the past decades, the world tourism has developed rapidly. In particular, the number of international tourists has grown year after year. As of 2017, tourism had become one of the fastest growing industries in the world economy. According to estimates of the World Tourism Organization (UNWTO), about 1.4 billion trips were made by international tourists in 2018, up by 6%. Tourism and the economic system formed around it have become the major drivers of the world economic growth, and contributed more than 10% to the global GDP. Tourism, as a universally recognized industry with low resource consumption, more job creation and high comprehensive benefit, has been determined by many countries as the focus of industrial structure adjustment and a major way to enhance the comprehensive competitiveness of a country. The weight of tourism in national economy has been on the rise. Simultaneously, tourism is no longer confined to an economic concept showing the collection of tourist relations, but evolves into a social phenomenon in contemporary relations between countries (regions), an active cultural cooperation manner between people from different countries and a natural result of the general trend of strengthening relationship between countries (regions). It has played a significant role in people – to – people and cultural exchanges. Nowadays tourism cooperation is increasingly becoming the trend of bilateral cooperation between countries and regional multilateral cooperation.

Chapter 5 Prospects of China – Georgia Tourism Cooperation under the Belt and Road Initiative Framework

I Conditions and Basis for China – Georgia Tourism Cooperation

Despite the remote distance and remarkable differences in natural landscape and customs between China located at the east coast of the Pacific Ocean and east of Asia and Georgia located at the central and western South Caucasus and along the Black Sea, the tourism cooperation between the two countries has accumulated certain basis and enjoyed broad prospects.

Firstly, stable and close China – Georgia bilateral relationship has created good political environment for the tourism cooperation and people – to – people exchange between them.

Tourism cooperation between countries is subject to friendly bilateral relations. China established diplomatic relations with Georgia on June 9, 1992, and thereafter, has always maintained good relations with Georgia. Various cooperations have developed smoothly, and the fields of cooperation have expanded continuously. China and Georgia have maintained good communication and coordination in international organizations like UN. In 2018, the volume of trade between China and Georgia reached 1.15 billion USD, up 17.3% year on year. So far, China is the fourth largest trading partner of Georgia, the third largest wine importer and investor of Georgia, while Georgia is the first Eurasian country establishing the free trade arrangement with China.

Secondly, both the Chinese government and Georgian government have devoted much attention to the development of their respective tourism, developed and implemented relevant planning and policies for development, and achieved phased results, which have paved a solid material foundation for their tourism cooperation.

Developing tourism has been deemed by Transcaucasian countries including Georgia as one of the major ways to realize sustainable development goals before 2030. Dmitry Kumsishvili, former minister of the Ministry of Economy and Sustainable Development of Georgia, pointed out that " (the Georgian government) planned to spare no effort to promote the tourism development, such as investing in the construction of tourism infrastructure, funding projects aiming at boosting the reputation of Georgia, etc. Georgian government is devoted to gradually diversifying the tourism market, boosting its reputation, assisting private departments to create excellent cheap tourism products, improving service quality and stimulating domestic tourism market to develop further". [1] George Kobulia, minister of the Ministry of Economy and Sustainable Development of Georgia, said that the Georgian government has always known that tourism will become a very powerful sector which can realize rapid development, but as a matter of fact, the reality exceeded our expectations. [2]

In order to practically promote development of tourism, the Ministry of Economy and Sustainable Development of Georgia together with the National Tourism Adminisration developed and began to implement the *Georgian Tourism Development Strategy 2025* under the financial and technical support of the WB. This Strategy aims to improve tourists'

---

[1] Манана Девидзе, Развитие туризма в Грузии: в интересах экономики и на благо граждан. https: //www. ictsd. org/bridges - news/% D0% BC% D0% BE% D1% 81% D1% 82% D1% 8B/news/% D1% 80% D0% B0% D0% B7% D0% B2% D0% B8% D1% 82% D0% B8% D0% B5 - % D1% 82% D1% 83% D1% 80% D0% B8% D0% B7% D0% BC% D0% B0 - % D0% B2 - % D0% B3% D1% 80% D1% 83% D0% B7% D0% B8% D0% B8 - % D0% B2 - % D0% B8% D0% BD% D1% 82% D0% B5% D1% 80% D0% B5% D1% 81% D0% B0% D1% 85 - % D1% 8D% D0% BA% D0% BE% D0% BD% D0% BE% D0% BC% D0% B8% D0% BA% D0% B8 - % D0% B8 - % D0% BD% D0% B0 - % D0% B1% D0% BB% D0% B0% D0% B3% D0% BE - % D0% B3% D1% 80% D0% B0% D0% B6% D0% B4% D0% B0% D0% BD.

[2] George Kobulia: The tourism development rate exceeded our expectations. http: //www. economy. ge/? page = news&nw = 995&s = giorgi - qobulia - turizmis - seqtoris - swrafma - ganvitarebam - molodins - gadaacharba.

satisfaction and develop the tourism sector of Georgia, create new jobs and eliminate poverty, and expects to accomplish 8 strategic objectives, namely:

(1) Respect elogical laws, realize sustainable development, rebuild and preserve Georgia's cultural and natural heritage;

(2) Create unique and real tourism experience on the basis of familiarity with natural and cultural heritage;

(3) Improve the industrial competitiveness by providing tourists with world – class service;

(4) Attract international tourists with strong consumption capacity by expanding and improving the effectiveness of tourism service marketing and promotion;

(5) Improve the capacity of collecting and analyzing tourism data and evaluating tourism efficiency;

(6) Increase the national and private investments in tourism agencies;

(7) Improve the business environment to increase domestic and foreign investments;

(8) Establish partnership necessary for accomplishing the aforesaid objectives with government, tourism agencies, non – governmental organizations and the public.

According to *Georgian Tourism Development Strategy 2025*, as of 2025, Georgia's tourism revenue will surge from 1.8 billion GEL (or 0.67 billion USD) to 5.5 billion GEL (or 2 billion USD), and the number of foreign tourists to Georgia will grow to 11 million. Moreover, in order to attract foreign tourists, Georgia has implemented relaxed visa policy. Currently, Georgia implements the visa – free policy to citizens from 94 countries and people with permanent residency in 50 countries, including the United

States, the United Arab Emirates, EU member states, Israel, etc. ①

In order to further implement the *Georgian Tourism Development Strategy 2025*, Georgia signed the *Memorandum on Establishing International College of Tourism* in April 2019. The College is dedicated to cultivating specialists in hotel management, catering service and cooking. Training courses will be available in Georgian and English languages, and follow the European and American practice. The certificates awarded will be internationally recognized. This College was established by Georgia to turn vocational training and improvement of the qualification of workforce into the new priorities of Georgia's economic growth strategy. ②

Moreover, the Ministry of Economy and Sustainable Development of Georgia and Chinese National Tourism Administration have jointly hosted the selection of the national tourism award named "Welcome to Georgia!" since 2015 to encourage development of Georgia's tourism and hotel sectors, boost the awareness of Georgia's tourism business and brand, and set up a good image of Georgia's tourism across the world. ③

Similar to Georgia, Chinese government also puts more emphasis on

---

① Source: Манана Девидзе, Развитие туризма в Грузии: в интересах экономики и на благо граждан. https://www.ictsd.org/bridges-news/%D0%BC%D0%BE%D1%81%D1%82%D1%8B/news/%D1%80%D0%B0%D0%B7%D0%B2%D0%B8%D1%82%D0%B8%D0%B5-%D1%82%D1%83%D1%80%D0%B8%D0%B7%D0%BC%D0%B0-%D0%B2-%D0%B3%D1%80%D1%83%D0%B7%D0%B8%D0%B8-%D0%B2-%D0%B8%D0%BD%D1%82%D0%B5%D1%80%D0%B5%D1%81%D0%B0%D1%85-%D1%8D%D0%BA%D0%BE%D0%BD%D0%BE%D0%BC%D0%B8%D0%BA%D0%B8-%D0%B8-%D0%BD%D0%B0-%D0%B1%D0%BB%D0%B0%D0%B3%D0%BE-%D0%B3%D1%80%D0%B0%D0%B6%D0%B4%D0%B0%D0%BD.

② Memorandum on Establishing International College of Tourism Signed. http://www.economy.ge/?page=news&nw=1118&s=turizmis-saertashoriso-kolejis-gaxsnstan-dakavshirebit-memorandumi-gaformda&lang=en.

③ George Kobulia: The tourism development rate exceeded our expectations. http://www.economy.ge/?page=news&nw=995&s=giorgi-qobulia-turizmis-seqtoris-swrafma-ganvitarebam-molodins-gadaacharba.

development of tourism, and promulgated the *Opinions of the State Council on Accelerating the Development of Tourism* (No. 41 [2009] of the State Council) on December 1, 2009, which proposed to develop tourism into a strategic backbone industry of the national economy and a more satisfactory modern service industry to the people. Thereafter, the State Council of the People's Republic of China further defined May 19 as China Tourism Day in 2011. According to the latest statistics released by the Data Center of Chinese National Tourism Administration, the growth of domestic tour exceeded expectations, and the inbound and outbound tours realized steady growth. As of the first half year of 2018, China had 69.23 million inbound tourists, including 14.82 million foreign inbound tourists, up 4%. The international tourism revenue reached 61.8 billion USD, up 2.8% year on year. Meanwhile, Chinese citizens took a total of 71.31 million outbound trips, up 15% year on year. ① Besides, the *Overview of 2018 Tourism Market* showed that the integration of culture and tourism started well in 2018. Adhering to the thoughts of integrating those fit for or capable of integration, promoting tourism through culture and manifesting culture through tourism, expand the development space of the tourism economy via culture, promote the development of high quality tourism via the supply side reform, and continuously enhance the public's sense of gain in tourism. Domestic tourism market has maintained the rapid growth. The inbound tourism market has steadily entered the slow recovery channel, while the outbound tourism market has developed steadily. The number of domestic tourists reached 5.539 billion, up 10.8% year on year; the number of inbound and outbound tourists reached 0.291 billion, up 7.8% year on year; the total tourism revenue amounted to 5.98 trillion yuan across

---

① *Statistics on Tourism in 2018HI*, website of the Ministry of Culture and Tourism of the People's Republic of China, August 22, 2018, http://zwgk.mct.gov.cn/ceshi/lysj/201808/t20180822_834337.html?keywords=.

the year, up 10.5% year on year. In 2018, the comprehensive contribution of tourism to GDP was 9.94 trillion yuan, accounting for 11.04% of the total GDP. The number of people directly employed in tourism reached 28.26 million, while the number of people directly and indirectly employed in tourism amounted to 79.91 million, accounting for 10.29% of the total employees in China. In terms of outbound tourism, about 149.72 million Chinese citizens travelled abroad, up 14.7% year on year. [1] China, as the world largest outbound tourism market, is willing to promote tourism cooperation together with other countries including Georgia, and share tourism market dividends. [2] The booming tourism of China and Georgia and the achievements made have paved a solid material foundation for tourism cooperation between the two countries.

Finally, the characteristic and varied tourism resources of China and Georgia have provided space and potential for tourism cooperation between China and Georgia.

Both China and Georgia possess abundant tourism resources which vary remarkably in kind, type and function of tourism resources. In terms of natural resources, Georgia known as the "God's garden" is famous for its diversified animal and plant resources, while China's natural resources are featured by magnificent and changeable geographical sceneries and climate wonders due to its vast territory and large latitudinal span. In terms of cultural resources, Georgia's relevant tourism resources bear distinctive features of Caucasian culture, while China as the center of the East Asia cultural circle, its relevant tourism resources have distinctive features of Confucian culture.

---

[1] Profile of the Tourism Market in 2018, website of the Ministry of Culture and Tourism of the People's Republic of China, February 12, 2019, http://zwgk.mct.gov.cn/auto255/201902/t20190212_837271.html?keywords=.

[2] New ambassador of Georgia to China visits the Ministry of Culture and Tourism of the People's Republic of China, China Culture.org, February 14, 2019, http://dy.163.com/v2/article/detail/E80CHDF60514A015.html

Moreover, from the perspective of function, Georgia enjoys strength in ecological and leisured tourism due to its charming mountain and ocean scenery, warm and moist climate, warm winter and cool summer, while China is better suited for development of various modern tourism products due to comprehensive tourism resources. The differences in tourism resources make China and Georgia rarely compete with each other while developing tourism, and can realize strength complementarity, and thus provide vast space for the tourism cooperation between the two countries.

II Deepening China – Georgia Tourism Cooperation

The sound foundation for the cultural and tourism cooperation between China and Georgia has been laid and some progress made. For example, both parties concluded the tourism cooperation agreement, cultural cooperation agreement and other documents, which have paved a solid foundation for both sides' cooperation in related fields. Moreover, Georgia's excellent artists and groups participated in a series of activities carried out in Beijing under the framework of the Dialogue of Asian Civilization in May 2019. Furthermore, Georgia's excellent young sinologists also attended the "Young Sinologists Training Program". Nevertheless, in order to deepen China—Georgia tourism cooperation and promote the high-quality development of China—Georgia tourism cooperation, there are several points to be focused.

Firstly, though Georgia is one of the countries whose tourism grows fastest across the world, there are still considerable differences and gap between Chinese and Georgian tourism markets.

According to statistics, from 2009 to 2013, the number of tourists to Georgia grew by more than 300%, surging from 1.5 million to 5.4 million;

the tourism revenue rose from 0.475 billion USD to 1.8 billion USD, more than 20 times above the global average. However, the average spending of each tourist in Georgia was only 74 USD per day, lower than the global average. According to statistics, the number of international tourists to Georgia exceeded 6.3 million in 2016, 45% above that in 2015, namely, 76,000. In the first 11 months of 2016, the volume paid by international tourists via foreign payment cards was about 1.50 million GEL (or 536,000 USD), up 10.1% year on year as compared with 2015. In 2016, Georgia had for the first time received about 2 billion USD from international tourism, 19% above 2015. According to the data released thereafter, from January to May 2017, more than 2.3 million foreign tourists visited Georgia, up 9.7% year on year as compared with 2016. ①

Though Georgia's tourism has realized rapid development over the past decade, it still has certain gap when comparing with China's tourism. According to *the Travel & Tourism Competitiveness Report 2017* released by the World Economic Forum in 2017, the comprehensive score of China's travel & tourism competitiveness was 4.72, ranking the 15th in the world and the 4th after Japan, Australia and Hong Kong SAR in Asia and the Pacific, while the comprehensive score of Georgia's travel & tourism competitiveness was 3.7, ranking the 70th in the world and the 2nd only next to Russia in Eurasia. Though the scores of Georgia in factors affecting

---

① Манана Девидзе, Развитие туризма в Грузии: в интересах экономики и на благо граждан. https://www.ictsd.org/bridges-news/%D0%BC%D0%BE%D1%81%D1%82%D1%8B/news/%D1%80%D0%B0%D0%B7%D0%B2%D0%B8%D1%82%D0%B8%D0%B5-%D1%82%D1%83%D1%80%D0%B8%D0%B7%D0%BC%D0%B0-%D0%B2-%D0%B3%D1%80%D1%83%D0%B7%D0%B8%D0%B8-%D0%B2-%D0%B8%D0%BD%D1%82%D0%B5%D1%80%D0%B5%D1%81%D0%B0%D1%85-%D1%8D%D0%BA%D0%BE%D0%BD%D0%BE%D0%BC%D0%B8%D0%BA%D0%B8-%D0%B8-%D0%BD%D0%B0-%D0%B1%D0%BB%D0%B0%D0%B3%D0%BE-%D0%B3%D1%80%D0%B0%D0%B6%D0%B4%D0%B0%D0%BD.

tourism development, such as business environment, safety and health, environmental sustainability, etc., are higher than those of China, its scores of factors decisive to tourism development, such as infrastructure, natural and cultural resources, etc., are lower than those of China, and this will to a certain extent have a negative impact on the tourism cooperation between China and Georgia.

Table 5 – 1   Comparison of Travel & Tourism Competitiveness Indexes between China and Georgia[1]

		China	Georgia
	Overall rank	4.72	3.7
Rank	World rank	15	70
	Regional rank	4 (Asia – Pacific)	2 (Eurasia)
Environmental conditions	Business environment	4.2	5.3
	Safety and security	5.0	6.0
	Health and hygiene	5.4	6.1
	Human resources and labor market	5.2	4.8
	ICT readiness	4.6	4.5
Policy conditions	Prioritization of travel & tourism	4.8	4.9
	International openness	3.0	3.1
	Price competitiveness	5.3	4.9
	Environmental sustainability	3.2	4.4
Infrastructure	Air transport infrastructure	4.3	2.2
	Ground and port infrastructure	4.0	3.3
	Tourist service infrastructure	3.2	4.0
Natural and cultural resources	Natural resources	5.3	2.4
	Cultural resources and business travel	6.9	1.6

Secondly, Georgia's tourism resources are homogenous with those of its

---

[1] Prepared according to *The Travel & Tourism Competitiveness Report 2017* of the World Economic Forum.

neighboring countries; meanwhile, Chinese tourists have low awareness of Georgia's tourism resources.

Since Georgia and its neighboring countries – Azerbaijan and Armenia have geographic similarities and historical common grounds, and homogenous natural and cultural tourism resurces while developing their respective tourism, which have to a certain extent reduced the uniqueness of Georgia's tourism products and weakened its competitiveness in the internatinal tourism market.

Moreover, China and Georgia are not each other's main source of tourists or tourist destination. According to statistics, in 2016, Georgia's internatonal tourists mainly came from Azerbaijan (1.523 million), Armenia (1.496 million) and Turkey (1.2 million). In addition, it is notable that the number of Russian tourists to Georgia had exceeded one million for the first time in 2016, reaching 1.03 million. Meanwhile, the number of tourists from EU member states has been on the rise. In the same year, the number of international tourists from Latvia, Lithuania, Czech, Bulgaria and Germany have maintained rapid growth, up 24%, 16%, 15%, 12% and 11%, respectively comparing with the same period of 2015. Though the number of Chinese tourists to Georgia rose remarkably by 116% due to the relaxed visa system, and China has gradually become Georgia's new source of international tourists, [1] Georgia's tourism products

---

[1] Манана Девидзе, Развитие туризма в Грузии: в интересах экономики и на благо граждан. https://www.ictsd.org/bridges – news/%D0%BC%D0%BE%D1%81%D1%82%D1%8B/news/%D1%80%D0%B0%D0%B7%D0%B2%D0%B8%D1%82%D0%B8%D0%B5 – %D1%82%D1%83%D1%80%D0%B8%D0%B7%D0%BC%D0%B0 – %D0%B2 – %D0%B3%D1%80%D1%83%D0%B7%D0%B8%D0%B8 – %D0%B2 – %D0%B8%D0%BD%D1%82%D0%B5%D1%80%D0%B5%D1%81%D0%B0%D1%85 – %D1%8D%D0%BA%D0%BE%D0%BD%D0%BE%D0%BC%D0%B8%D0%BA%D0%B8 – %D0%B8 – %D0%BD%D0%B0 – %D0%B1%D0%BB%D0%B0%D0%B3%D0%BE – %D0%B3%D1%80%D0%B0%D0%B6%D0%B4%D0%B0%D0%BD.

are still less attractive for Chinese tourists. According to the data released by China National Tourism Administration, Georgia has not been on the list of Top 17 tourist source markets of China 2017. ①

Thirdly, continuous domestic tensions and frequent protests have undermined to a certain extent the image of Georgia's tourism, and hindered the tourism cooperation between China and Georgia.

Safety is one of the key considerations when tourists select tourism products. But Georgia has been caught in protracted turbulence after the outbreak of the "Rose Revolution" in 2003, and had military conflict with Russia in 2008. The continuous unrests at home and abroad have damaged the tourism image of Georgia, and negatively influenced its tourism development and tourism cooperation with other countries.

Ⅲ Tentative Thoughts on China – Georgia Tourism Cooperation Strategies

In view of the sound foundation for China – Georgia tourism cooperation and existing considerable problems and obstacles, it is necessary to take targeted measures in light of the reality to change potential into result and practically promote the practical cooperation between the two countries in tourism:

Firstly, promote China and Georgia to jointly develop the third party market of international tourism under the Belt and Road Initiative framework.

Market is one of the key factors affecting China – Georgia tourism cooperation, but the lack of market momentum and expectation on low profitability in the future have directly resulted in the weak attractiveness of

---

① Chinese National Tourism Administration: Nationwide tourism revenue reaches 5.40 trillion yuan in 2017, XINHUANET, February 6, 2018, http://www.xinhuanet.com/travel/2018 – 02/06/c_1122376586.htm.

investment in China – Georgia tourism cooperation projects. Under such circumstances, it is necessary to strengthen China and Georgia's joint development of the third party market of international tourism products by relying on the Belt and Road Initiative, so that expand the market channel of China – Georgia tourism cooperation and enhance the attractiveness of investment in the cooperation projects.

Secondly, make use of the geographical characteristics of Georgia to promote cross – border (regional) tourism cooperation and build characteristic regional tourism cluster.

Georgia has the conditions and possibility to develop regional tourism clusters with its neighboring countries, such as Azerbaijan, Armenia, etc. The development of tourism projects across borders and regions cannot only partially solve the problem of homogenization of tourism resources between Georgia and its neighboring countries, but also reduce redundant construction of similar projects, which can reduce even avoid unnecessary cutthroat competition and further deepen regional economic cooperation while cutting down the international tourism costs and raising the performance – price ratio to a certain extent.

Thirdly, introduce third party payment platform and promote Internet payment to facilitate payment of tourism consumption.

Tourism is a comprehensive economic activity integrating food, accommodation, transportation and entertainment, in which, one of the most important links is consumer payment. It is necessary to know China's tourism market to develop China's outbound tourism market, and develop tourism products and services catering to the consumptive habits of Chinese tourists. Along with the popularity of mobile payment in China, Chinese tourists have got used to the cashless consumption manner. Therefore, China and Georgia shall strengthen cooperation in financial payment while carrying out tourism cooperation, promote more convenient mobile payment methods, and thus indirectly stimulate the spending power of tourists.

Finally, emphasize marketing, and take new approaches like new media and popular TV shows to recommend respective tourism products.

Nowadays, the world has entered the 5G era. Life is closely connected with the Internet. Therefore, it is suggested to adopt new media such as Internet and mobile APPs to recommend respective tourism products, and make use of popular variety shows, films and TV dramas to enable potential tourism product consumers from China and Georgia to get a preliminary understanding of respective culture and tourist spots, and thus drive the consumption of tourist products.

To sum up, despite certain obstacles to China – Georgia tourism cooperation, China – Georgia tourism cooperation has already had a good foundation in terms of political environment, policy support and resource complementarity, and enjoys broad prospects. As for concrete strategies for the cooperation implementation, it is suggested to adopt such measures as joint development of third party market, development of regional tourism cluster, facilitation of consumption payment, diversification of product promotion, etc. in light of the industrial characteristics and existing cooperative conditions and obstacles to promote the tourism cooperation between China and Georgia, and make it become a highlight in China – Georgia cooperation and a model in the Belt and Road cooperation.

Chapter 6

Exchanges and Studies of Chinese and Georgian Literature in the Belt and Road Context

Wang Yuhuan

Confucius Institute at Tbilisi Open Teaching University

China and Georgia have a long history of cultural exchanges. The spread and research of Georgian literature in China has changed with the change of certain historical periods, such as the disintegration of the Soviet Union. Chinese literature in Georgia is also affected by national policy. There are opportunities and challenges. After the Belt and Road Initiative was put forward, cultural and educational exchanges between the two countries have become increasingly close. This paper aims to sort out the general situation of literary communication and research between the two countries, summarize the characteristics of Georgia's cultural market, and analyze the response to the development of literary exchanges between the two countries in the context of the Belt and Road Initiative.

I Introduction

People-to-people bond is one of the "five focuses" in the construction of the Belt and Road Initiative. It can enhance mutual understanding, trust and friendship between China and target countries, and is the fundamental destination of the Belt and Road Initiative. As Chinese President Xi Jinping has emphasized on multiple diplomatic occasions, friendship, which drives from close contact between the people, holds the key to sound state-to-state relations. Over the years, China and Georgia have always focused on discovering each other's profound historical and cultural accumulation, constantly expanding cultural and educational exchanges and cooperation between the two countries, and promoting cultural integration and people – to – people exchanges. It can be said that it is the time – honored Chinese – Georgian cultural exchanges that have enhanced the mutual understanding between the people of the two countries, promoted the cultural integration between the two countries and the common sense of the people, and provided a solid support for determining the future direction of cooperation between the two countries.

Literature, as an important humanities discipline, also plays an important role in the cultural and people – to – people exchanges between China and Georgia. Literature is the carrier of life, and it can reflect a country's national character, social contradictions, customs, aesthetic tastes, etc. It can be said that literature is the most convenient way to understand a country and the most direct window into the soul of a nation. China and Georgia have a long history and splendid cultures, and both have vast literary works. These literary works are like ambassadors for cultural exchanges, allowing the peoples of the two countries to understand and communicate with each other, promote cultural exchanges and further realize the communication between the two peoples.

Georgia has a long history of more than 3,000 years and is located in the junction of Europe and Asia. For the Chinese, Georgia is a small country in the Trans – Caucasus (69,700 square kilometers, with a population of 4.5 million), but it is no stranger. Georgia is the hometown of former Soviet Union leader Stalin. A well – known writer in China, Mr. Mao Dun wrote an article "Underground Printing House in Tbilisi", which described the story of Stalin's revolutionary activities in Georgia during his youth. The article was once included in the textbooks of middle schools in China, and is widely circulated. It can be said that literary works have filled the Chinese people with longing for Georgia.

On June 9, 1992, China and Georgia formally established diplomatic relations. China became one of the first countries in the world to recognize Georgia's independence and establish diplomatic relations with it. On June 3, 1993, the two countries signed the *Agreement on Cultural Cooperation between the Government of the People's Republic of China and the Government of Georgia*, proposing that the two sides encourage and support the protection of literature, drama, music, fine arts, cultural relics, and library and museum organizations and institutions between the two countries. Since the establishment of diplomatic relations 28 years ago, China and Georgia have strengthened mutual political trust and deepened cooperation in various fields such as culture and education.

In 2013, the Belt and Road Initiative brought new opportunities for cultural exchanges between the two countries. The Georgian people's need for understanding of China is increasing. The literary and artistic groups of the two countries move more frequently, and official or private exchange activities are increasing. Among them, the two local Confucius Institutes— the Confucius Institute at the Tbilisi Open University and the Confucius Institute at the Free University of Tbilisi bridge the cultural and educational development of China and Georgia, and have promoted cultural exchanges between the two sides, lectures by writers, experts and scholars. Activities such as cultural gatherings and cultural and art exhibitions have also contributed to the literary exchanges between the two countries.

II Dissemination and Research of Georgian Literature in China

Georgian literature has its origins in the 5th century, and has undergone a long historical development process. Based on the progressive thought of each historical period, it is based on history and real life. Based on the true feelings of the writers, Georgian history is depicted. The social features of the period and the life scenes of thousands of worlds have comprehensively presented the development of the country, which is of great reference value for researchers to deeply understand Georgia's social history and national culture. Since the 20th century, Georgia has undergone many historical changes. Joining the Soviet Union in 1922, the disintegration of the Soviet Union in 1991, and the Georgian War in Russia in 2008. These historical events have brought many changes to Georgia, and literary works have also presented a new trend of thought and popular psychology.

1. Georgian Literature Overview [1]

Georgian literature has a long history. From ancient times, folk songs, stories, myths, heroes and legends have been circulating in the folk. With the development of feudal society and the introduction of Christianity, ecclesiastical literature appeared in the 5th century. The 12th century Shota Rustavari's long narrative poem "Tiger Warrior" is full of patriotism and has

---

[1] Weng Yiqin, "A Glimpse of Georgian Literature", *Soviet Literature*, Issue 3, 1988, pp. 77 – 78.

a profound influence.

The invasion of foreign forces hindered the development of Georgian literature for a long time, and it only gradually recovered in the 17th century. In the 17th to 18th centuries, getting rid of slavery and striving for liberation became the subject of Georgian literature. The long poem "The Scourge of Georgia" by Da Gulamishvili (1705—1792) describes the tragic events in Georgia in the first half of the 18th century. The works of Sue Alberiani and Vyabashvili (1750—1791) reflect Georgia's desire to break free from Persian and Turkish rule.

In 1801, Georgia was incorporated into Tsarist Russia. The national oppression of Greater Russia has caused dissatisfaction among the Georgian people. The dominant romantic genres of the 1830s and 1940s reflected this social mood. The poetry of its founder, A. Chafcawaze (1786—1846), is imbued with the ideas of national freedom and social justice. The poetry of Nibaratashvili (1817—1845) linked the idea of individual freedom with the goal of national liberation.

In the second half of the 19th century, Georgia's feudal autocracy disintegrated into the period of capitalism, class struggle intensified, and the realist genre took advantage of literature. This trend was shown in the plays of Gua Eristavi (1811—1864), the novels of La Aldaguiani (1815—1870), and Da Chankazer (1830—1860). The works of La Elistavi, Ni Lomouri, Ye Gabashvili and others describe the miserable life of farmers. The long poem "Phantom", "The Bandit Kako" and the novel "Is He Human?" expose social disadvantages and attack the autocratic system and the serf system. The poetry of Al - Zerejeri (1840—1915) reflects the struggle of the Georgian people for freedom and independence.

From the 1890s to the beginning of the 20th century, with the rise of the proletarian revolutionary movement, writers such as Da Krtiyashvili (1862—1931) continued to reflect the tragic life of the people; Ai

Ninoshvili (1859—1894) and other writers reflected the ideas of the peasant revolution in their works; I. Yevdoshvili (1873—1916) first described the scenes of cruel exploitation and oppression of workers in Georgian poetry, calling on the people to fight in unity. After the failure of the first revolution in Russia, some writers' works were full of pessimism and despair, while writers such as Shadatiani (1874—1959), Neil Koldipanyze (1880—1944), described the struggle of the Georgian people after the Revolution of 1905—1907 and its failure.

After Georgia established the Soviet regime, literature entered a new era. The collection of poems "Time" (1930), "Revolutionary Georgia", and "World March" by Ga Tabitzer (1892—1959) praises the October Revolution and the labor of the people. I. Abbasid (1909—), A. Mirzhurawa, West Chekovany (1902—1966), Sang Shanshi Ashvili, Jay Sengelaya, and Gleón. The works of writers such as Nietzsche (1899—1966) and Yi Mosashvili describe the collapse of the old world, praising the new Georgia, socialist builders and people's leaders, and reflecting the course of rural socialist transformation.

During the Patriotic War, the poems of Ga Tabizze, "The Song of David Gulamishvili" by Si Chekovany, "Caucasus with Victory" by Ge Abbasidze, Ge Mdiwani's "Going West" all condemned German fascism and expressed patriotism. After the war, old writers such as Ge Abbasidze, G. Mdivani, I. Abbasid, and San Shanghi Ashvili continued to publish their works, while young authors such as Le Japaridze, Noum Dumbazer, Ann Kalandadze, Shao Nisnyaniez, Jacques Chalkiani, and Taziladze began to make a figure. In their works, they describe the history of Georgia, expressing the Patriotic War, and some touch the problems of contemporary society.

After the 1950s, modern novels dominated. Ko Gamsahurgia's novel Vine Flowers (1956), Ah Beliashvili's novel Rustavi (Parts 1, 2 1959—

1960), and Shived "Kasha" (1960—1961), etc., praised the people's achievements in fighting and labor. Dumbadze's novels "White Flag" (1974) and "The Law of Eternity" (1980, received the Lenin prize in the same year), exposed all the disadvantages and bad habits of society, and were valued by the society.

Since Georgia announced its independence in 1991, Georgia has experienced many historical changes. It joined the Commonwealth of Independent States in 1993, and the Georgian war broke out on August 8, 2008. Georgia decided to withdraw from the CIS on August 14, the same year, and in August 2009, the formalities were completed on the 18th, and Georgia officially withdrew. The literary works at this stage focus on the impact of the war on the Georgian people, and show the social trend of thoughts about Georgia's "out of Asia and entering Europe".

2. The Spread and Research of Georgian Literature in China

Throughout the study of Georgian literature by domestic scholars, we can find that obvious chasm has appeared in the time period. The research boom period focused on the late 1980s, that is, before the collapse of the Soviet Union, Georgian literature was frequently translated and reviewed. Some appear in mainstream publications such as "Soviet Literature" and "Russian Literature". However, after the disintegration of the Soviet Union in 1991, Georgia as an independent country had very little research on its literature in China. It is worth mentioning that, after the Belt and Road Initiative was launched, Georgia has set off a "Chinese fever". The teachers and volunteer teams of the two local Confucius Institutes in Georgia have continued to grow, and they have also contributed to the study of Georgian literature.

At present, domestic research on Georgian literature is mainly reflected in three forms.

The first is a general introduction, such as "A Glimpse of Georgian

Literature" written by Weng Yiqin, which roughly shows the development of Georgian literature from ancient times to the present, representative writers, and representative works;

The second is translated works, such as Li Zuo's "Anthology of Contemporary Poems in Georgia", "Nor Dunbaze: I See the Sun" translated by Zhang Jingming, etc. ;

The third is text analysis. The text analysis research on Georgian literature is mainly focused on one work, that is, the long narrative poem "Tiger Warrior" by Shaw Rustavili, born in the 12th century.

In summary, the existing domestic research results have three characteristics. First, the research time is mainly focused on the study of Georgian literature as a part of Soviet literature before the disintegration of the Soviet Union; second, Georgia's modern and contemporary literature is rarely involved; third, the text studies on analysis, social history, and comparative literature are lacking.

If Georgian literature is not regarded as a part of Soviet literature, but as a separate national literature, foreign studies of Georgian literature are rare, mainly reflected in the research and exploration of Georgian scholars on their own literature. But it also mainly focuses on ancient literary works such as epic and folklore, and it is rare to discuss modern and contemporary literature. For example, Bela Mosia's "The Symbols of the Fire in Georgian Folklore in Comparison With Global Experience", mainly interprets Georgia's older literary works such as folklore from the perspective of cultural symbols, religion, etc. , which has certain reference and research value for non – Georgian researchers.

However, with the proposition of the Belt and Road Initiative in 2013, the Georgian people's enthusiasm for learning Chinese has increased, which has also contributed to the development and growth of Confucius Institutes in Georgia. At present, there are two Confucius Institutes in Georgia and the teachers and volunteers of the two Confucius Institutes indirectly undertake the task of studying Georgian literature through essays and other channels, such as the author of the "Analysis of China through the Tiger Warrior" is the volunteer of the Confucius Institute. At the same time, with more and more domestic literature research on countries along the Belt and Road, Georgian literature has also received increasing attention. Some domestic universities and research institutes have strengthened their research on Georgian literature, such as the National Library of Contemporary Literature Translation Library series has incorporated the representative of the famous Georgian writer Gulam Otysaria, "The President's Cat".

Ⅲ Dissemination and Research of Chinese Literature in Georgia

Since the 7th century, Georgia has understood Chinese literature from European literature. Georgians believe that China is a magical fairy – tale world, and people here are full of goodwill. Historically, Georgia and the North Caucasus, Mongolia, Persia, and Turkey have had wars, but there has been no conflict with China. This friendly and beautiful impression of China has always existed in the hearts of Georgians and is expressed in words. There is a word in Georgian that means "a beautiful light in your eyes", which is related to China. Until the 9th century, a Chinese book was translated and introduced, and Georgian talents had a general understanding of China. Most of Georgia's understanding of Chinese literature came from the Soviet Union period, but most of it knew about some mainstream literature, and knew little about folk literature. Georgia has a fixed research team with Chinese literature, mainly local Chinese scholars and university sinology research institutes. After the Belt and Road Initiative was proposed, the demand for Georgian people to learn Chinese has increased, which has also indirectly promoted Chinese literature's dissemination and research in Georgia.

1. Survey of Georgian Sinology and Chinese Literature

Before the disintegration of the Soviet Union, the Tbilisi Foreign Languages Institute of Georgia had added a social teaching department and taught Chinese in 1984, but it was suspended for various reasons. After the collapse of the Soviet Union in 1991, Georgia became independent. China was one of the first countries to recognize Georgia's independence and autonomy. In 1992, the Embassy of the People's Republic of China in Georgia was established. Among Georgian universities, the Tbilisi Institute of Asia and Africa was the first to start sinology research and Chinese language teaching. The Tbilisi Asian – African National Academy is a higher education institution affiliated with the Georgian Oriental Institute, and the Georgian Oriental Institute is one of the most famous institutions in the world. The Tbilisi Asian – African National Academy is a center dedicated to teaching and research in Eastern languages. In addition to Chinese, he is currently teaching and researching other oriental languages and related history. The Asian – African National College officially established the Chinese Department in Georgia in 1992, providing a good foundation for Georgian students to learn Chinese. At this point, Georgian's Sinology research and Chinese teaching have been able to write a new page. Young people interested in Chinese culture and language are beginning to choose this profession. However, at the time, the Sino – African College was a newly established Sinology major, so it was relatively small. [1]

Liu Guangwen, an overseas Chinese who has lived in Georgia for a long time, played a vital role in the development of Georgian sinology and

---

[1] Marina Gibraze, "Georgian Sinology Development and Chinese Teaching", *World Chinese Teaching*, Vol. 4, 2004, pp. 109 – 111.

Chinese literature research. Most of Georgian sinologists learnt from her. Liu Guangwen's grandfather, Liu Junzhou, is the founder of Georgia's "Liu Cha". Georgia, located on the coast of the Black Sea, has never had tea production before. At the end of the 19th century, at the invitation of a Russian tea merchant, Liu Junzhou had repeatedly tested and cultivated excellent tea varieties for the Caucasus. "Chinese Tea King of the Caucasus". Because of his ancestors, Liu Guangwen came to Tbilisi from Beijing to study in 1958, studied watercolor painting, and married a local painter. Liu Guangwen is currently a professor at the Tbilisi Free University, a professional painter, the founder and chairman of the "Gezhong Silk Road Cultural Center", and a well-known Chinese in Georgia. In 1986, Liu Guangwen took the lead in setting up Chinese language teaching at the Oriental Institute in Tbilisi to teach Chinese, the history of Chinese literature, and Chinese history to locals. The Georgian Chinese talents it has cultivated have covered all walks of life in Georgia. In 1992, Liu Guangwen founded the "Gezhong Silk Road Cultural Center" and served as its chairman, with more than 50 members. Since 1995, members of the Center have compiled nearly 20 books including "Chinese Classical Poetry", "Sun Tzu's Art of War", "Chinese Culture in Time and Space", "China in the Eyes of Georgians", and "Mo Yan's Short Stories". Liu Guangwen has translated many Chinese works such as Pu Songling's "Liao Zhai" and Mo Yan's "Frog" into Georgian. In 2017, the book "Silk Road and the Caucasus", authored by Liu Guangwen was published.

Georgian sinologists generally combine research with teaching, and almost have individual or collective research topics. Sinology research topics cover a wide range. For example, Georgian and Chinese idioms, Chinese literature, the Analects of Confucius, culture, philosophy, Chinese religion, early Chinese feudal literature and commentary, Chinese cultural history, Chinese contemporary (poetry) literature, Hange dictionary,

Tang and Song poetry (Chinese translation case), Tao Te Ching (Chinese translation case), China's economic system and reform, China's regional economy, China's state and politics, Georgia – China relations, China's diplomatic relations, the return of Hong Kong and Macau to China, China in the 21st century, etc.

In recent years, with the Belt and Road construction, the two countries have been getting closer and closer. Chinese books have become more and more popular in Georgia. Mo Yan, Rauma and many other outstanding Chinese writers' works have been translated and published in Georgia. In September 2015, a collection of short stories by Chinese writer Rauma was published in Georgia and appeared on the cover of the country's highest – level magazine, which featured large – scale publications of Rauma's novels. In 2017, at the 25th anniversary of the establishment of diplomatic relations between China and Georgia, the Georgian National Library established a Chinese Book Corner, which also provided a platform for the translation of Chinese and Georgian literary works.

2. Approaches of Chinese Literature to Georgia

Georgia translator, writer, and associate professor of Ilya State University Anna once said that many Georgians speak European languages such as Russian, German, French, but few people understand Chinese, and for Georgians, reading Chinese literature is very difficult. Georgian readers do not know much about Chinese names and place names and it is difficult to understand Chinese metaphors. European literary works are mostly based on one person, while Chinese literary works are mostly scenes with many characters. Due to the limitations of the translator's translation level, or the incorrect cultural information, Georgian readers cannot understand the original intention well. If the translators cooperate with translators who understand Chinese culture, it will achieve good results. ①

Professor Anna's opinion pointed out the difficulties and obstacles that Chinese literature will face overseas. Georgia's unilateral research team on Chinese literature has limited strength, so the development of literary exchanges between the two countries requires the joint efforts of both parties. In recent years, the Chinese book publishing industry has also made various attempts in the field of Chinese literature going abroad. At present, there are three main ways for Chinese literature to go overseas: first, the copyright transaction between domestic and foreign publishers; second, the National Press and Publication Administration through foreign projects such as the "China Book Promotion Program" to fund translation by foreign translators and publishers; and third, foreign publishers have directly obtained authorization from Chinese writers for translation and publishing. The first two methods account for about 90% and are the main channels for Chinese literature to "go global".

According to related reports, in order to promote the "going out" of Chinese literature, China Publishing and Media Holdings Co., Ltd. has launched a "Chinese Program for Foreigners Writing" and invited a group of foreign scholars and sinologists who understand China and love China, such as Gu Bin, B. R. Deepark, and Giray Fidan, to tell their "Chinese story" and write books on Chinese themes. Currently, they have collaborated with India, Turkey, Georgia and Poland and signed contracts with 19 sinologists and experts on Chinese issues from these countries. In 2018, at the 20th Tbilisi International Book Fair, China National Import and Export (Group) Corporation brought a series of outstanding contemporary Chinese books such as "Xi Jinping: The Governance of China" and "Xi Jinping Telling

---

① Arranged from Associate Professor Anna of Ilya State University of Georgia to give an academic lecture for the Summer School of Lanzhou University. Lanzhou University website: http://news.lzu.edu.cn/c/201907/58477.html

Stories" to the book exhibition for the first time. Following the widespread attention of the local media and the public, this participation in the local book fair is also a useful attempt to "go global" for Chinese literature.

In addition, Chinese literature has entered into Georgia, and it is inseparable from the promotion of Georgia's local publishing culture market. An in-depth understanding of Georgia's publishing market is also conducive to the local promotion of Chinese literature. According to reports, as of 2015, there were about 100 registered publishers in Georgia, of which 55 were active. Most of these publishers are small publishers, and large and medium-sized publishers have a smaller share of the book publishing market in Georgia. Moreover, most of Georgia's current publishing activities are concentrated in Georgia's capital and the political, economic, cultural and educational center of Tbilisi. Most of the 55 active publishers operate in Tbilisi, and two more are in southwestern Georgia, near Batumi on the Black Sea. In 2015, Georgia served as the guest of honor for the Frankfurt Book Fair, which led the world's attention to Georgia's publishing and cultural markets.

Since 2013, the Georgian book market has shown an overall growth trend. The number of books published has increased every year, with an average annual increase of about 100. According to the statistics of the National Assembly Library of Georgia, Georgia published 4,100 books in 2015, of which 1,491 books were published by major publishers, including various types of literature and imported books, with a total revenue of about 43.7 million USD. From 2013 to 2015, Georgian publishers' sales revenue mainly came from literary books, and textbooks also contributed a significant portion of the revenue stream. Among literary books, 55% are Georgian native literary works, and the remaining 45% are imported literary works.

In terms of imported books, Georgia's imported books are mainly

English books, followed by German, French, Russian, and other languages such as Nepali. It is worth noting that in the past three years, Georgia's number of imported literary books has soared five times compared to its output.

In terms of online sales, Georgia currently has two of the largest and long-standing online bookstores: saba. com. ge and lit. ge. These two websites have more than 2,500 books on sale, and they are rich in variety. These books are original from Georgia and imported. The highest price of these books sold online is around 20 lari (about 50 yuan), and the lowest is as low as 0.25 lari (about 0.7 yuan). Readers can also download free e-books on the website. On lit. ge, readers can download more than 2500 different types of e-books. The price of these e-books is as high as 13.9 lari (about 35 yuan) and as low as 0.2 lari (about 0.5 yuan). [1]

In online bookstores, readers can easily search for relevant Chinese books in Georgian, such as biography of Mao Zedong, historical biography of Genghis Khan, Chinese Buddhism, Lao Tzu's Tao Te Ching, Confucius' Analects, and so on. Georgia's online bookstore has a large collection of books, complete functions, and is very popular among young readers. Therefore, for Chinese literature, online promotion is also a good way to enter Georgia.

IV Conclusion

As Yue Bin, the former Chinese ambassador to Georgia, said, China and Georgia have many similarities and good development prospects in the "five focuses". China and Georgia are both ancient civilizations, with

---

[1] Data source: George Glize, "Chinese books are becoming more and more popular in Georgia", *International Publishing Weekly*, 2018.

thousands of years of history and profound cultural heritage. In the long development process, many outstanding figures have emerged in the two countries, leaving behind cultural monuments, which have made great contributions to the progress of human civilization, and also left their nations with valuable wealth. Both countries have unique languages, with unique grammar and writing systems, and are recognized as difficult languages in the world. The literary treasures of the two countries are also starry and shining, leaving a strong record in the history of world literature.

Since the establishment of diplomatic relations, China and Georgia have witnessed rapid development of cooperation in the humanities, including education, culture, and tourism, and have achieved fruitful exchanges and cooperation. After the Belt and Road Initiative was put in place, the exchanges between the two countries embarked on a new journey and cooperation has become closer. The exchanges and mutual learning of the literature of the two countries have continuously changed with the change of a specific historical period. They have different characteristics before and after the collapse of the Soviet Union and the Belt and Road Initiative. The friendship between the peoples of the two countries promotes the healthy development of relations between the two countries, promotes all – round cooperation between the two countries, and achieves win – win development of the two countries.

At the same time, we should also see that the Chinese and the Georgian are both relatively difficult languages, and the differences are very large. Therefore, in the process of translation and dissemination, the original style is not easy to retain, and the translation of the work will inevitably cause a large loss of the original work. How to make the work still classic when presented in another language so as to truly tell the "Chinese story" and help "connect people with the heart" is also a challenge to the translator's native language level and even the ability to rewrite and re –

create. It is worth mentioning that in recent years, following the Belt and Road Initiative, Georgia's "Chinese fever" has risen. From elementary school students to social adults, more and more Georgians have made learning Chinese as a goal. The Confucius Institute also provides support for the promotion of local Chinese. With the continuous improvement of local students' Chinese level, high - level translators will continue to increase. This will promote the exchange and development of literature between the two countries. And exchange and development will become increasingly prosperous.

References

Weng Yiqin, "A Glimpse of Georgian Literature", *Soviet Literature*, Issue 3, 1988.

Marina Gibraze, "Georgian Sinology Development and Chinese Teaching", *World Chinese Teaching*, 2004.

George Glize, "Chinese Books are Becoming More and More Popular in Georgia", *International Publishing Weekly*, 2018.

Associate Professor Anna of Ilya State University of Georgia gave an academic lecture to the Summer School of Lanzhou University, Lanzhou University website: http://news.lzu.edu.cn/c/201907/58477.html

"Going out, Chinese literature is flourishing", China Reading Daily http://epaper.gmw.cn/zhdsb/html/2017 - 09/20/nw.D110000zhdsb_20170920_1-06.htm

"Chinese Ambassador to Georgia Yue Bin: The Silk Road Economic Belt will witness a better tomorrow for Sino - Georgian cooperation", Xinhuanet: http://www.xinhuanet.com/world/2015 - 04/21/c_1115043641.htm

Chapter 7

Cultural Exchange and Cooperation between China and Georgia in Belt and Road Initiative

Wang Hui

Confucius Institute of Tbilisi Open Teaching University

Exchange between China and Georgia has a long history. As early as two thousand years ago, the ancient Silk Road has closely linked the people of the two countries. After China and Georgia formally established diplomatic relations in 1992, the relationship between the two sides has been developing smoothly. In 2013, after China proposed the Belt and Road Initiative, China – Georgian relations have achieved great development and improvement, and further strengthened the exchanges and cooperation between the people of the two countries in humanities and education.

Georgia has actively participated in the Belt and Road Initiative from the beginning, and is also one of the first countries to sign a memorandum of cooperation under the Belt and Road Initiative. In view of the special significance of Georgia to China, it is necessary to study the cultural exchange and cooperation between China and Georgia in the construction of the Belt and Road.

I Introduction

The Belt and Road is the abbreviation of Silk Road Economic Belt and 21st Century Maritime Silk Road. It is a cooperation initiative proposed by Chinese President Xi Jinping in September and October 2013, respectively. This great idea aims to promote cooperation and exchanges between China and the countries along the Belt and Road. To build a community of shared interests, shared responsibilities and a shared destiny with political mutual trust, economic integration, and cultural inclusive, and further build a global community of shared future. It can be said that in the Belt and Road Initiative, economic integration is only the focus, and cultural exchange and development are the core. Chinese culture has a long history and is extensive and profound. It has not only played an important role in enhancing the friendship between Chinese and foreign people, but also provided a better environment for public opinion in China's long – term strategic development.

Georgia is located at the crossroads of Eurasia, and is also one of the important countries along the Belt and Road. In June 1992, China established diplomatic relations with Georgia. Since the establishment of diplomatic relations between the two countries, bilateral relations have developed smoothly. China's friendly development has laid a solid foundation. In April 2006, Georgian General Saakashvili visited China, which opened a new chapter in Georgia's interaction with China in the new century. In September 2015, Chinese Premier Li Keqiang met with Georgian President Gali Bashvili in Dalian, which further promoted the development of the two countries. In June 2016, Deputy Prime Minister Zhang Gaoli visited Georgia and met with President and Prime Minister of Georgia, accelerating the negotiation of the free trade agreement between the two sides, and promoting the negotiation process of the China – Georgia Free Trade Agreement. On January 1, 2018, the China – Georgia Free Trade Agreement came into effect. This is the first free trade agreement signed by China and countries in Eurasia. It is also the first free trade agreement signed and implemented by China after the Belt and Road Initiative was proposed. In May 2019, Chinese State Councilor and Foreign Minister Wang Yi visited Georgia. This is the first visit by a Chinese Foreign Minister to Georgia in 23 years, which is of landmark significance.

As one of the important countries along the Belt and Road, Georgia will play an important role in the implementation of the Belt and Road Initiative as the exchanges between the two countries become more frequent. Since the reform and opening-up, China's economy has developed rapidly, people's lives have changed with each passing day, and their overall national strength has grown stronger. Therefore, it is very necessary for us to take Georgia as an example to study the exchange and cooperation between the two sides in the construction of the Belt and Road.

In the context of the Belt and Road Initiative, especially since the entry into force of the China – Georgian Free Trade Agreement, China and Georgia have made substantial economic development and achieved mutual benefit. However, in the current research on the Belt and Road, there are many studies involving exchanges and construction in the political, economic, and trade fields between China and foreign countries. There are few studies in the field of cultural exchange and construction in China.

Political and economic and trade relations between nations have always been a matter of widespread concern in the international community, but with the process of globalization, intercultural relations have become increasingly prominent. On the one hand, with the deepening of the Belt and Road Initiative, China has paid more and more attention to cultural exchanges with foreign countries, and cultural soft power is also playing a more and more important role in establishing national prestige, enhancing the image of the country, and enhancing the country's external influence. On the other hand, in order to make the Belt and Road Initiative more smoothly and create a good external environment, people in countries along the Belt and Road can more easily accept and support it, and thus achieve "people-to-people bond". Therefore, studying the cultural exchange and cooperation between China and Georgia in the context of the Belt and Road is of great significance for the sustainable development of China's cultural exchange strategy.

There are many studies on culture and cultural soft power in foreign countries. For example, Samuel Huntington explained the role of cultural soft power from the perspective of "clash of civilizations" in the "Clash of Civilizations and Reconstruction of the World Order" and proposed that in the process, the role of culture is indispensable. The game of countries around the world is based on economic aspects, but actually is based on culture. As early as the 1990s, Joseph Nye's "soft power" is defined in this way: "soft power is a capability that achieves its purpose through attraction rather than intimidation or use. This attraction comes from a country's culture, political values, and foreign policy."

Since the Belt and Road Initiative was first proposed by China, there is not much research abroad on this initiative, and most of them are based on the ancient Silk Road to explore the characteristics and impact of the Belt and Road in the new era. A more representative example is the historian Peter Fracopan of Oxford University, who recounted the history of the Belt and Road in the new era through the reinterpretation of world history in "Silk Road: A New World History". Emphasizing that the Belt and Road is quietly weaving together the communication network on the roof of Asia, and the brilliant history of the "Silk Road" may be rewritten.

Regardless of whether the research level of foreign scholars is based on the cultural field or the Belt and Road background, most of them focus on the international political level, involving less cultural exchange and construction between countries, which also provides greater research for this article space.

For a long time, research on the relations between China and Georgia has been studied since the 1960s. Earlier studies, such as Feng Zhongping and Sun Xiaoqing's "China's Policy Research Report on Central and Eastern European Countries", which mainly discusses the status quo of Eastern Europe, makes analysis and research on its status, role, and internal and external adjustments in the development process, and puts forward its own views on the further development of China's relations with Central and Eastern European countries.

Since the Belt and Road Initiative was put forward, many domestic experts and scholars have started extensive research and discussion on the countries along the Belt and Road, and many related research results have emerged. But looking at these research works, most of the research focuses on countries with a long history and close relations. For example, Liang Fuxing and Luo Dan's "Research on the Cooperative Development of Luoyue Cultural Tourism Industry between China and Vietnam under the Background of the Belt and Road" elaborates that China and Vietnam have good tourism cooperation foundations and realistic conditions, and puts forward that the development of cultural tourism innovation forum and project investment and cooperation have promoted the development of the cultural tourism industry in the two countries; Wang Mengdong's "Strategic Study on the Development Strategy of Sino – Italian Economic, Trade, and Cultural Cooperation Projects under the Belt and Road Initiative focuses on cultural industry, medical and health safety, and aerospace technology.

At present, domestic research on China and Georgia in the Belt and

Road is mainly focused on politics, economy, trade and education, and there are very few research results on cultural exchanges and construction between China and Georgia. Therefore, this article has important research value.

II Theoretical Analysis of Cultural Exchanges and Cooperation

Cultural exchange and cooperation are important ways to promote development between countries, and the Belt and Road Initiative has made special historical contributions to cultural exchanges and cooperation in the new era. Cultural exchanges and cooperation between China and Georgia can not only promote the promotion of mutual understanding and deepen mutual feelings between the two countries, but also promote the development of modern culture of the two countries.

1. Definition of Culture

"Culture" is a very broad concept and it is difficult to give it a precise scientific definition. The record of the word "culture" was first seen in the hexagrams of the "Book of Changes", "Rigid – flexible interlaced, astronomical; civilized, humanistic. It is about astronomy to detect changes in time, and humanity has become a world". Later, in the Western Han Dynasty, Liu Xiang combined "wen" and "hua" for the first time in "Shuo Yuan · Zhi Wu", and proposed that "the rule of the sages also governs the world, the first is morality and then the military, and the prosperity of all martial arts is unconvinced". "Culture" here means "education through culture", which refers to the cultivation of human nature and the cultivation of moral character. Later, culture developed into two concepts of broad sense and chivalry. In a broad sense, culture refers to "the sum of material and spiritual wealth created in the practice of the human word society"; in the narrow sense, it refers to "the sum of the social and spiritual life forms in which a certain mode of material production occurred and developed in history". The British writer Taylor put forward the classic culture theory in "Primitive Culture", that is, "the cultural stone includes the complex whole of knowledge, belief, art, morals, law, custom" and the ability and habits of anyone as a member of society.

It can be seen that the definition of culture is different in different periods because people have different perceptions of culture. Here, we take culture as a broad ideology of thought, value, tradition, or similar.

2. Forms of Cultural Exchanges and Cooperation

According to the different subjects of cultural behavior, we divide it into two forms: official and folk.

Official cultural exchanges and cooperation are led by the government and implemented through official government cultural exchange projects, such as official agreements, international cultural conferences, visits between personnel in the cultural sector, cultural business development, and exhibitions of cultural achievements.

And folk cultural exchanges and cooperation is a kind of folk behavior. Literature and art exhibitions, language and culture teaching, news media reports, folk art personnel exchanges, sports and cultural exchanges, cultural heritage protection, and cultural industry trade are all folk cultural exchanges and cooperation. By carrying out folk cultural exchanges, it not only will promote Chinese culture be "going out", but more importantly, "going in" and "incorporating" and truly implements it will make Chinese culture the "community" and "cultural mutual learning".

III Basic Forms of Cultural Exchanges and Cooperation between China and Georgia

As early as more than 2,000 years ago, the "Silk Road" closely linked the people of China and Georgia, and many good talks have flowed in the history of friendly exchanges between China and Georgia. In the 12th century AD, a famous Georgian poet wrote in his book "The Tiger Skin Knight": At the end of the 19th century, the Chinese with the surname Liu had cultivated "Liu Tea" suitable for the local climate and soil conditions on the Black Sea coast of Georgia. This kind of tea has also been extremely welcomed by the local and surrounding people.

1. Official Contacts

After the two countries formally established diplomatic relations in 1992, cultural exchanges and cooperation between the two sides became increasingly extensive.

(1) Early Stage (1992—1999)

The 1990s were an early stage of development of cultural exchanges and cooperation between the two sides, and the two countries carried out a series of official delegation visits.

From June 2 - 4, 1993, the head of state of Georgia and the chairman of the parliament, Shevardnadze, paid an official visit to China. The two sides signed a joint statement on the cooperation protocol between the two foreign ministries, the agreement on economic and trade cooperation between the two governments, the agreement on encouragement and protection, and science and culture. 17 documents including cooperation agreements in the fields of health, agriculture, tourism, customs, sports, post and telecommunications have laid the foundation for the development of bilateral relations. Georgia's Minister of Culture Asatiani visited China in July 1998, and from September 8 – 15, 1998, the chairman of the Georgian Parliament's Immigration and Georgian Affairs Committee Saradze visited China. Georgia's early official visit to China has further strengthened friendly relations between China and Georgia.

(2) Development Stage (2000—2012)

Since the beginning of the 21st century, cultural exchanges between China and Georgia have entered a new era. On April 12 – 14, 2001, then Vice Premier Li Lanqing of the State Council paid an official friendly visit to Georgia and met with Georgian President Shevardnadze, Speaker Zhivania, and Minister of State Arsenishvili. The two sides signed economic, cultural and educational agreements. On May 26 – 27, at the invitation of the Georgia Association for Foreign Friendship and Cultural Relations, a delegation from Quzhou City, Zhejiang Province visited Georgia. The discussions and the signing of a series of letters of intent on economic and cultural cooperation between the two cities opened a precedent for urban exchanges between China and Georgia.

In October 2003, the head of the Georgian Tourism Board, Vazha Shubradze, traveled to the World Tourism Annual Conference in Beijing.

On April 10 – 14, 2006, President Saakashvili paid a state visit to China. Then Chinese President Hu Jintao held a welcoming ceremony in the Great Hall of the People. The two countries discussed and reached consensus on bilateral relations and international issues. The conference promoted all – round cooperation in the political, economic, trade, cultural, and tourism fields of both sides, which in turn benefited the peoples of the two countries. On June 24, 2008, the "Silk Road" Georgia – China Friendship Association and the Chinese Embassy in Georgia jointly hosted the launch of the Georgian version of "Chinese Culture in Time and Space" in Tbilisi. "Chinese Culture in Time and Space" is a book jointly compiled by Ms. Liu Guangwen and Georgian sinologists, sponsored and published by the

Chinese Embassy in Georgia, and is the first Georgian work to comprehensively introduce Chinese history, religion, philosophy, art, and literature. On July 9, the opening ceremony of Chinese bronzes was held at the National Museum of Tbilisi, Georgia. Chinese ambassador to Georgia Wang Kaiwen, Georgian Culture Minister Cheval Ishvili, and Georgian National Museum curator Lorky Kipanidze, government officials, and people from all walks of life attended the event. This exhibition lasted two months in Tbilisi and played an important role in promoting mutual understanding and friendship between the people of China and Georgia.

On December 22, 2009, the "Chinese Kaleidoscope – Modern Life in Every Face" picture opening ceremony to celebrate the 60th anniversary of the founding of the People's Republic of China was held at David Kakabaze Gallery in Kutaisi, western Georgia. Chinese ambassador to Georgia Gong Jianwei, Kutaisi's mayor, Goldena Ruzer, delivered a speech respectively, and the people highly appreciated the Chinese pictures. This photo exhibition has achieved a complete success.

On September 28, 2010, the opening ceremony of Chinese art was held at Sova Amilanashvili, a subsidiary of the National Museum of Georgia. The art exhibition was jointly organized by the Chinese Embassy and the National Museum of Georgia on the eve of the 61st anniversary of the founding of New China More than 120 exhibits on display are art treasures collected by the National Museum of China in different periods, including ivory crafts, traditional costumes, porcelain, silk fabrics, paintings, sculptures, Buddha statues, etc. This art exhibition has promoted Chinese-Georgian culture. On November 23, Chinese Ambassador to Georgia Chen Jianfu met with Georgian Minister of Culture Nikolos Rurua. The two sides exchanged views on strengthening cooperation and exchanges between the cultures of the two countries. The cultural construction of the city has taken a new step.

In September 2012, Georgian Minister of Culture Rurua visited China and attended the "Georgia Culture Day" event. Cai Wu, Minister of Culture and Tourism of China met with Rurua in Beijing. The two sides signed an agreement on cultural cooperation, which opens up new ideas for the construction of cultural relations between the two countries, and further promotes the common development of official and folk cultural exchanges between the two countries, and it has laid the foundation for the two countries to consolidate a solid friendship.

(3) New Development Stage (2013—2020)

With the proposition of the Belt and Road Initiative, cultural exchanges between China and Georgia have continued to deepen, and the scope of cooperation has continued to expand.

On November 4, 2013, Chinese Ambassador to Georgia Yue Bin met with Georgian Minister of Culture and Monuments Ogisalia. Both parties talked about the ancient Silk Road as a cultural link and closely linked the cultural relations between the two countries. With the joint efforts of both sides, new progress will surely be made in cultural cooperation between China and Georgia.

On October 14 – 16, 2015, the first Silk Road Forum co-organized by China and the Georgian government was held in Tbilisi. Government representatives from 38 countries and 12 international organizations represented more than 150 Chinese companies participated in the forum. This forum let the ancient Silk Road exude vitality and vitality, which is of great significance to the economic and trade and cultural construction of countries along the Silk Road.

On February 6, 2016, Ji Yanchi, Chinese Ambassador to Georgia, held the first Chinese New Year reception at the Palings Hotel in Hualing. Georgia's Minister of Education and Science, Sani Kidze, and Deputy Minister Shavarshdze, Ministry of Foreign Affairs and Culture, officials from the Ministry of Sinologists Association, the Silk Road Cultural Research Center, the Confucius Institute at the Free University of Tbilisi, leaders of universities and colleges in Georgia, mainstream media and Chinese students attended the event. On April 9, Chinese Ambassador Ji Yanchi met with the Chairman of the Silk Road Cultural Research Center, Professor Liu Guangwen, and other representatives from the center. Ambassador Ji encouraged the Silk Road Center to include countries along the Silk Road as the center's research content and to continuously enrich the Silk Road Economic Belt spiritual connotation. This meeting played an important role in the good public opinion basis of China and Georgia.

On January 26, 2017, the Chinese Ambassador to Georgia Ji Yanchi held the second Sinologist Reception at the Hualing Hotel. Georgian Foreign Minister Janelidze, Chairman of the Parliamentary Committee on Culture and Education, Yahi, Chairman of the Partnership Fund Saganelidze, officials of the Ministry of Foreign Affairs, Education and Culture, Sinologists Association, Silk Road Cultural Research Center, Confucius Institute at Tbilisi Free University, Chinese Language Teaching Center, and more than 130 people attended the meeting. The reception promoted the development of Sino – Georgia education and culture, and brought the development of Chinese teaching and the spread of Chinese culture to a new level. On November 28, the second Belt and Road International Forum was held in Tbilisi. More than 2,000 dignitaries, think tank scholars and business representatives from more than 60 countries and international organizations attended the forum. Outside China, the first Belt and Road summit forum hosted by the Central Government demonstrated Georgia's strong support for the Belt and Road Initiative, and also demonstrated Georgia's determination to conduct exchanges and construction with China.

On May 24, 2019, Chinese State Councilor and Foreign Minister Wang Yi visited Georgia and met with Georgian Prime Minister Mamuka

Bakhtadze, Georgian President Salome Zurabishvili, and Georgian Foreign Minister Zarkalyani. The two sides reached a consensus on strengthening trade relations between China and Georgia, deepening the pragmatic cooperation between the two countries, and promoting cultural exchanges. On June 29, the award ceremony of the "Etalon Chinese Year" middle school student knowledge contest was held in Georgia. Held by the Ministry of Education, Culture and Sports, Zuo Hongbo, the temporary ambassador to Georgia, Georgia's Deputy Minister of Education Abladze, Georgian Parliamentary Committee Chairman Jash and other school teachers and students attended. This competition is the largest national knowledge competition in Georgia. It attracted more than 40,000 students from more than 20,000 middle schools, and played a significant role in promoting the development of Chinese language and the spread of Chinese culture. On July 1, Premier Li Keqiang met with Georgian Prime Minister Bakhtadze in Dalian, expressing support for co – construction of the Belt and Road, expanding the scale of bilateral trade, deepening exchanges and cooperation in the humanities, and continuously promoting the friendship between the two countries and achieve mutual benefit and win – win results. On October 23, the 3rd Silk Road International Forum successfully concluded in Tbilisi. In this forum, strengthening cooperation with China and actively connected with the Belt and Road Initiative become a public forum for representatives of participating countries. On December 27, the National Collection Exhibition of the National Museum of Georgia officially opened. More than 100 people, including Li Yan, Chinese Ambassador to Georgia, Rod Kipanidze, Director of the National Library of Georgia, art lovers from all walks of life, and representatives of the Confucius Institute of Chinese – funded enterprises attended the opening. As a carrier of Chinese culture, Chinese collections are of great significance to Georgian people's understanding of Chinese culture and to promote friendship between the two countries.

On January 13, 2020, Chinese Ambassador to Georgia Li Yan met with Georgian Minister of Science, Education, Culture and Sports Qihengli and exchanged views on bilateral relations and cooperation in science, education, culture and sports. The talks promoted the development and growth of Chinese teaching in Georgia and the cooperation and exchanges in the humanities between the two countries.

2. Folk Culture Exchanges

(1) Early Stage (1992—1999)

"Friendship, which drives from close contact between the people holds the key to sound state to state relationship. " Through the exchange of folk cultures, people promote mutual understanding and trust, and promote dialogue between the minds, thereby building a bridge of friendship and cooperation.

1998 was a very active year for cultural exchanges between China and Georgia. In August, the Mtatsminda Song and Dance Troupe came to China to participate in the Fourth International Folk Art Festival in China; in October, the China Coal Mine Art Troupe went to Georgia to participate in the Second International Arts Festival. The artistic activities of these two visits laid the foundation for the exchange and cooperation of Chinese and Georgian folk culture.

(2) Development Stage (2000—2012)

After the Chinese – Georgian folk cultural exchanges entered the development stage, the channels for cultural exchanges gradually expanded, and a basic pattern of cultural cooperation was formed.

In October 2002, China's photo exhibition was held in Tbilisi, Georgia. In July 1 – 6, 2005, the famous Chinese female wheelchair painter Qin Bailan's personal exhibition was successfully held in Tbilisi Gallery. Chinese Ambassador to Georgia Wang Kaiwen and Georgian Deputy Minister of Culture Kvariani co – chaired the opening ceremony of the painting, which attracted hundreds of people from the Georgia – China Friendship Association, Georgian culture circle, the press, and the overseas Chinese in Georgia.

From September 29 to October 26, 2006, "China's Jingdezhen Porcelain Exhibition" and "'Dancing Beijing' Picture Exhibition" were held at the Tbilisi History Museum. The art exhibition was extremely enthusiastic among the people of Georgia. The public praised the superb craftsmanship of Chinese porcelain, and marveled at the achievements of Beijing's construction. This exhibition deepened the understanding of Georgian people about Chinese tradition and modernity. The radio, newspapers and other media all praised this event. The exhibition gave high praise and called the exhibits "Chinese Miracles".

On July 23, 2008, Tbilisi, Georgia's capital, held a "China Theme Day" folk performance event. This performance was held in the folk village. Little actors from the Tianjin Huaxia Future Children's Art Troupe and actors from the Sichuan Opera Troupe were special. The audience presented exquisite performances of songs and dances, music, martial arts, and dragon and lion dances. The wonderful folk art programs with Chinese characteristics such as "Changing the Face" produced extraordinary results in the folklore world.

On February 13, 2010, the Chinese Embassy held the first 2010 Chinese Embassy, Chinese – funded Institutions and Chinese Overseas Chinese Spring Festival Gala in Tbilisi. The entire Spring Festival Gala was full of a strong festive atmosphere. On September 27, the Georgian edition of the classic Chinese classic "Liao Zhai Zhi Yi" was first launched in Tbilisi. The book was proposed and chaired by Professor Liu Guangwen, a well – known Chinese in Georgia and the director of the Silk Road Georgia – China Cultural Exchange Center. The Chinese Embassy sponsored the publication. Ms. Liu Guangwen has made important contributions to promoting cultural exchanges between China and Georgia. With her efforts, the Georgian version of "The Art of War" and "Chinese Culture" have also been published. On November 25, Tbilisi Education and Training School for the Mentally Handicapped held the "China Day" event. The school's students with intellectual disabilities prepared carefully a scene play that changed the theme of Chinese folktales, and brought the national anthem and "Two Tigers" song in Chinese. The "China Day" event was very successful.

On January 30, 2011, the 2nd Chinese New Year Gala was held at the "Muse" International Cultural Center in Tbilisi. All the programs of the party were self – written and performed, singing and dancing, opera, musical instruments, poetry recitals and sketches, etc. Students from the Confucius Institute at the Free University of Tbilisi also brought wonderful harmony and singing and dancing programs. The soprano singer of the Tbilisi Conservatory of Music also sang the songs "Jasmine" and "Beautiful Nightingale" in Chinese. This party not only created the atmosphere of the Spring Festival, but also evoked the pride of overseas Chinese and overseas Chinese to the motherland.

In December 2012, in order to celebrate the 20th anniversary of the establishment of diplomatic relations between China and Georgia, the two ministries of culture of the two governments agreed to hold cultural days. The large – scale dance drama "Dunhuang Rhyme" brought by the Opera House of Gansu Province depicts the prosperity of the Chinese Tang Dynasty and expresses the Chinese people's history. This cultural day event has brought the relationship between the two countries to a new level of history.

(3) New Development Stage (2013—2020)

With the ever – increasing cultural exchanges between China and Georgia, and the great achievements that have been made, after entering a new stage of development, a new prelude to the cultural exchange between China and Georgia has begun.

On March 27 - 28, 2013, the Wushu team of Lanzhou University was invited to have a martial arts cultural exchange with the Georgian Martial Arts Association. The two sides jointly held a "China - Georgia Martial Arts Exchange Conference". Chinese martial arts is a reflection of Chinese culture and national spirit. The exchange meeting stimulated the enthusiasm of Georgian people to learn martial arts, and also promoted the cultural exchange and construction of Chinese and Georgian martial arts. On September 9th, the opening ceremony of the "Dialogue of Terracotta Warriors - EU and Chinese Sculptor Works Tour" was held in Chav. The exhibition was jointly organized by the Shaanxi Provincial Museum of China, the "Modern Sculpture Center" of Belgium, the Georgian Silk Road Group and other units. It exhibited a total of 30 works by Chinese and European artists. The exchange is of great significance and the friendship between each other is promoted through silent artistic language. On December 7, the Christmas Charity Bazaar organized by Youge Women's Club opened at the Sheraton Hotel in Tbilisi. It is full of products with Chinese characteristics and delicious snacks. The Georgian people have a keen interest in Chinese culture.

On July 5, 2014, the "Nanjing Youth Olympics Cultural Exchange - China and Georgia" event was held at the Fifth Senior School in Nanjing. This event opened the school level between China and Georgia prelude to teaching cooperation.

On October 11, 2015, Yue Bin, Chinese Ambassador to Georgia, participated in the first Georgia "China Day" event. Georgian Minister of Education and Technology Sanigidze, Tbilisi Mayor Narmania, and Director of Georgia National Tourism Administration Qiao together with 10,000 people participated in Govarzee and Georgia, and the successful holding of the

"China Day" event is a milestone in Chinese – Georgian folk cultural exchanges, which will help the people of Georgia to have close contact with Chinese culture and foster more Chinese – Georgian cultural exchanges. The communicator of friendship is of great significance.

On March 13, 2016, at the graduation concert of the National Theatre Orchestra 2015—2016, Georgian female pianist Tiya Bunyatishvili collaborated with the orchestra's chief conductor Lu Jia at the concert. The Schumann Piano Concerto was played on the stage, and after the concert, a Chinese tour was opened to let more Chinese people understand Georgian art and culture; On June 22, the Georgian Wine Festival was held at the Shanghai Roosevelt Mansion to let Chinese people learn about Georgian wine history and culture. On October 10, Tina Ting, Sisinashvili, the First Secretary of the Georgian Embassy in China, paid a visit to the Chinese Artists Association. The meeting laid the tone for the exchanges between the Chinese and Georgian art circles, and laid a solid foundation for the long – term and in – depth cooperation between the two sides.

In response to China's Belt and Road Initiative, on January 11, 2020, the Georgian Chinese Institute of Foreign Education held an opening ceremony and ribbon – cutting ceremony to provide Georgians with more opportunities to learn Chinese and understand Chinese culture.

3. Cultural and Educational Construction of Confucius Institute

The Confucius Institute is a Chinese – foreign cooperative non – profit organization for Chinese language learning and the promotion of Chinese culture in order to satisfy the world's passion for learning Chinese. It is an educational platform developed through the establishment of both parties through the form of Chinese – foreign cooperation. In order to meet the needs of Georgians to learn Chinese and understand Chinese culture, the Confucius Institute Headquarters successively established the Confucius Institute at the Tbilisi Free University and the Confucius Institute at the

Tbilisi Open University.

(1) Early Stage (1992—1999)

Chinese was officially introduced to Georgia as early as the Tsarist period. After the development, the number of Chinese learners has reached a certain scale. In 1991, the Georgian Asian – African College was established. It became the first institution of higher learning with a Chinese major in Transcaucasian. In 1992, the number of Georgian learners in Georgia increased gradually after the establishment of diplomatic relations between China and Georgia. In the early days of the establishment of the Chinese Department, due to the lack of Chinese teachers and learning materials, Chinese courses faced many difficulties in the development of the course. In 1992, Ms. Liu Guangwen was invited to be a teacher of the Chinese Department of the Asian – African College, which laid the foundation for the future establishment of the Confucius Institute.

(2) Development Stage (2000—2012)

After entering the 21st century, with the widespread rise of the "Chinese fever" around the world, in 2002, the Georgian Ministry of Education applied to China, hoping that China could send Chinese teachers to teach Chinese in Georgia. In the future, there will be 1 – 2 teachers each year in Tbilisi Free University to teach Chinese; since 2010, Georgia elementary and middle schools have also applied for Chinese teachers from the Ministry of Education, hoping that they can teach in middle schools and teach Chinese courses; on November 26, 2010, the opening ceremony of the Confucius Institute was held. The establishment of the Confucius Institute provided a broad platform for the people of Georgia to learn Chinese and understand Chinese culture. On February 6, 2012, the 2012 Confucius Institute Spring Festival Tour of Lanzhou University was held in Tbilisi, Georgia. In the first performance, the Chinese Ambassador to Georgia Chen Jianfu, the Georgian Ministry of Foreign Affairs, the Ministry of Science and Technology, the Ministry of Culture and Heritage, the Georgia – China Friendship Association, Chinese and Overseas Chinese, and Chinese – funded enterprises altogether more than 500 people participated in the event. The event provided an opportunity for exchanges between Chinese and Georgian folk performing arts and it is a bridge that transcends national boundaries, nations and times.

(3) New Development Stage (2013—2020)

After the Belt and Road Initiative was put forward, cultural exchanges between China and Georgia have reached a new level in history.

On November 23, 2013, the sixth "Confucius Institute Cup" Wushu Sanda was opened. The Wushu Sanda competition was jointly organized by the Confucius Institute at the Free University of Tbilisi and the Georgian Wushu Association. The participating martial arts Sanda players came from Georgia and Iran. The competition has had a profound impact on the spread of Chinese martial arts culture.

On January 27, 2014, the Free University of Tbilisi hosted the Spring Festival Gala. As a major annual event of the Confucius Institute, it not only provided a platform for Chinese students to show themselves, but also effectively spread Chinese language and culture. On September 26, on the eve of the 65th anniversary of the founding of the People's Republic of China, the University of St. Andrea organized a "China Day" event. Students from the "Chinese Club" produced promotional films and photo exhibitions on Chinese history and culture and contemporary development. They performed traditional Chinese dance, and received unanimous praise from the participants. On September 30, the Chinese Ambassador to Georgia Yue Bin attended the event that Tbilisi Free University Confucius Institute was established for four years. It has achieved excellent results in the promotion of Chinese culture, and has also made significant contributions to cultural cooperation and exchanges between China and Georgia.

Chapter 7 Cultural Exchange and Cooperation between China and Georgia in Belt and Road Initiative

On January 29, 2015, the Confucius Institute at the Free University of Tbilisi hosted the second "Chinese Georgian Elementary and Middle School Knowledge Contest", which attracted more than 500 students from 12 primary and secondary schools to participate, effectively expanding the spread of Chinese in Georgia. On February 5, the Confucius Institute at the Free University of Tbilisi held a "Chinese New Year Gala for the Year of the Sheep"; on April 17, the final of the first "Sound of China" Chinese Song Contest was held at the Confucius Institute at the Free University of Tbilisi Held. The Chinese Ambassador to Georgia Yue Bin presented awards to the champions. This song competition allows more Georgians to understand Chinese song culture. On May 15th, the Confucius Institute at the Free University of Tbilisi hosted the fourth session of Georgian Chinese Poetry, and more than 200 people including Yue Bin, Chinese ambassador to Georgia, Chicowani, president of the Free University of Georgia, and officials of the Ministry of Foreign Affairs of Georgia participated in the event. The poetry contest showcased China's poetry culture and was well received by the Georgian public; The Georgian Final of the 8th "Chinese Bridge" Chinese Proficiency Competition for Middle School Students was held in Georgia. This is the First time the competition entered Georgia. Students participated in the competition to showcase their Chinese learning results, and also promoted cultural exchanges between China and Georgia. On October 11, the "Confucius Institute Day" series of activities, "Chinese Culture Entering the Community" activity held in Dedaena Park. The event was jointly organized by the Chinese Embassy in Georgia, the Tbilisi City Government, and the Confucius Institute at the Free University of Tbilisi, which attracted more than 10,000 people from Georgia.

On March 31, 2016, Shan Jixiang, President of the Beijing Museum, held a cultural lecture entitled "The World of the Palace Museum, The

Palace of the World" at the Confucius Institute at the Free University of Tbilisi. Learned the cultural heritage behind the Forbidden City Collection and the development of related cultural industries. From August 16 to 29, Lanzhou University hosted a cultural visit to China by some principals of Georgia and Chinese project leaders. This project is to consolidate and broaden Chinese teaching sites. Promote the education of high – level leaders' understanding of Chinese culture and actively rent them; On August 27, the "2016 Georgian Student Cultural Tour Summer Camp" opened a two – week cultural tour in China, deepening Georgian students' knowledge of the Chinese people and Chinese culture. This understanding has gradually improved the friendship between Chinese and foreign teachers and students.

On January 24, 2017, the Confucius Institute at the Free University of Tbilisi hosted a seminar on Georgia and the Belt and Road. Chinese Ambassador to Georgia Ji Yanchi attended and delivered a speech. He introduced the achievements of China and Georgia in the construction of the Belt and Road, and emphasized the importance of cultural exchanges for the mutual communication between the two peoples. The Confucius Institute contributed to the cultural construction of China and Georgia in the Belt and Road. On November 16, the opening ceremony of the Confucius Classroom at the Tbilisi Open University was held. This is the first Confucius Classroom in Georgia. Zuo Hongbo, Chinese Counselor to Georgia, officials from the Ministry of Education, Pan Baotian, Vice President of Lanzhou University, teachers and students from the Open University, and overseas Chinese attended the opening ceremony. The Confucius Classroom will build a bridge for Georgians to learn Chinese and Chinese culture, and further promote the exchange of education and culture between China and Georgia. With the promotion of the Belt and Road Initiative, and the increase of China's influence in Georgia, Georgian government officials are paying more and more attention to Chinese learning. Since the establishment of the Confucius

Classroom, Chinese courses have been successively provided for Georgian officials, and more and more Chinese – Georgian friendly ambassadors have been trained. On December 23, Tbilisi opened a Chinese painting class at the Confucius Classroom at the University made the Georgian people enthusiastic.

On February 10, 2018, the first Spring Festival Gala of the Confucius Classroom at the Tbilisi Open University kicked off. This Spring Festival Gala not only provided a platform for Chinese students to show themselves, but also showcased Chinese art and culture to Georgians. After the establishment of the Confucius Classroom, a series of cultural activities including "Chinese Culture Enters the Campus" will be formed. These cultural exhibitions have played a positive role in promoting Chinese culture, promoting Chinese – Georgian cultural exchanges, and improving the influence of Confucius Classrooms. The Lantern Festival was made to make students feel the atmosphere of traditional Chinese festivals. In order to meet the needs of Georgian people to learn Chinese culture, Confucius Classroom teachers planned and launched a series of cultural events on Saturdays based on the actual situation of students. Every Saturday, calligraphy, painting, Chinese knot, paper cutting, martial arts, tea art and other Chinese Cultural activities will be held. It has gradually formed their own distinctive brand of the Confucius Classroom, and has continued to do so. On April 3, the Confucius Classroom held the first final of the Chinese Song Contest. This competition not only tested the teaching level of the Confucius Classroom, but also spread it. Confucius Classroom held the first "Confucius Classroom Cup" Go contest on April 26. This contest not only provided a platform for Go fans to learn about chess skills, but also to further promote Chinese Go culture and promote education in both countries. On May 7 – 8, the Belt and Road International Forum in a Global Perspective co – sponsored by Tbilisi Open University and Lanzhou University was held at Tbilisi Open University.

Experts and scholars from various countries have established a platform for exchanges and cooperation, which helps to promote the Belt and Road and promote the exchange and development of education and culture in China; On May 9 - 10, Lanzhou University co - constructed a Confucius Institute Classroom Joint Conference and the 2018 Council was held at the Open University of Tbilisi. The meeting was successfully held for China and Georgia. The development of culture and education has made outstanding contributions. On October 22, the Belt and Road 5th Anniversary of China - Georgia Cooperation New Roundtable held by the Chinese Academy of Social Sciences, Tbilisi Open University and Confucius Classroom was held in Confucius Classroom. This meeting provided an opportunity for experts to communicate in depth and wrote a new chapter in China - Georgia cooperation. On November 24, Confucius Classroom hosted a forum for Chinese language teaching principals in primary and middle schools. This forum not only guided the development and construction of Chinese language teaching sites in primary and secondary schools, but also laid the foundation for the scientific development of Confucius Classrooms. On November 24, the classroom also held the first anniversary celebration. Looking back on the first anniversary since the establishment of the Confucius Classroom, a total of more than 20,000 Chinese students have been covered, covering 22 teaching sites in Georgia University, Elementary School, and Primary School, and more than 30 cultural events have been held. Excellent results have been achieved in teaching and cultural promotion. On December 15, the first "Chinese style" fun sports meeting was held in the Confucius Classroom. This event promoted Chinese culture in a form of good news and received unanimous praise from the local people.

On February 2, 2019, the Confucius Classroom held the 2019 Spring Festival Gala, which enabled the people to learn about the Chinese Spring Festival customs and increase their enthusiasm and interest in learning

Chinese culture. On March 16, the Confucius Classroom hosted the first elementary school Chinese element drawing competition, and this competition is to integrate students into hobbies and to narrow the distance between students and Chinese culture. On May 18, the second "Confucius Classroom Cup" Go contest kicked off in Confucius Classroom. Compared with the "Confucius Classroom Cup", the players of this Go competition are higher and further promote the Chinese Go culture. On June 15, the 12th "Chinese Bridge" Chinese Proficiency Competition for Middle School Students was held in the Confucius Classroom. This is the first time that the Confucius Classroom has hosted the "Chinese Bridge" competition since its establishment. It has been well received by all sectors of society and expanded the influence of the Confucius Classroom. On July 15 – 28, 2019, the Confucius Classroom went to the China Summer Camp to launch language and culture in China. The summer camp activity provides a chance for students to understand Chinese culture; on November 16, the Confucius Classroom held the second Chinese Song Contest. The competition is higher than the first Chinese language and the performance is more mature, which is of great significance to the promotion of Chinese culture. On December 14, the Confucius Classroom held the second "Chinese Style" Fun Games; on December 21, the second anniversary of the establishment and the unveiling ceremony of the Confucius Institute were ushered in. Chinese Ambassador to Georgia Li Yan, Georgian Ambassador to China Archil Kalandia, Georgian President of Rustaveli National Academy of Sciences Zwad Gabsenia, the principals of Tbilisi's primary and secondary school teaching sites and Chinese – funded enterprises in Georgia participated in the ceremony. The Confucius Institute has become a window for Georgia to understand China, and has made outstanding contributions to the exchange and development of education and culture between the two countries.

IV Conclusion

Since the Belt and Road Initiative was put forward, China and the countries along the Belt and Road have attracted much attention from the national community in areas such as political ties, economic and trade integration, education and cultural exchanges. "Friendship, which drives from close contact between the people, holds the key to sound state to state relationship." The Silk Road has left us a rich historical heritage. In the new era of the 21st century, the Belt and Road has not only inherited the Silk Road and Business Road has also been given a new era connotation, that is, the "road to connect people".

As one of the important countries along the Belt and Road, Georgia attaches great importance to cooperation and exchanges with China in various fields. The two sides carried out a series of cultural exchange activities through official platforms, non-governmental organizations, and Confucius Institutes, which not only created a good international image for China, but also provided an important window for the Georgian people to understand China. Today, China and Georgia have carried forward the Silk Road spirit of "peace and cooperation, openness and inclusiveness, mutual learning and mutual benefit" through cultural exchanges and cooperation. At the same time, they have also created political mutual trust, economic integration, and cultural inclusion.

Although in the process of cultural exchanges between China and Georgia, some difficulties and challenges were encountered, the two sides strengthened cooperation in education, tourism and culture, improved the cultural industry cooperation mechanism, and innovated the new situation of cultural cooperation through various forms of cultural exchanges to realize the culture. Exchanges and cooperation continue to develop.

In summary, China and Georgia have made great achievements in the process of cultural exchanges and construction. Especially after the Belt and Road Initiative was proposed, the areas of cultural exchanges between the two sides have been further expanded. At the same time, we should also face objectively. Existing challenges, building a new pattern of cultural exchanges between China and Georgia, ensuring the safety and smoothness of the Belt and Road, and thus realizing the "Chinese dream" of the great rejuvenation of the Chinese nation.